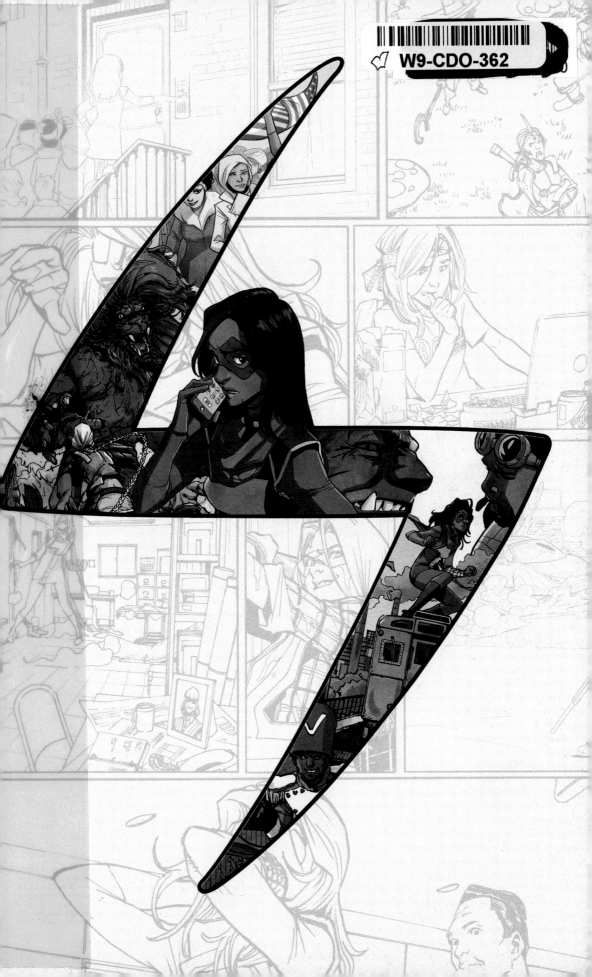

MS. MARVEL VOL. 7: DAMAGE PER SECOND. Contains material originally published in magazine form as MS. MARVEL #13-18. First printing 2017. ISBN# 978-1-302-90305-3. Published by MARVEL WORLDWIDE, INC., a subsidiary of MARVEL ENTERTAINMENT, LLC. OFFICE OF PUBLICATION: 135 West 50th Street, New York, NY 10020. Copyright © 2017 MARVEL No similarity between any of the names, characters, persons, and/or institutions in this magazine with those of any living or dead person or institution is intended, and any such similarity which may exist is purely coincidental. **Printed in the U.S.A.** DAN BUCKLEY, President, Marvel Entertainment; JOE QUESADA, Chief Creative Officer; TOM BREVOORT, SVP of Publishing; DAVID BOGART, SVP of Business Affairs & Operations, Publishing & Partnership; C.B. CEBULSKI, VP of Brand Management & Development, Asia; DAVID GABRIEL, SVP of Sales & Marketing, Publishing; JEFF YOUNGQUIST, VP of Production & Special Projects; DAN CARR, Executive Director of Publishing Technology; ALEX MORALES, Director of Publishing Operations; SUSAN CRESPI, Production Manager; STAN LEE, Chairman Emeritus. For information regarding advertising in Marvel Comics or on Marvel.com, please contact Vit DeBellis, Integrated Sales Manager, at vdebellis@marvel.com. For Marvel subscription inquiries, please call 888-511-5480. **Manufactured between 5/26/2017 and 6/27/2017 by QUAD/GRAPHICS WASECA, WASECA, MN, USA.**

10 9 8 7 6 5 4 3 2 1

MS. MARVEL

writer
G. WILLOW WILSON

artists
MIRKA ANDOLFO (#13), **TAKESHI MIYAZAWA** (#14-17)
& FRANCESCO GASTON (#18)

color artist
IAN HERRING

letterer
VC's JOE CARAMAGNA

cover art
JOËLLE JONES & RACHELLE ROSENBERG (#13)
AND **NELSON BLAKE II & RACHELLE ROSENBERG** (#14-18)

assistant editor
CHARLES BEACHAM

associate editor
MARK BASSO

editor
SANA AMANAT

collection editor
JENNIFER GRÜNWALD
assistant editor
CAITLIN O'CONNELL
associate managing editor
KATERI WOODY

editor, special projects
MARK D. BEAZLEY
vp production & special projects
JEFF YOUNGQUIST
svp print, sales & marketing
DAVID GABRIEL

editor in chief
AXEL ALONSO
chief creative officer
JOE QUESADA
president
DAN BUCKLEY
executive producer
ALAN FINE

PREVIOUSLY

WHEN A STRANGE TERRIGEN MIST DESCENDED UPON JERSEY CITY,
KAMALA KHAN WAS IMBUED WITH POLYMORPH POWERS. USING
HER NEW ABILITIES TO FIGHT EVIL AND PROTECT JERSEY CITY,
SHE BECAME THE ALL-NEW

SINCE GAINING HER POWERS, MS. MARVEL'S WORKED HARD TO
EMULATE THE HEROES SHE LOOKS UP TO, BUT A RECENT DISPUTE IN THE
SUPER HERO COMMUNITY CAUSED HER TO QUESTION EVERYTHING.
KAMALA EVENTUALLY FOLLOWED HER HEART, BUT NOT BEFORE SHE
LOST THE TRUST OF HER PERSONAL HERO, CAPTAIN MARVEL, AND
DESTROYED HER RELATIONSHIP WITH HER BEST FRIEND BRUNO.

LOSING EVERYTHING CAUSED KAMALA TO REEVALUATE WHAT BEING
A HERO MEANS TO HER. AND WHILE SHE'S MORE RESOLVED THAN EVER,
DEALING WITH THE LOSS STILL HURTS...

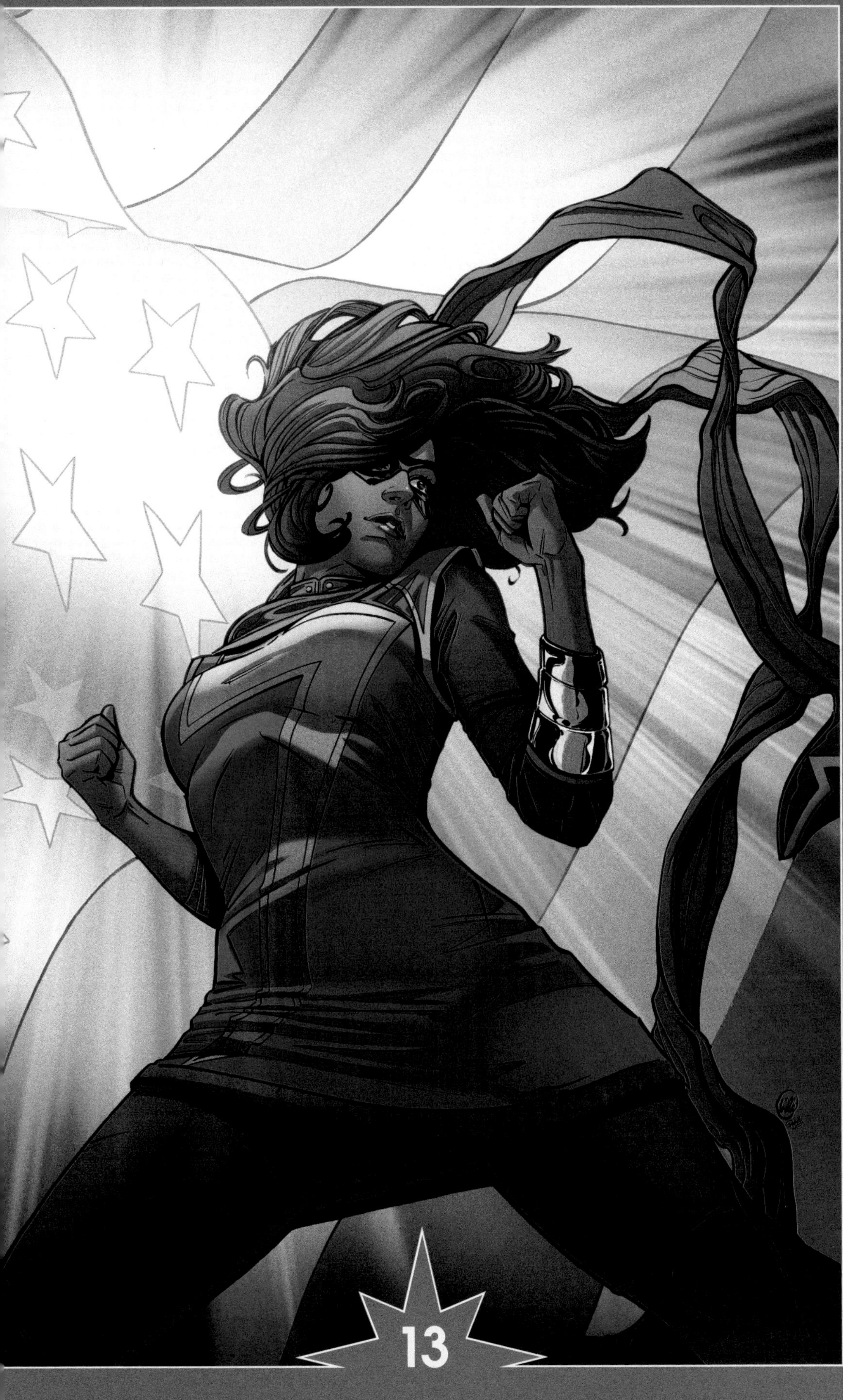

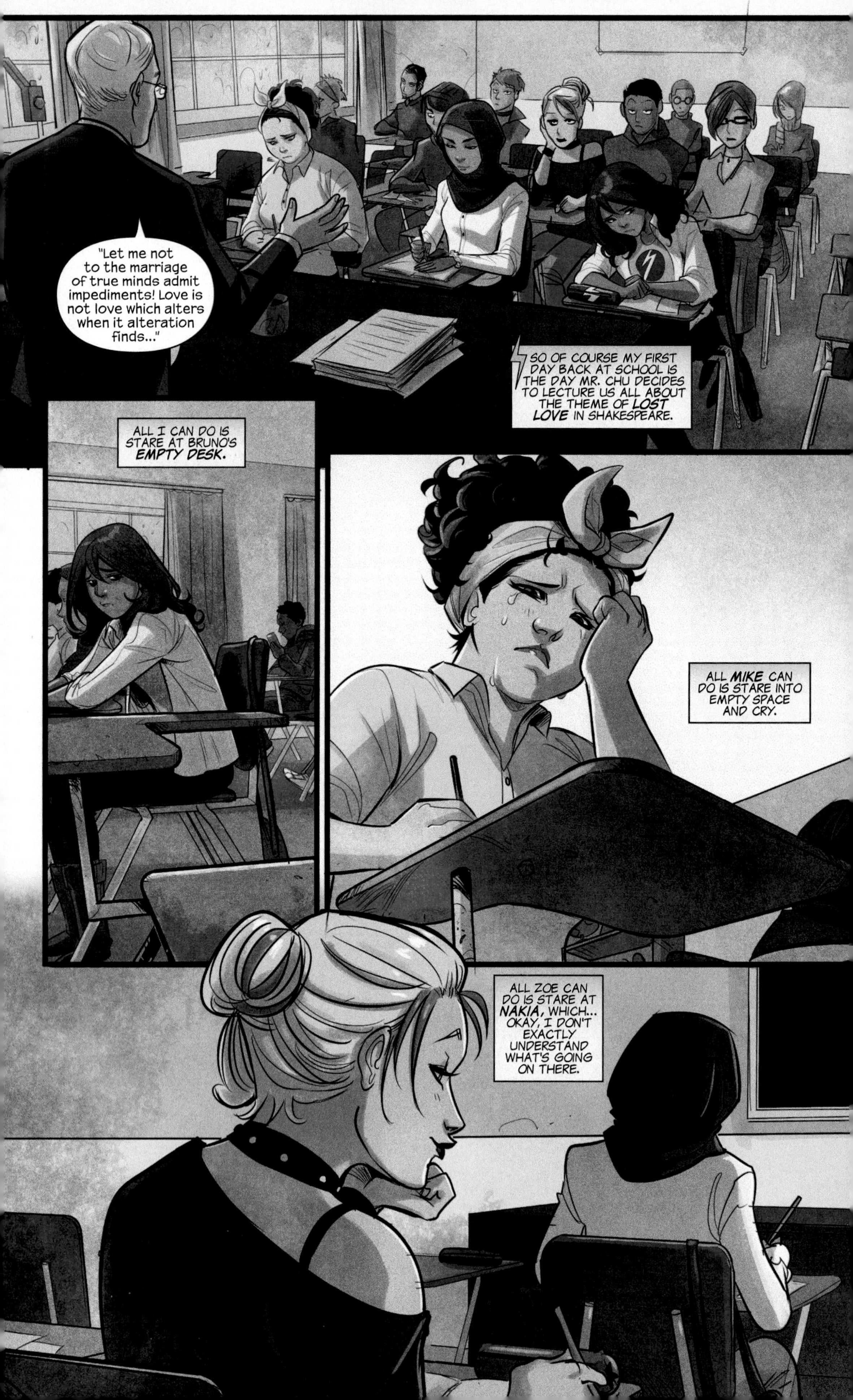
"Let me not to the marriage of true minds admit impediments! Love is not love which alters when it alteration finds..."
SO OF COURSE MY FIRST DAY BACK AT SCHOOL IS THE DAY MR. CHU DECIDES TO LECTURE US ALL ABOUT THE THEME OF LOST LOVE IN SHAKESPEARE.
ALL I CAN DO IS STARE AT BRUNO'S EMPTY DESK.
ALL MIKE CAN DO IS STARE INTO EMPTY SPACE AND CRY.
ALL ZOE CAN DO IS STARE AT NAKIA, WHICH... OKAY, I DON'T EXACTLY UNDERSTAND WHAT'S GOING ON THERE.

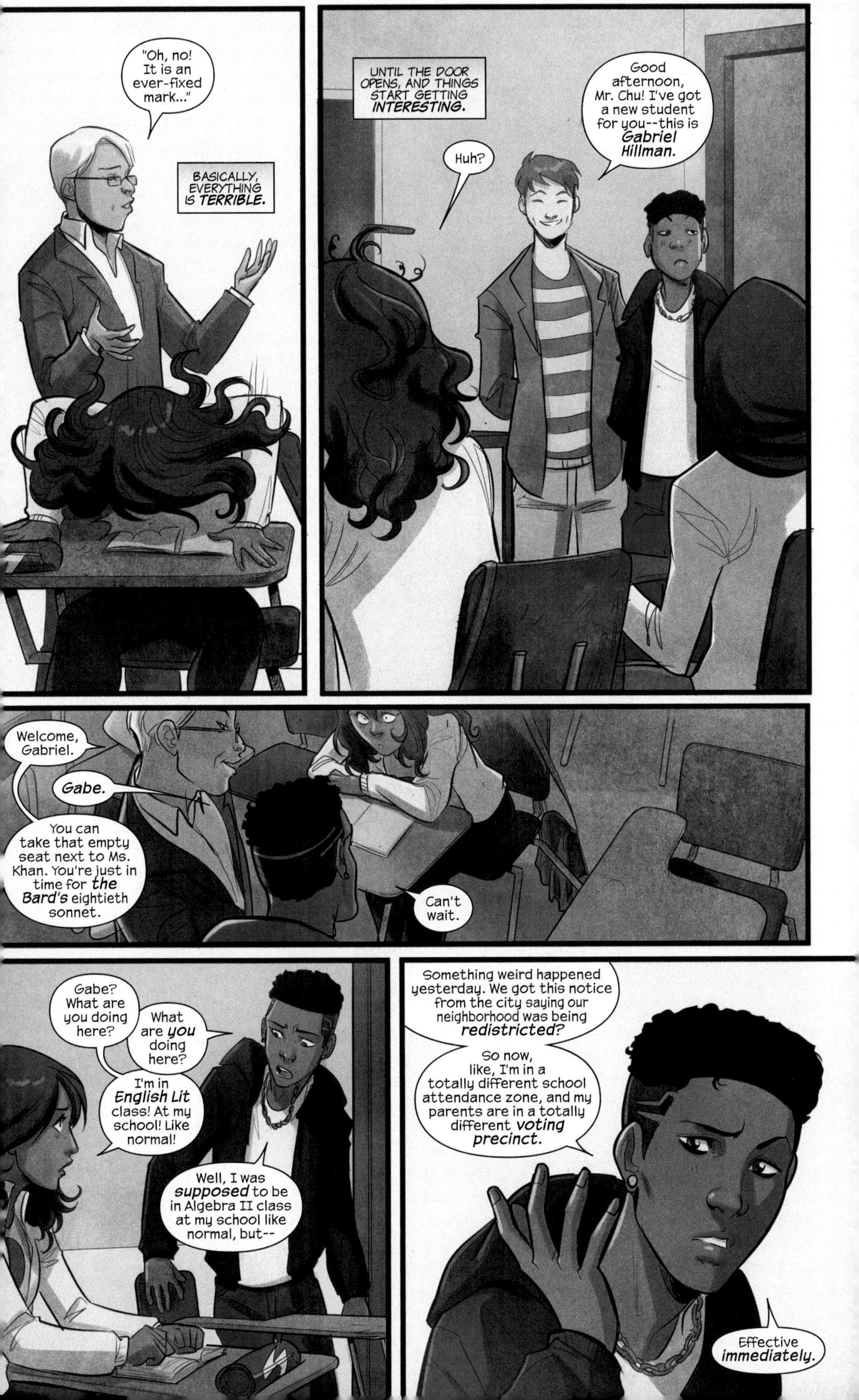
"Oh, no! It is an ever-fixed mark..."
BASICALLY, EVERYTHING IS TERRIBLE.
UNTIL THE DOOR OPENS, AND THINGS START GETTING INTERESTING.
Good afternoon, Mr. Chu! I've got a new student for you--this is Gabriel Hillman.
Huh?
Welcome, Gabriel.
Gabe.
You can take that empty seat next to Ms. Khan. You're just in time for the Bard's eightieth sonnet.
Can't wait.
Gabe? What are you doing here?
What are you doing here?
I'm in English Lit class! At my school! Like normal!
Well, I was supposed to be in Algebra II class at my school like normal, but--
Something weird happened yesterday. We got this notice from the city saying our neighborhood was being redistricted?
So now, like, I'm in a totally different school attendance zone, and my parents are in a totally different voting precinct.
Effective immediately.

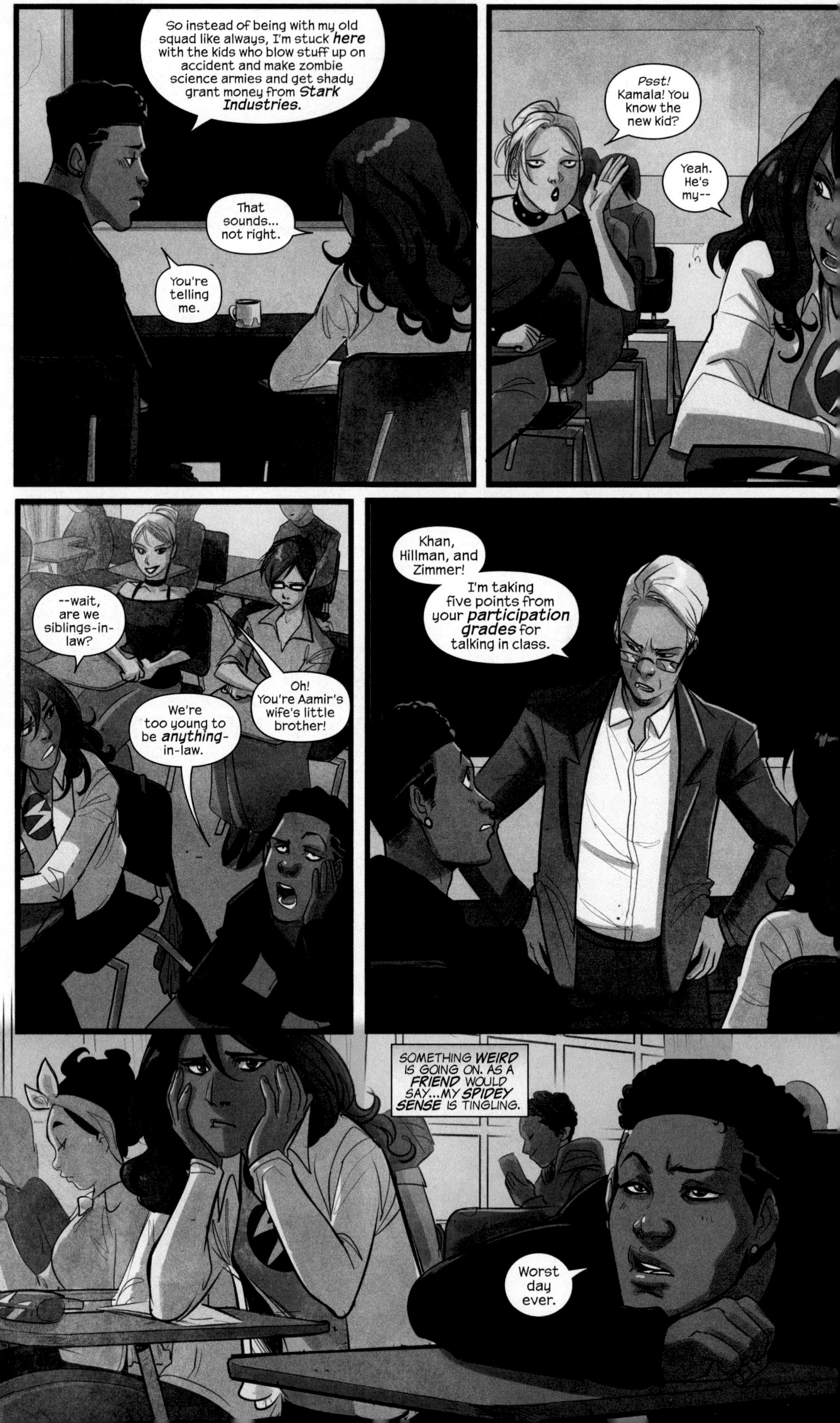
So instead of being with my old squad like always, I'm stuck *here* with the kids who blow stuff up on accident and make zombie science armies and get shady grant money from *Stark Industries*.
That sounds... not right.
You're telling me.
Psst! Kamala! You know the new kid?
Yeah. He's my--
--wait, are we siblings-in-law?
Oh! You're Aamir's wife's little brother!
We're too young to be *anything*-in-law.
Khan, Hillman, and Zimmer!
I'm taking five points from your *participation grades* for talking in class.
SOMETHING *WEIRD* IS GOING ON. AS A *FRIEND* WOULD SAY...MY *SPIDEY SENSE* IS TINGLING.
Worst day ever.

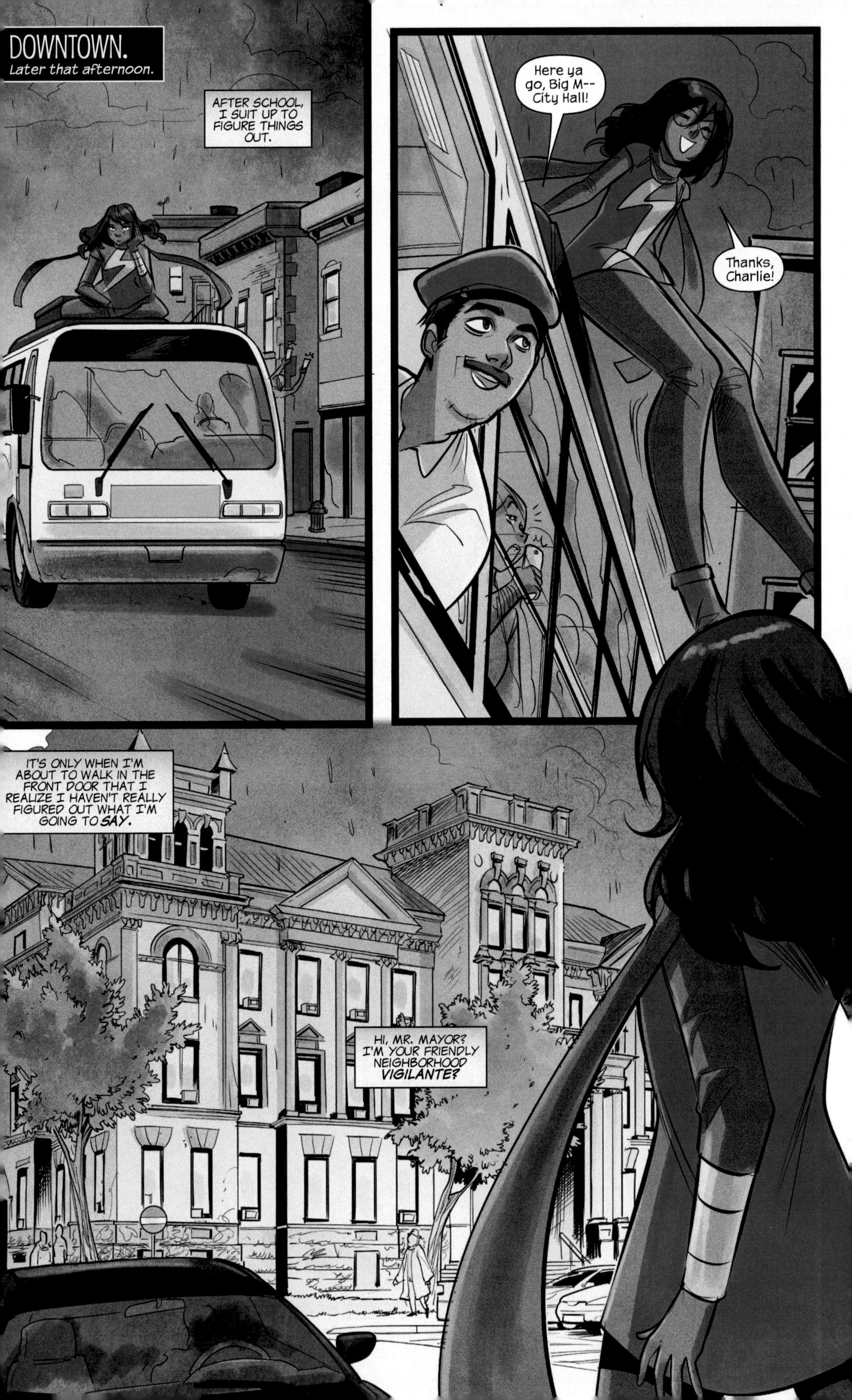
DOWNTOWN.
Later that afternoon.
AFTER SCHOOL, I SUIT UP TO FIGURE THINGS OUT.
Here ya go, Big M-- City Hall!
Thanks, Charlie!
IT'S ONLY WHEN I'M ABOUT TO WALK IN THE FRONT DOOR THAT I REALIZE I HAVEN'T REALLY FIGURED OUT WHAT I'M GOING TO SAY.
HI, MR. MAYOR? I'M YOUR FRIENDLY NEIGHBORHOOD VIGILANTE?

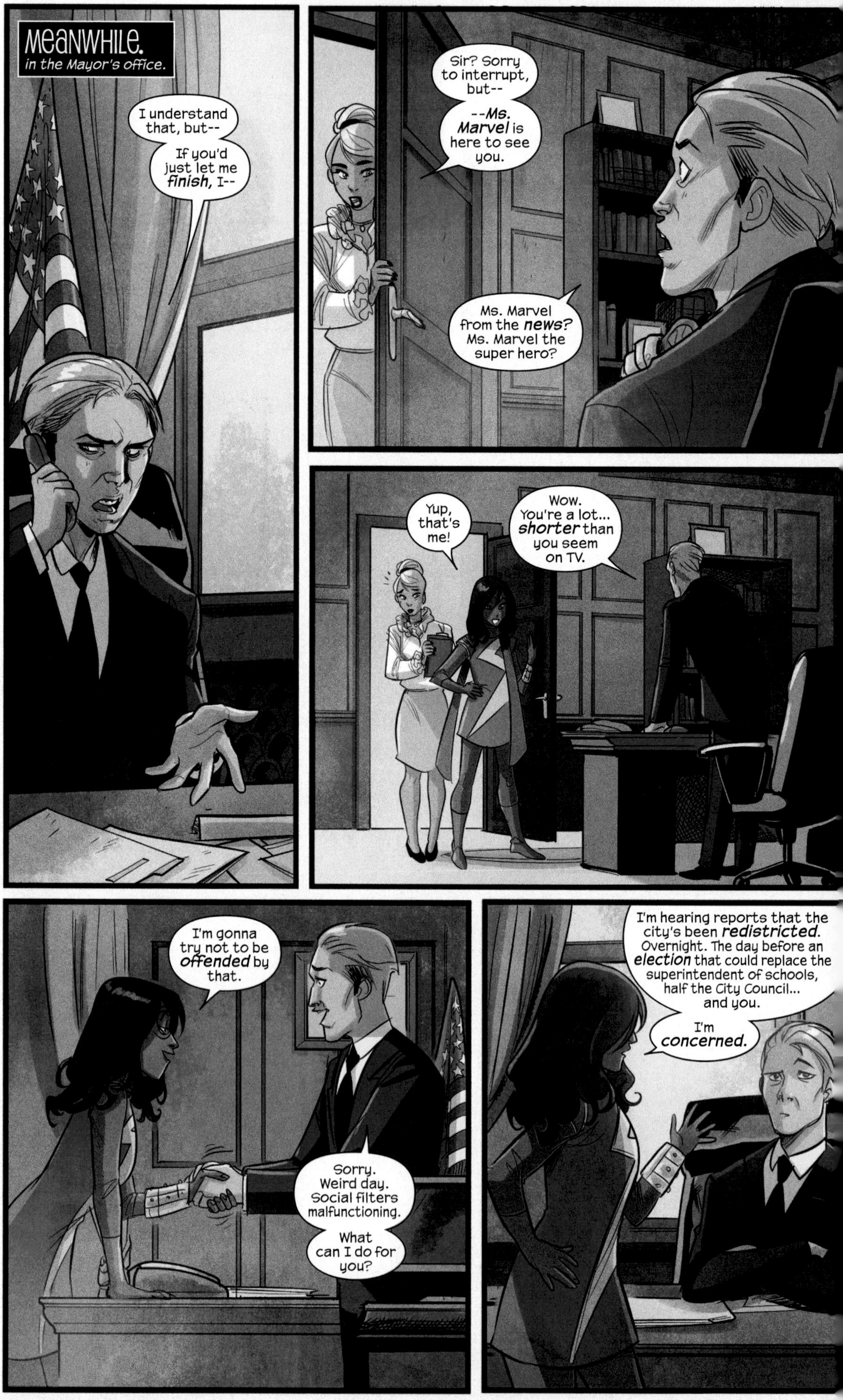
MEANWHILE.
in the Mayor's office.
I understand that, but--
If you'd just let me *finish,* I--
Sir? Sorry to interrupt, but--
--*Ms. Marvel* is here to see you.
Ms. Marvel from the *news?* Ms. Marvel the super hero?
Yup, that's me!
Wow. You're a lot... *shorter* than you seem on TV.
I'm gonna try not to be *offended* by that.
Sorry. Weird day. Social filters malfunctioning.
What can I do for you?
I'm hearing reports that the city's been *redistricted.* Overnight. The day before an *election* that could replace the superintendent of schools, half the City Council... and you.
I'm *concerned.*

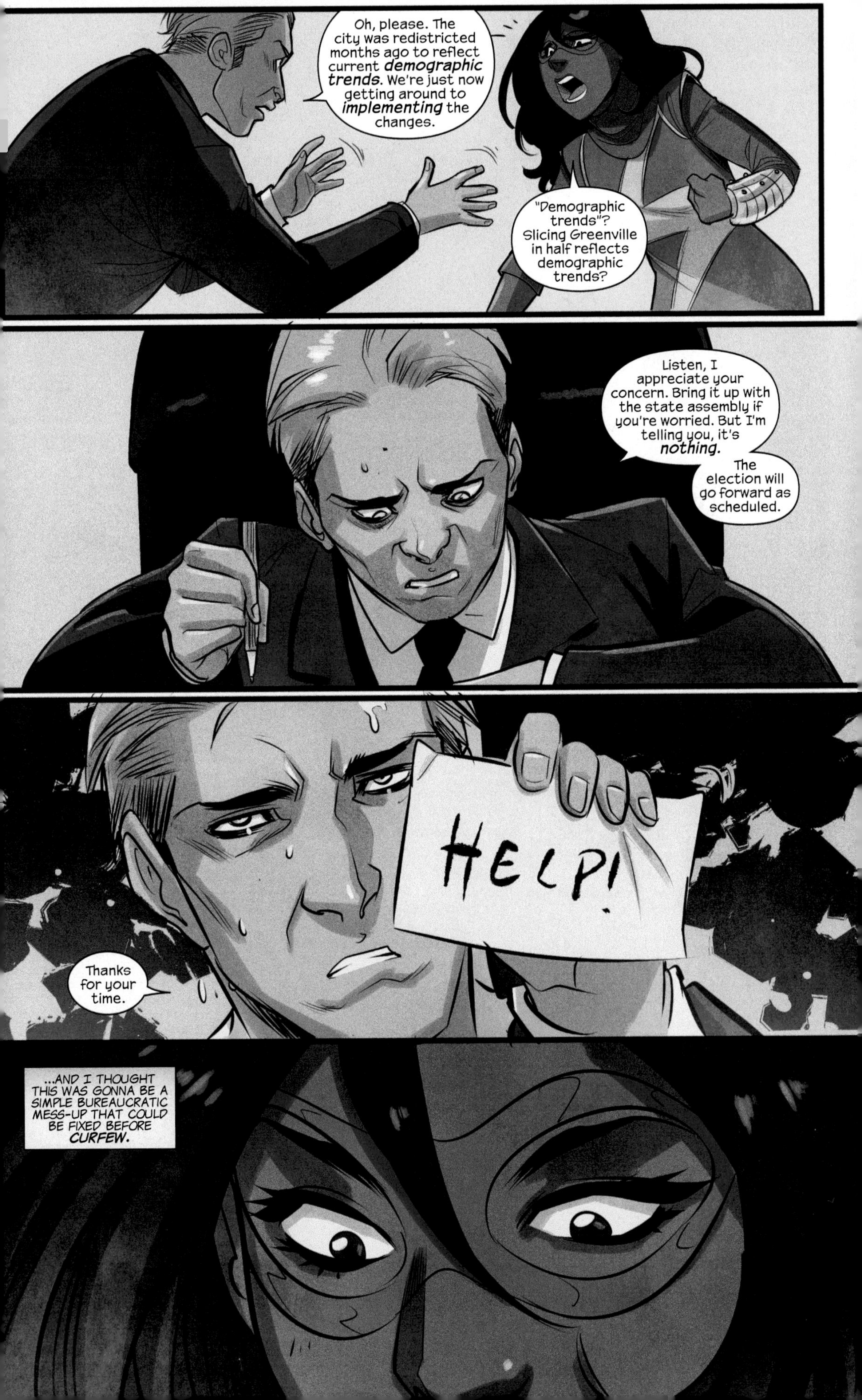
Oh, please. The city was redistricted months ago to reflect current *demographic trends.* We're just now getting around to *implementing* the changes.
"Demographic trends"? Slicing Greenville in half reflects demographic trends?
Listen, I appreciate your concern. Bring it up with the state assembly if you're worried. But I'm telling you, it's *nothing.*
The election will go forward as scheduled.
HELP!
Thanks for your time.
...AND I THOUGHT THIS WAS GONNA BE A SIMPLE BUREAUCRATIC MESS-UP THAT COULD BE FIXED BEFORE *CURFEW.*

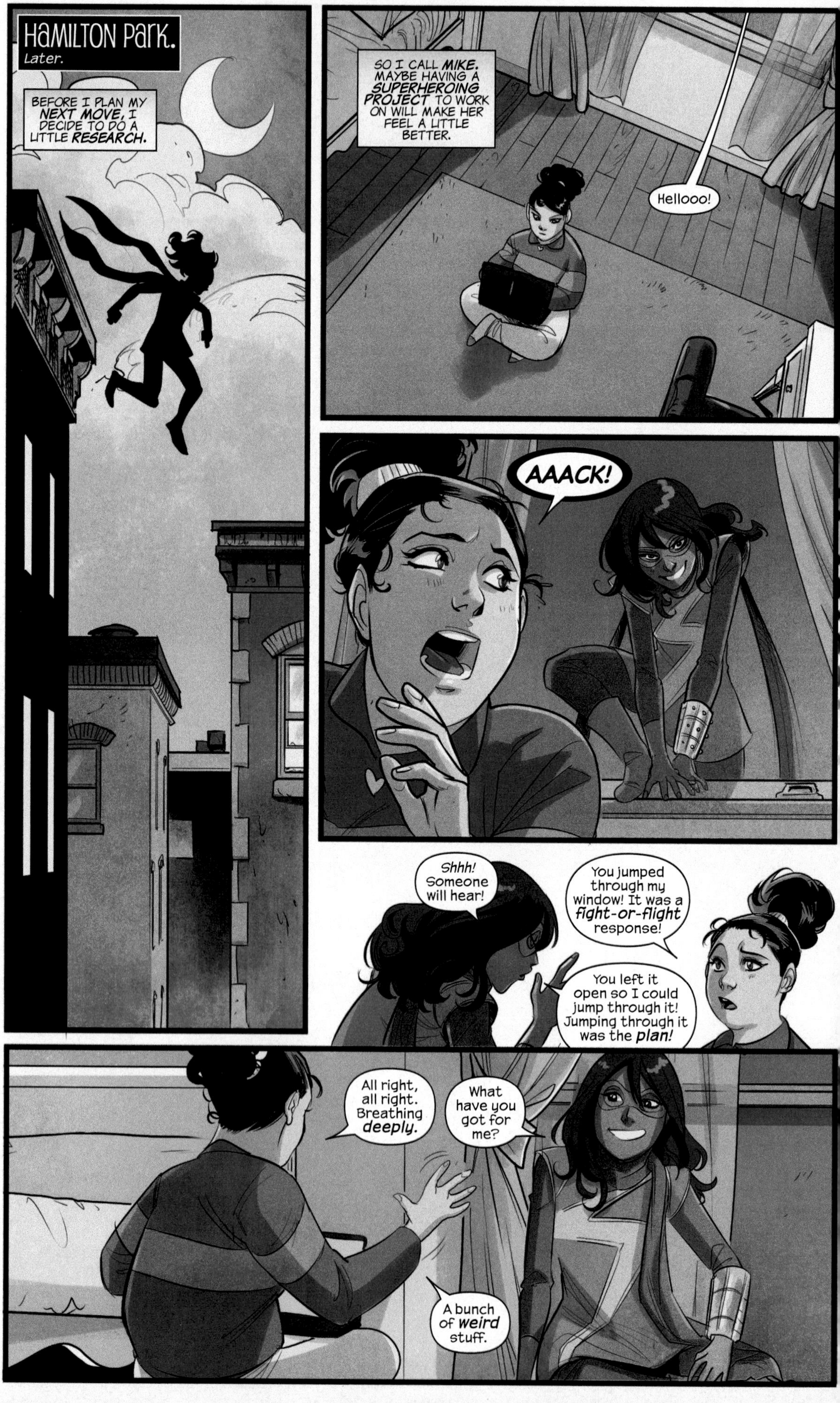

HAMILTON PARK.
Later.
BEFORE I PLAN MY NEXT MOVE, I DECIDE TO DO A LITTLE RESEARCH.
SO I CALL MIKE. MAYBE HAVING A SUPERHEROING PROJECT TO WORK ON WILL MAKE HER FEEL A LITTLE BETTER.
Hellooo!
AAACK!
Shhh! Someone will hear!
You jumped through my window! It was a fight-or-flight response!
You left it open so I could jump through it! Jumping through it was the plan!
All right, all right. Breathing deeply.
What have you got for me?
A bunch of weird stuff.

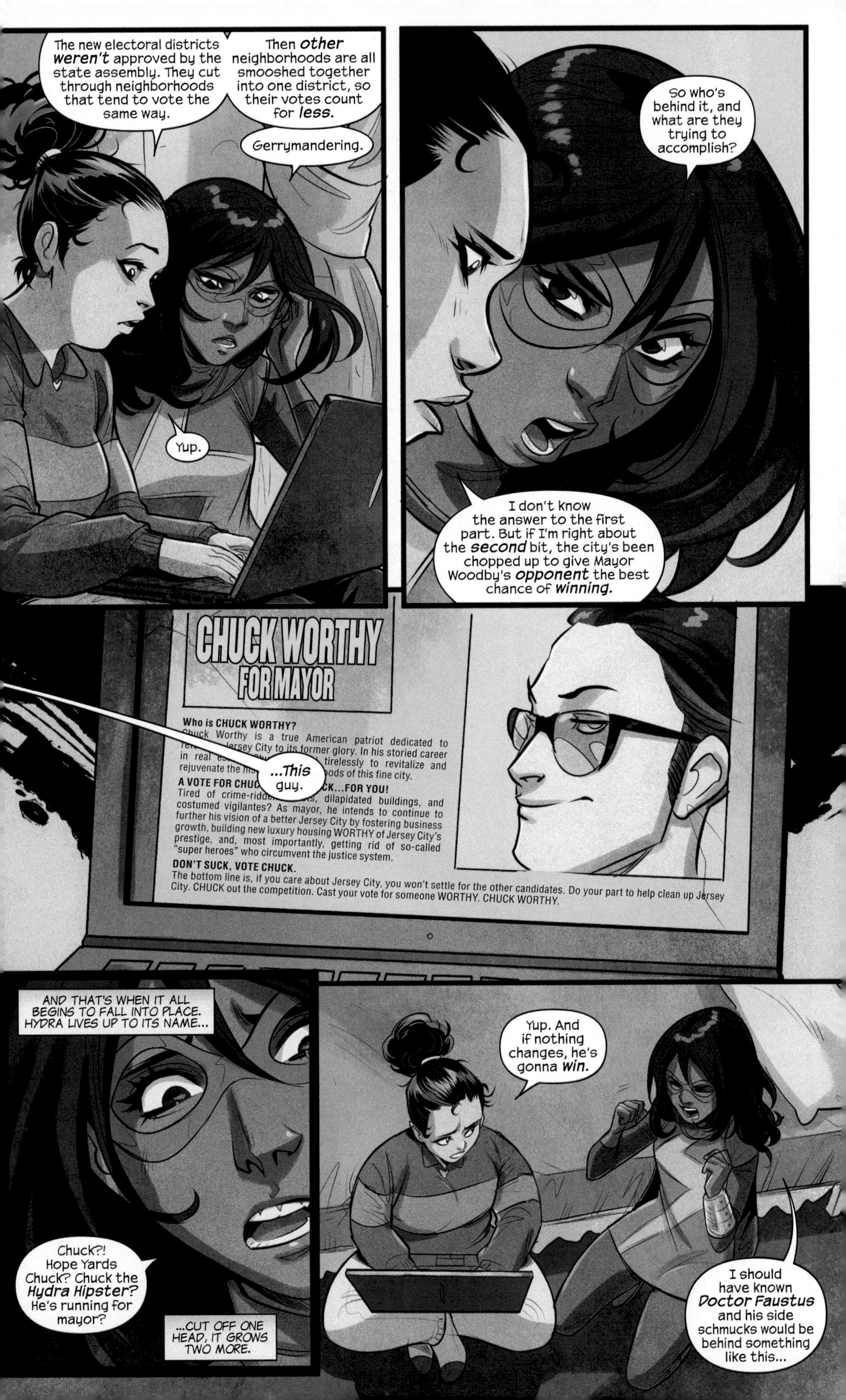
The new electoral districts weren't approved by the state assembly. They cut through neighborhoods that tend to vote the same way.
Then other neighborhoods are all smooshed together into one district, so their votes count for less.
Gerrymandering.
Yup.
So who's behind it, and what are they trying to accomplish?
I don't know the answer to the first part. But if I'm right about the second bit, the city's been chopped up to give Mayor Woodby's opponent the best chance of winning.
CHUCK WORTHY
FOR MAYOR
Who is CHUCK WORTHY?
Chuck Worthy is a true American patriot dedicated to
Jersey City to its former glory. In his storied career
in real es
tirelessly to revitalize and
rejuvenate the
oods of this fine city.
A VOTE FOR CHUC
CK...FOR YOU!
Tired of crime-ridden
dilapidated buildings, and costumed vigilantes? As mayor, he intends to continue to further his vision of a better Jersey City by fostering business growth, building new luxury housing WORTHY of Jersey City's prestige, and, most importantly, getting rid of so-called "super heroes" who circumvent the justice system.
DON'T SUCK, VOTE CHUCK.
The bottom line is, if you care about Jersey City, you won't settle for the other candidates. Do your part to help clean up Jersey City. CHUCK out the competition. Cast your vote for someone WORTHY. CHUCK WORTHY.
...This guy.
AND THAT'S WHEN IT ALL BEGINS TO FALL INTO PLACE. HYDRA LIVES UP TO ITS NAME...
Chuck?! Hope Yards Chuck? Chuck the Hydra Hipster? He's running for mayor?
...CUT OFF ONE HEAD, IT GROWS TWO MORE.
Yup. And if nothing changes, he's gonna win.
I should have known Doctor Faustus and his side schmucks would be behind something like this...

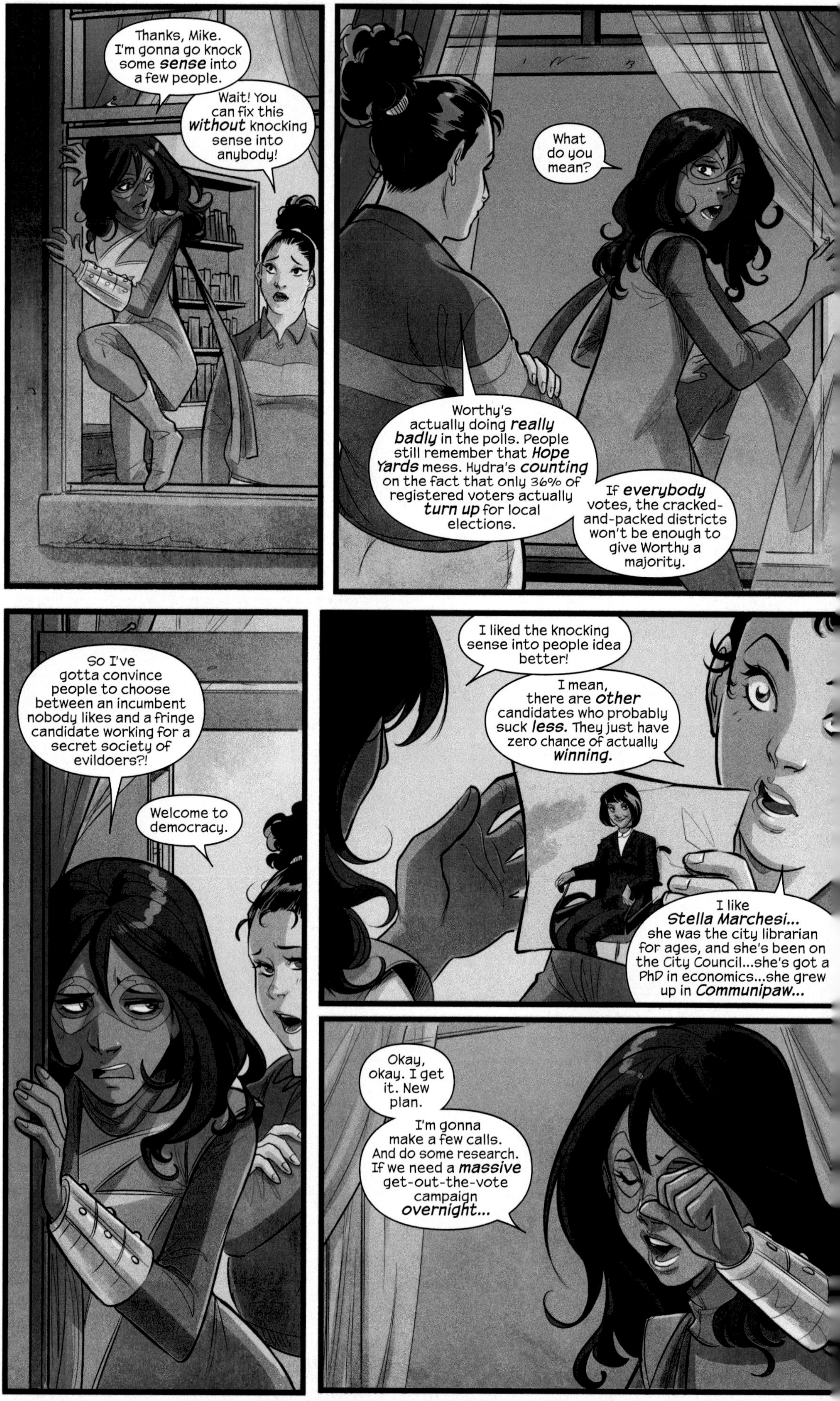

Thanks, Mike. I'm gonna go knock some sense into a few people.
Wait! You can fix this without knocking sense into anybody!
What do you mean?
Worthy's actually doing really badly in the polls. People still remember that Hope Yards mess. Hydra's counting on the fact that only 36% of registered voters actually turn up for local elections.
If everybody votes, the cracked-and-packed districts won't be enough to give Worthy a majority.
So I've gotta convince people to choose between an incumbent nobody likes and a fringe candidate working for a secret society of evildoers?!
Welcome to democracy.
I liked the knocking sense into people idea better!
I mean, there are other candidates who probably suck less. They just have zero chance of actually winning.
I like Stella Marchesi... she was the city librarian for ages, and she's been on the City Council...she's got a PhD in economics...she grew up in Communipaw...
Okay, okay. I get it. New plan.
I'm gonna make a few calls. And do some research. If we need a massive get-out-the-vote campaign overnight...

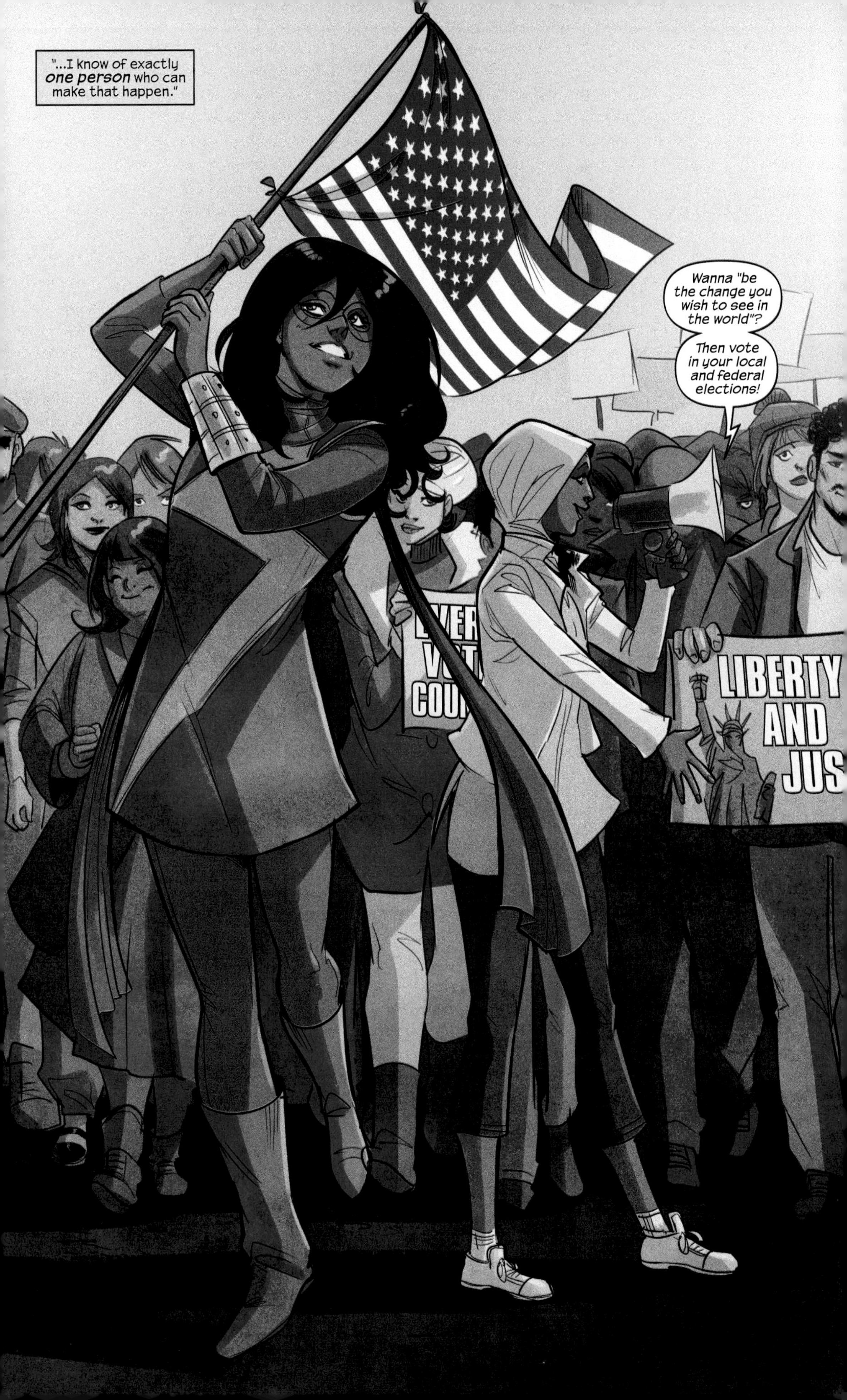

"...I know of exactly **one person** who can make that happen."
Wanna "be the change you wish to see in the world"?
Then vote in your local and federal elections!
LIBERTY AND JUS

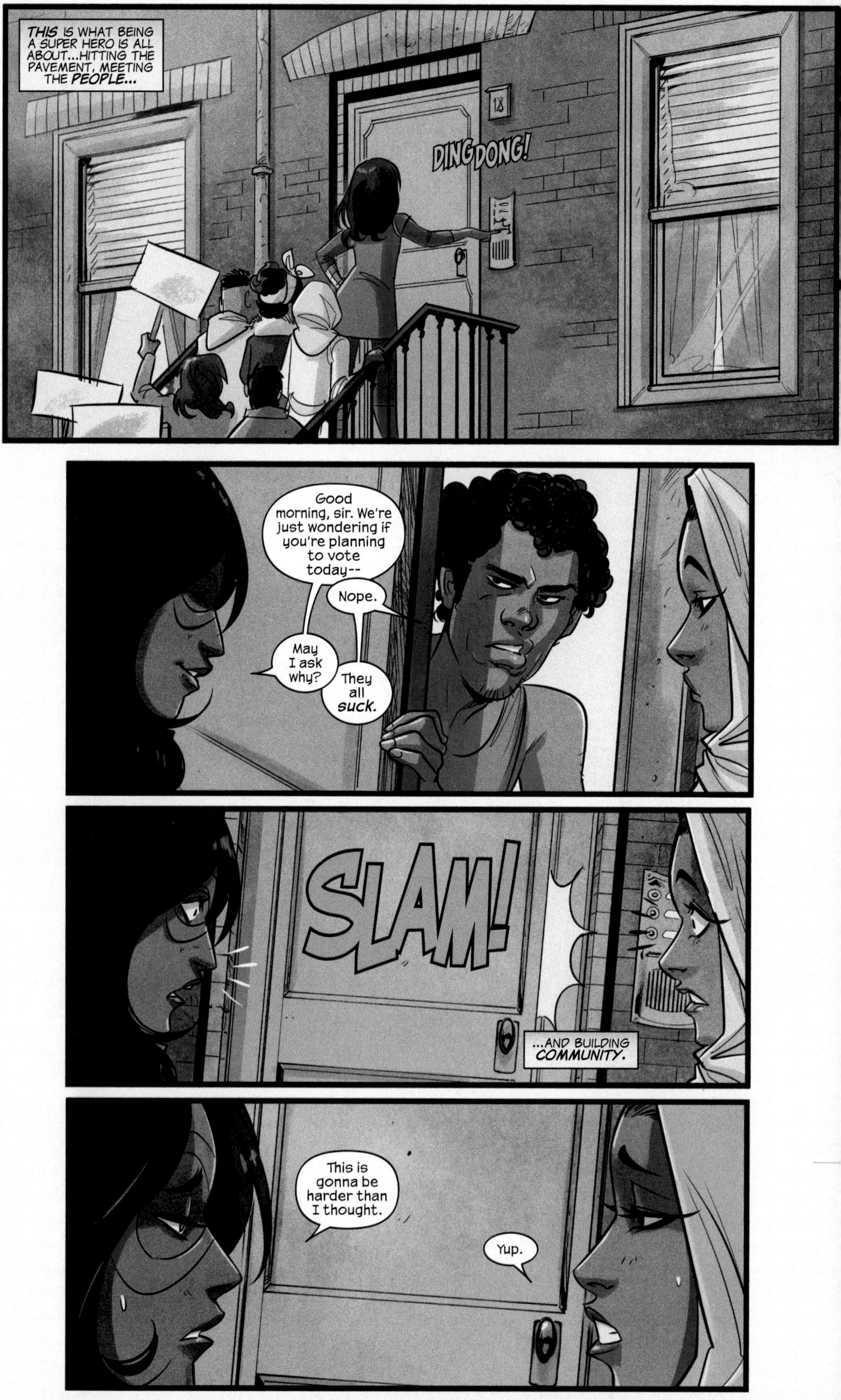
THIS IS WHAT BEING A SUPER HERO IS ALL ABOUT...HITTING THE PAVEMENT, MEETING THE PEOPLE...
DING DONG!
Good morning, sir. We're just wondering if you're planning to vote today--
Nope.
May I ask why?
They all suck.
SLAM!
...AND BUILDING COMMUNITY.
This is gonna be harder than I thought.
Yup.

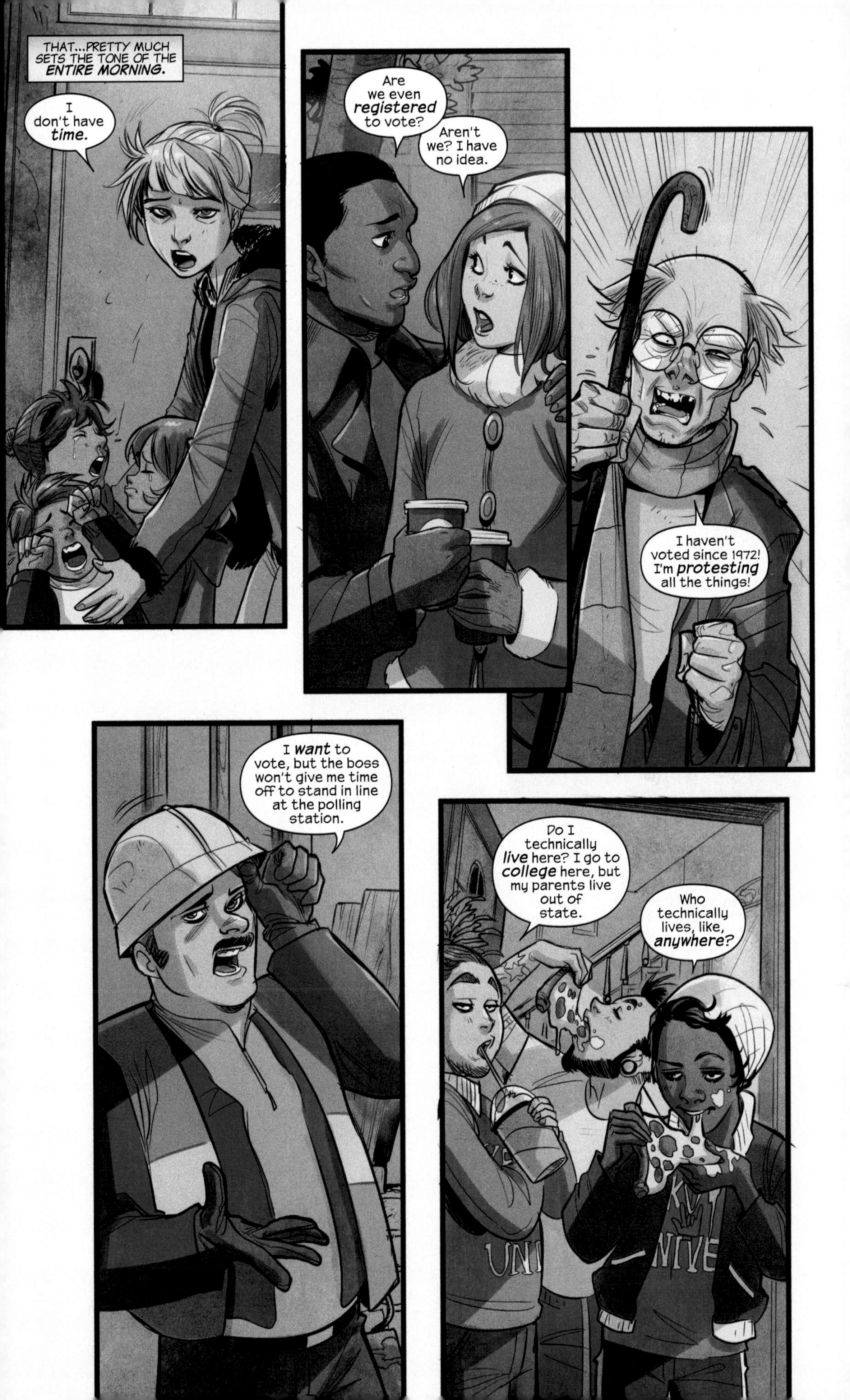
THAT...PRETTY MUCH SETS THE TONE OF THE ENTIRE MORNING.
I don't have time.
Are we even registered to vote?
Aren't we? I have no idea.
I haven't voted since 1972! I'm protesting all the things!
I want to vote, but the boss won't give me time off to stand in line at the polling station.
Do I technically live here? I go to college here, but my parents live out of state.
Who technically lives, like, anywhere?

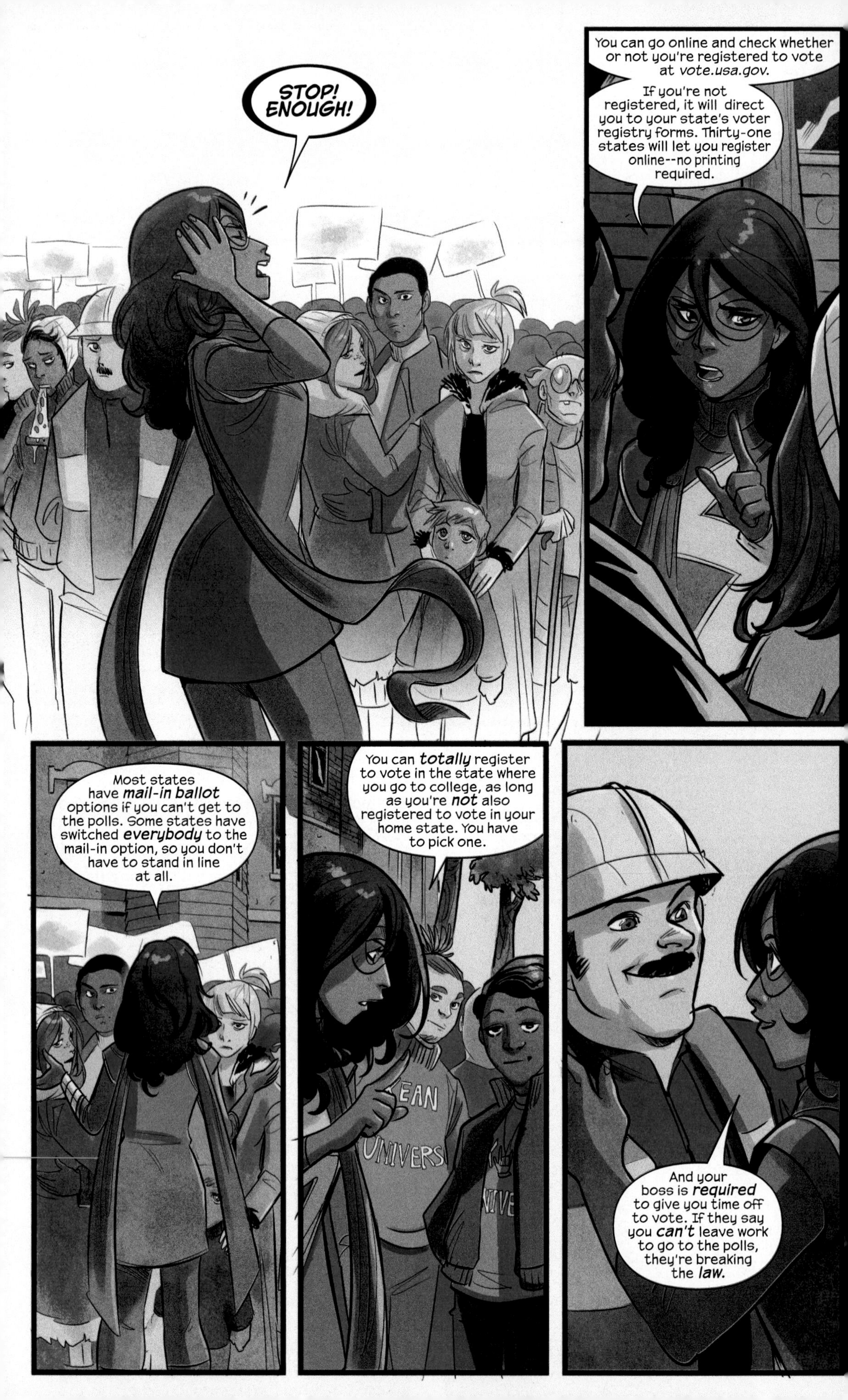
STOP! ENOUGH!
You can go online and check whether or not you're registered to vote at vote.usa.gov.
If you're not registered, it will direct you to your state's voter registry forms. Thirty-one states will let you register online--no printing required.
Most states have mail-in ballot options if you can't get to the polls. Some states have switched everybody to the mail-in option, so you don't have to stand in line at all.
You can totally register to vote in the state where you go to college, as long as you're not also registered to vote in your home state. You have to pick one.
And your boss is required to give you time off to vote. If they say you can't leave work to go to the polls, they're breaking the law.

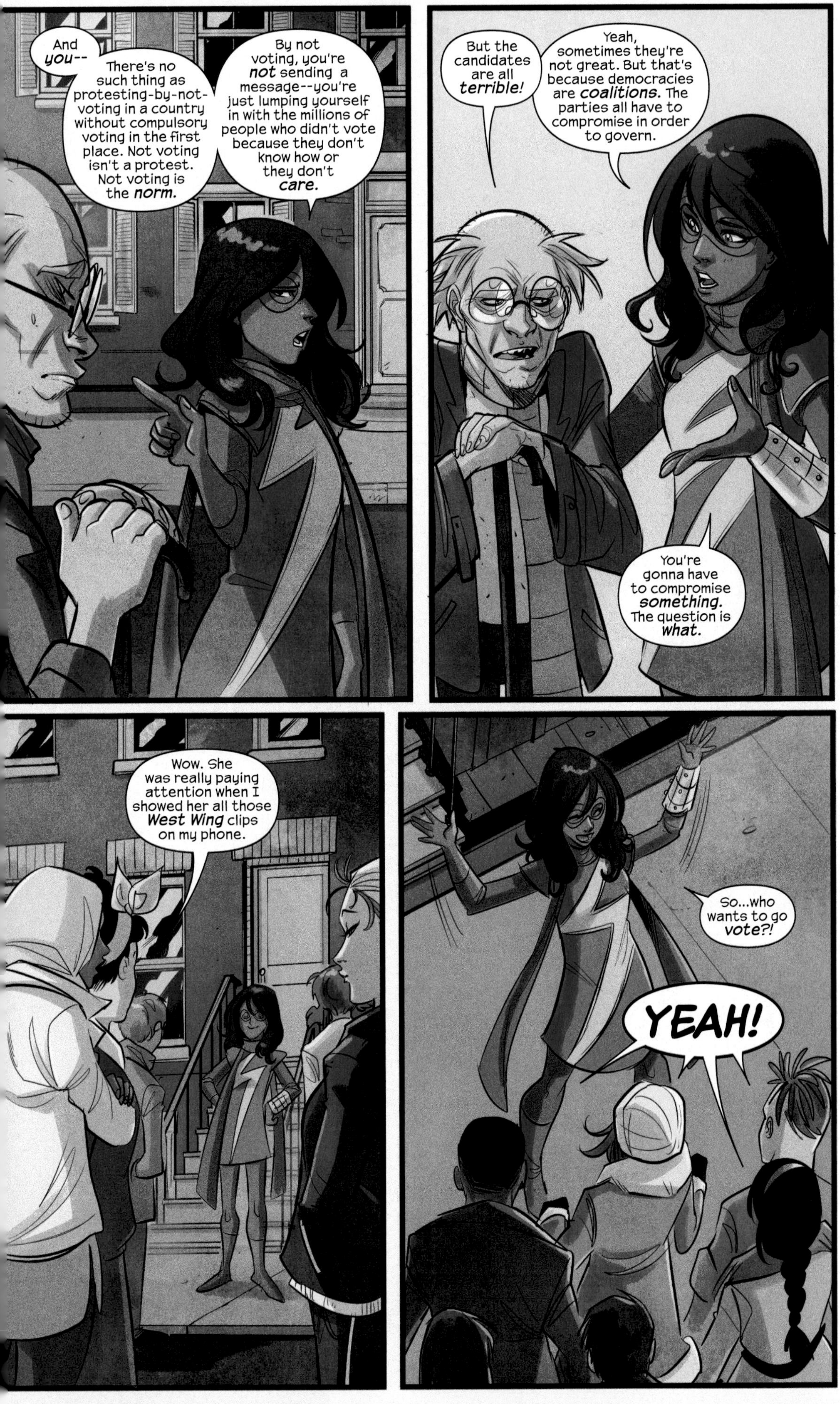
And you--
There's no such thing as protesting-by-not-voting in a country without compulsory voting in the first place. Not voting isn't a protest. Not voting is the norm.
By not voting, you're not sending a message--you're just lumping yourself in with the millions of people who didn't vote because they don't know how or they don't care.
But the candidates are all terrible!
Yeah, sometimes they're not great. But that's because democracies are coalitions. The parties all have to compromise in order to govern.
You're gonna have to compromise something. The question is what.
Wow. She was really paying attention when I showed her all those West Wing clips on my phone.
So...who wants to go vote?!
YEAH!

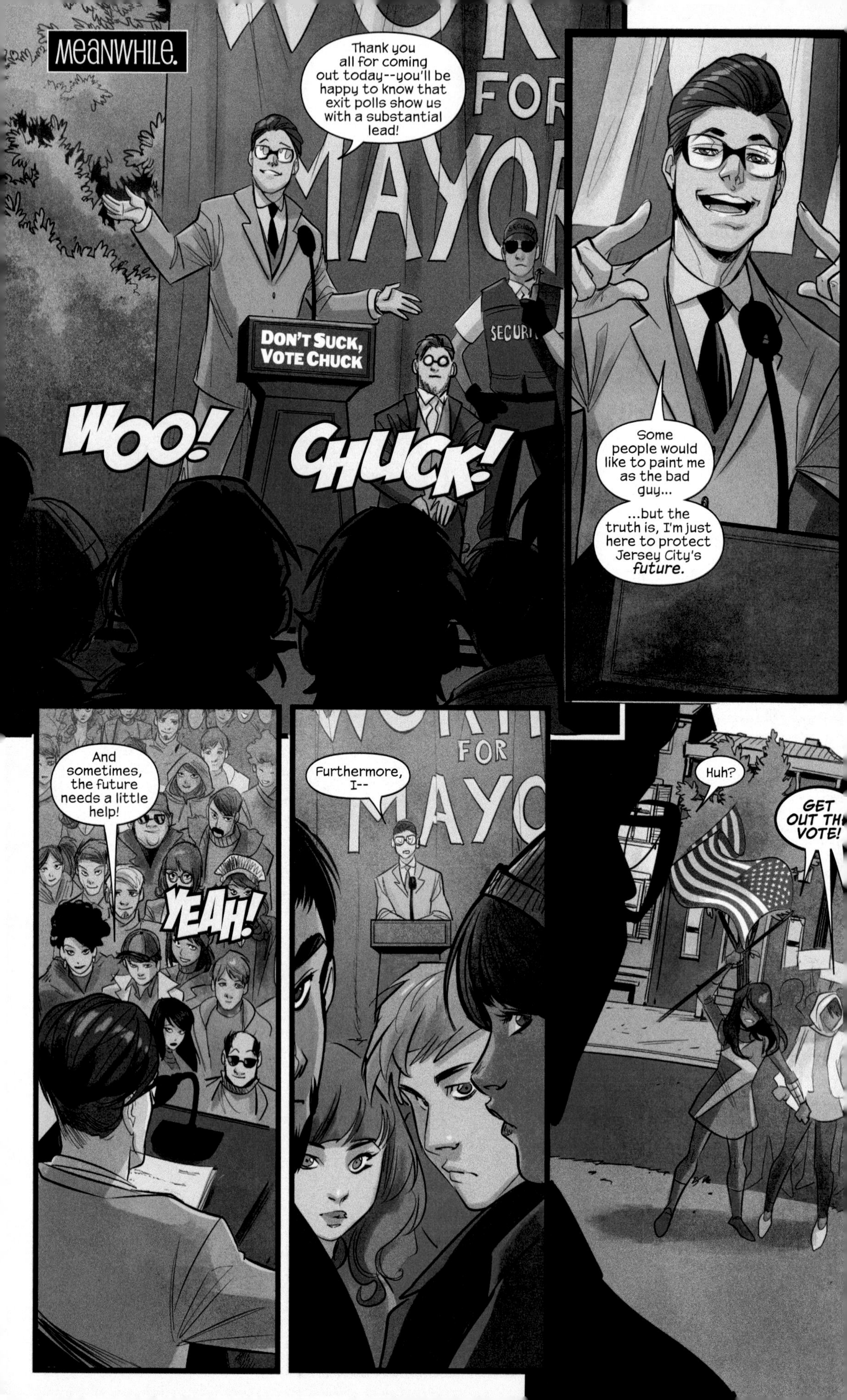
MEANWHILE.
Thank you all for coming out today--you'll be happy to know that exit polls show us with a substantial lead!
DON'T SUCK, VOTE CHUCK
WOO!
CHUCK!
Some people would like to paint me as the bad guy...
...but the truth is, I'm just here to protect Jersey City's *future.*
And sometimes, the future needs a little help!
YEAH!
Furthermore, I--
Huh?
GET OUT TH VOTE!

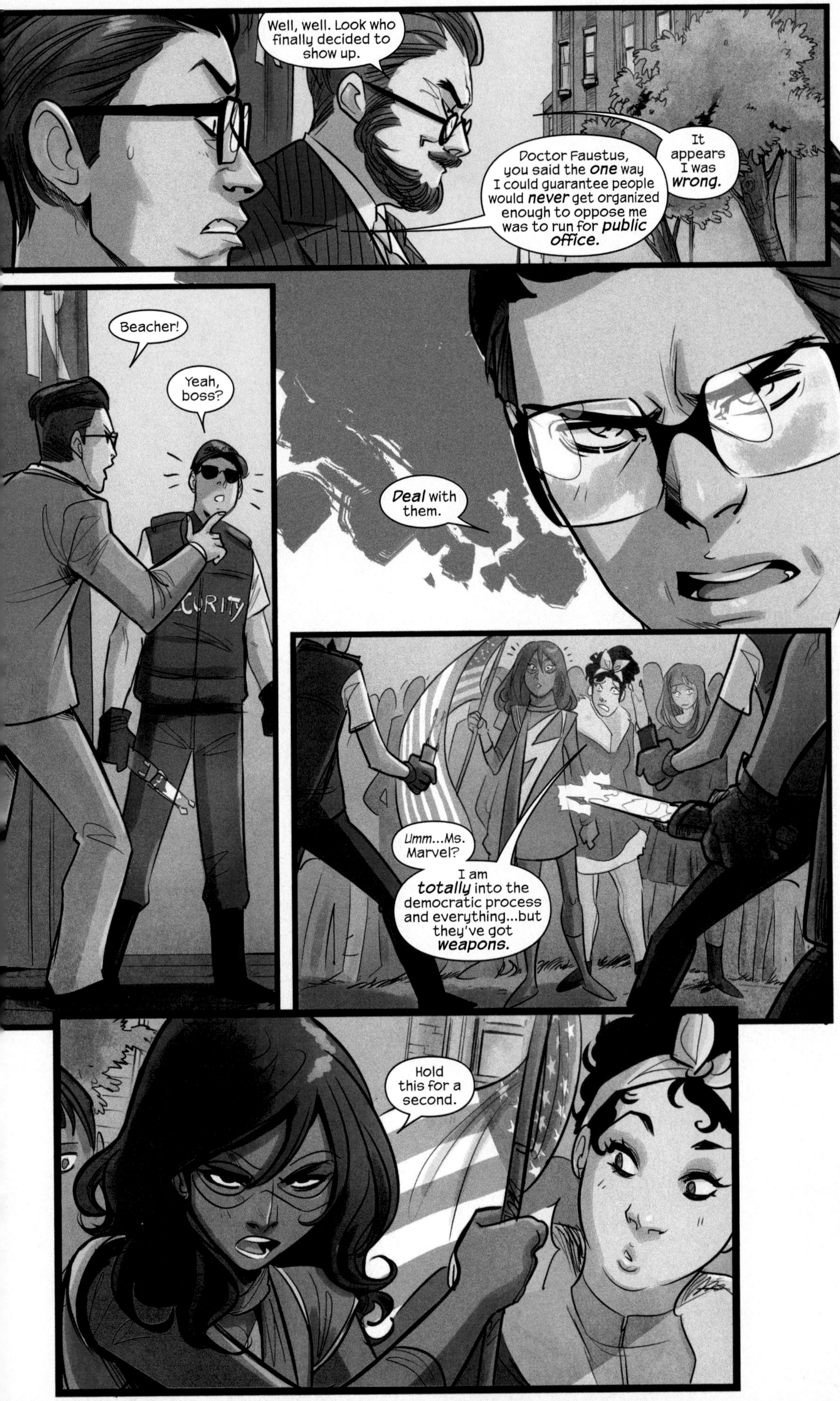
Well, well. Look who finally decided to show up.
It appears I was wrong.
Doctor Faustus, you said the one way I could guarantee people would never get organized enough to oppose me was to run for public office.
Beacher!
Yeah, boss?
Deal with them.
Umm...Ms. Marvel?
I am totally into the democratic process and everything...but they've got weapons.
Hold this for a second.

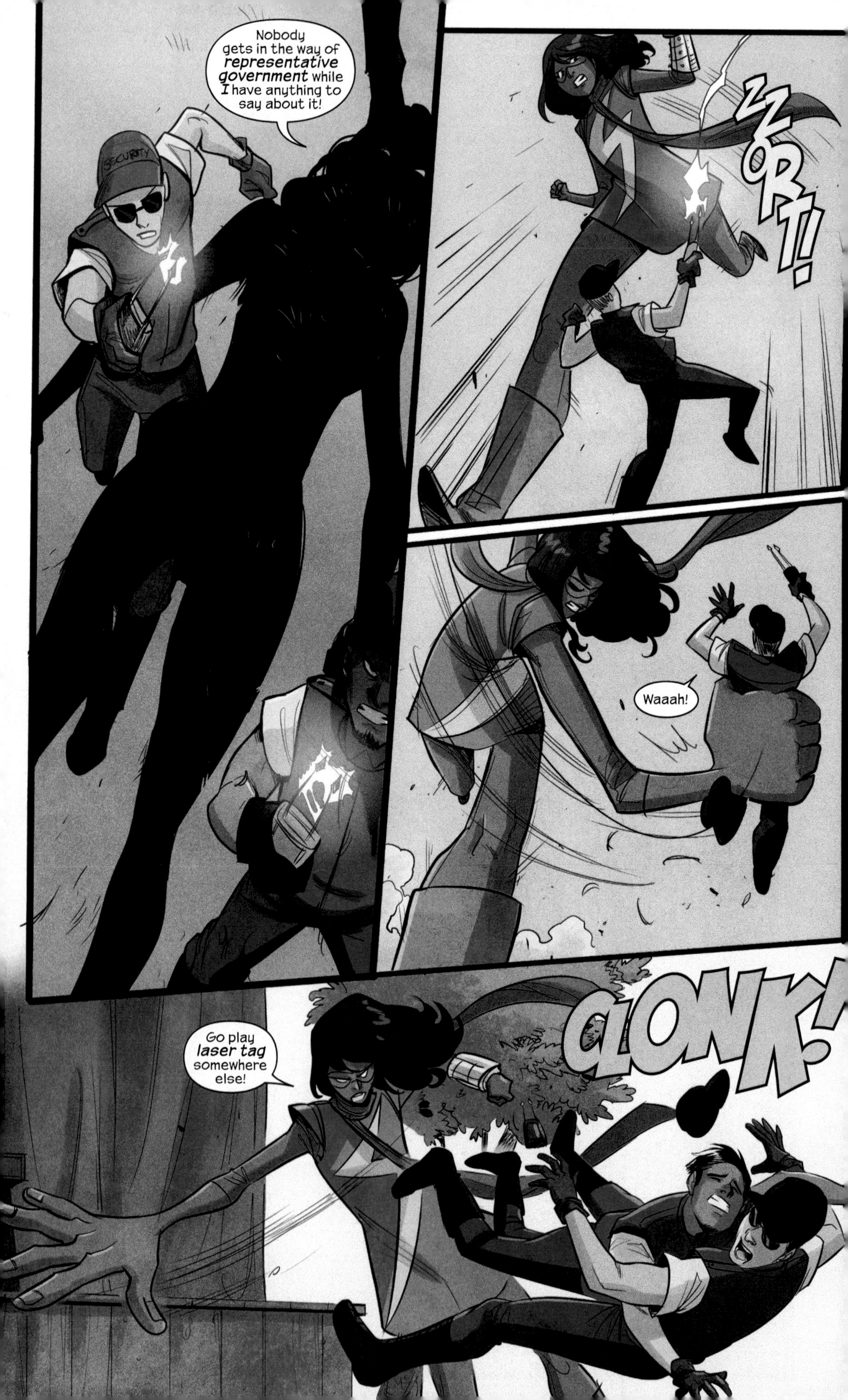
Nobody gets in the way of *representative government* while *I* have anything to say about it!
ZZORT!!
Waaah!
CLONK!
Go play *laser tag* somewhere else!

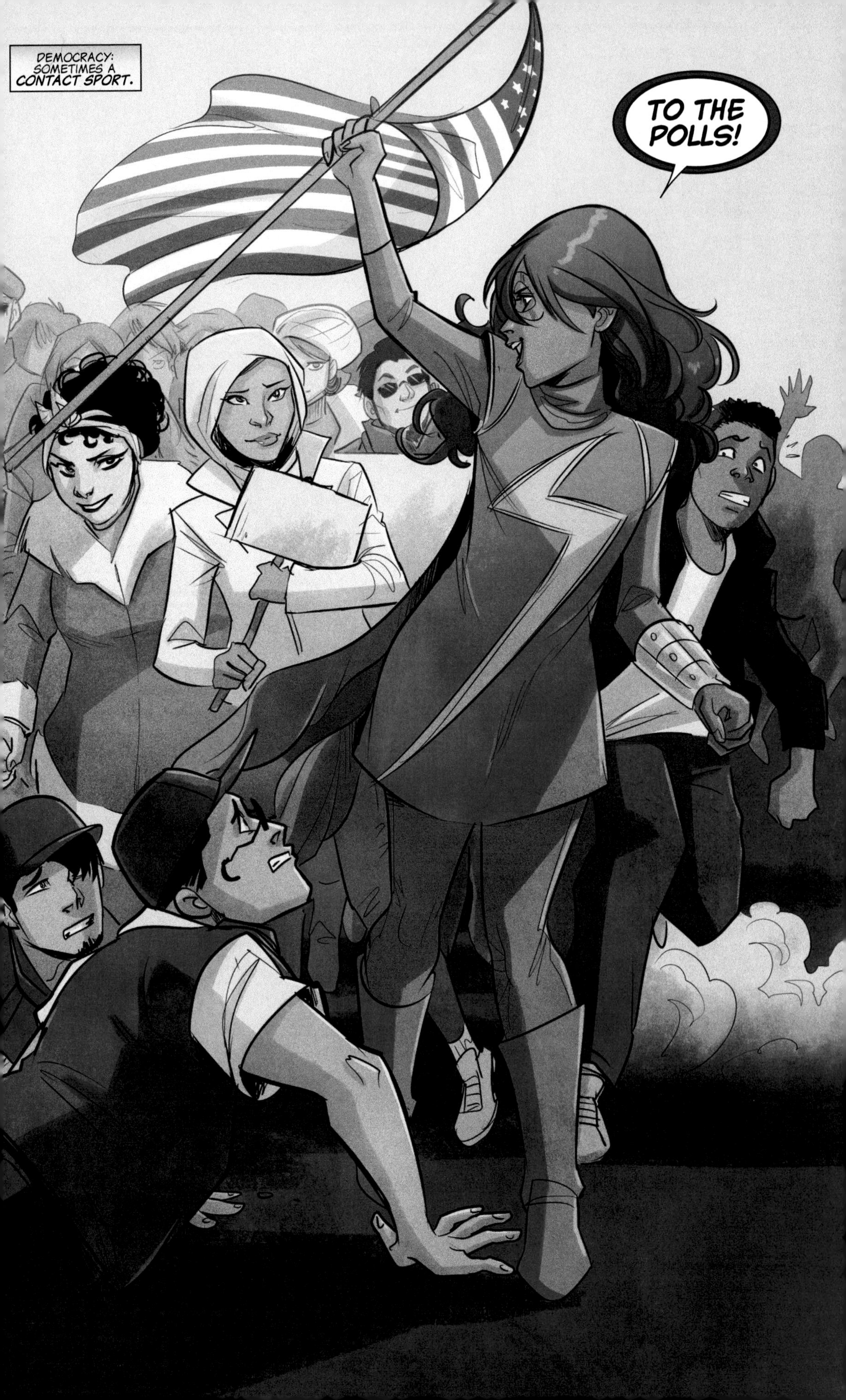
DEMOCRACY: SOMETIMES A CONTACT SPORT.
TO THE POLLS!

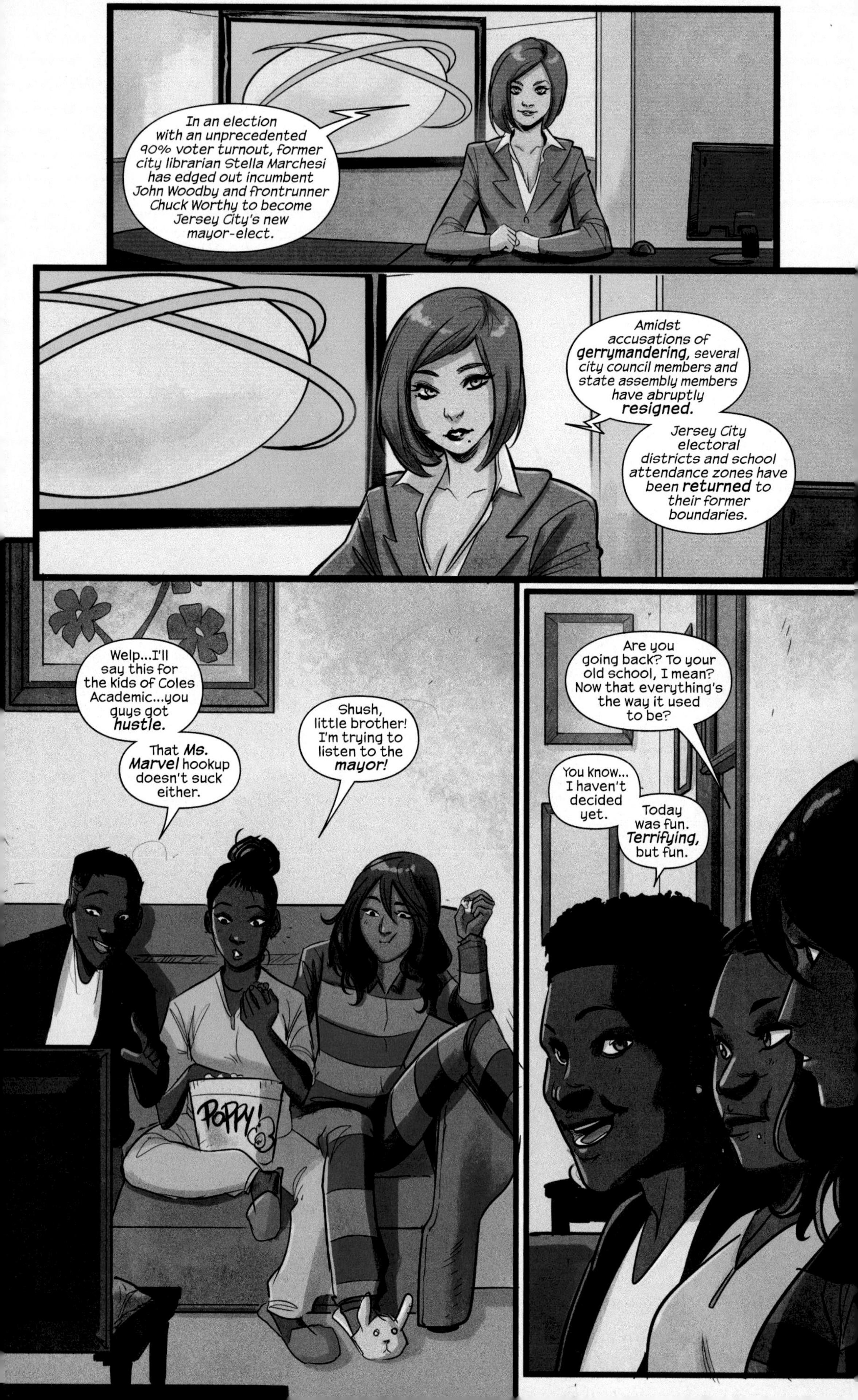
In an election with an unprecedented 90% voter turnout, former city librarian Stella Marchesi has edged out incumbent John Woodby and frontrunner Chuck Worthy to become Jersey City's new mayor-elect.
Amidst accusations of gerrymandering, several city council members and state assembly members have abruptly resigned.
Jersey City electoral districts and school attendance zones have been returned to their former boundaries.
Welp...I'll say this for the kids of Coles Academic...you guys got hustle.
That Ms. Marvel hookup doesn't suck either.
Shush, little brother! I'm trying to listen to the mayor!
POPPY!
Are you going back? To your old school, I mean? Now that everything's the way it used to be?
You know... I haven't decided yet.
Today was fun. Terrifying, but fun.

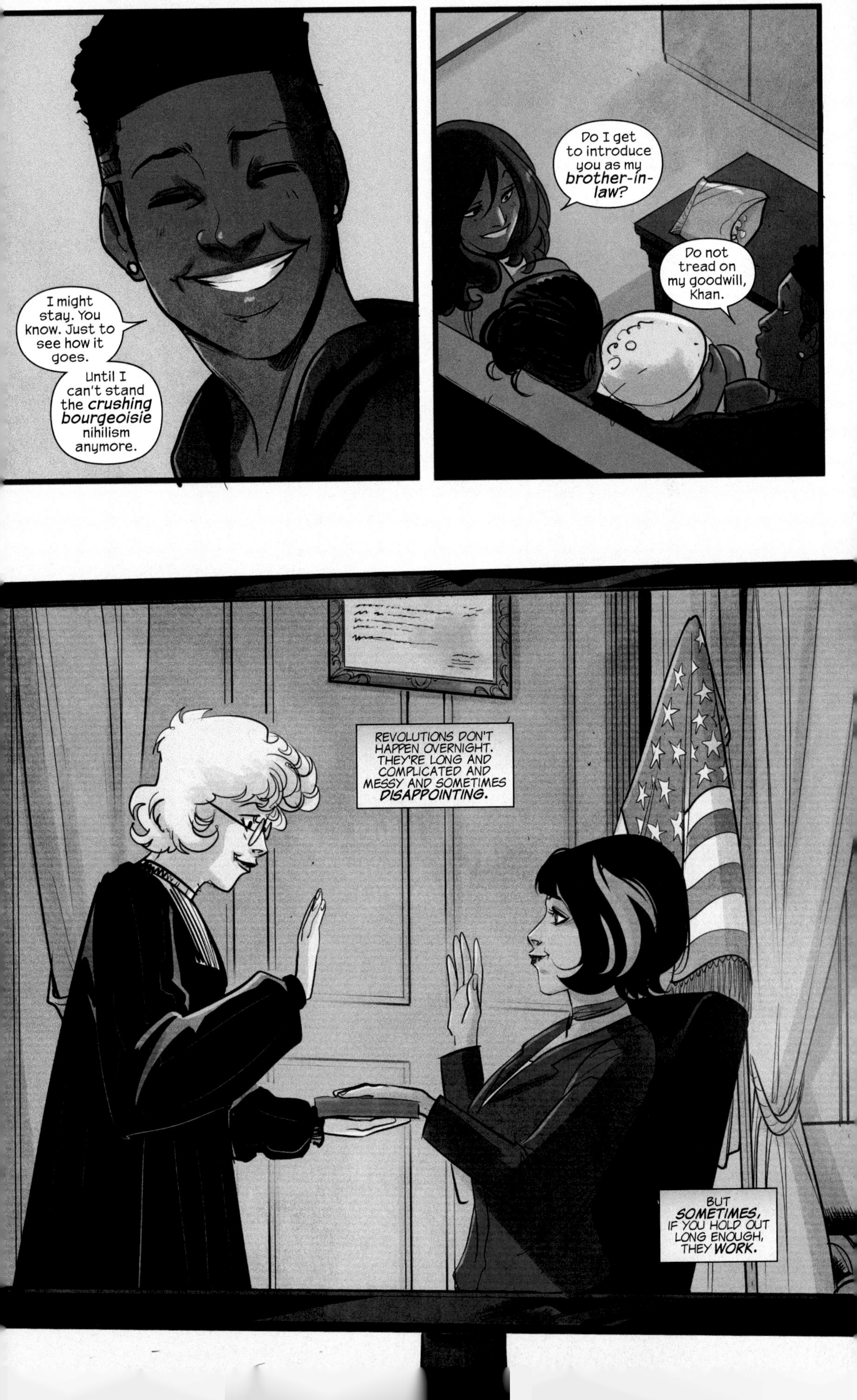
I might stay. You know. Just to see how it goes.
Until I can't stand the *crushing bourgeoisie* nihilism anymore.
Do I get to introduce you as my *brother-in-law?*
Do not tread on my goodwill, Khan.
REVOLUTIONS DON'T HAPPEN OVERNIGHT. THEY'RE LONG AND COMPLICATED AND MESSY AND SOMETIMES *DISAPPOINTING.*
BUT *SOMETIMES,* IF YOU HOLD OUT LONG ENOUGH, THEY *WORK.*

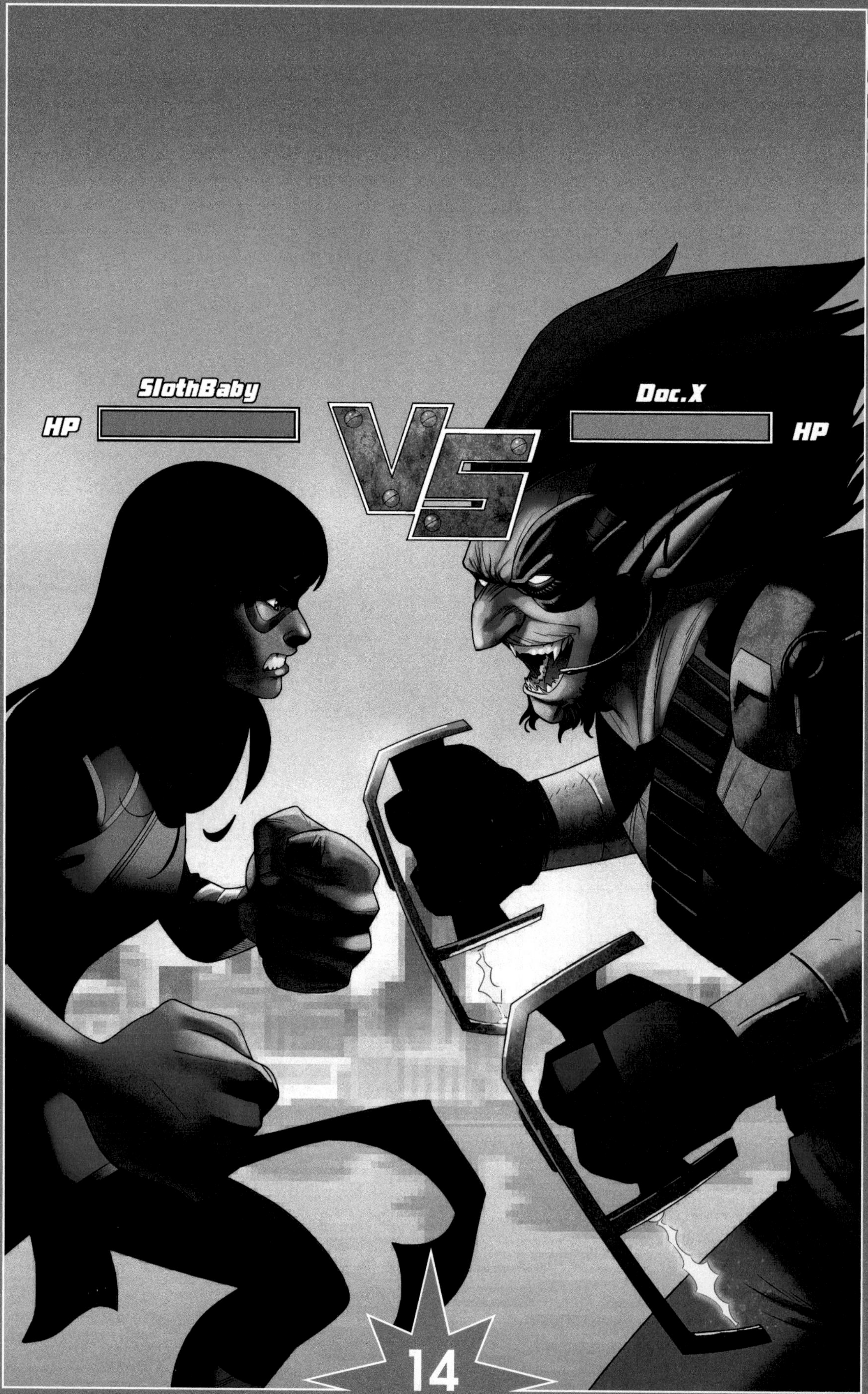
SlothBaby
HP
VS
Doc.X
HP
14

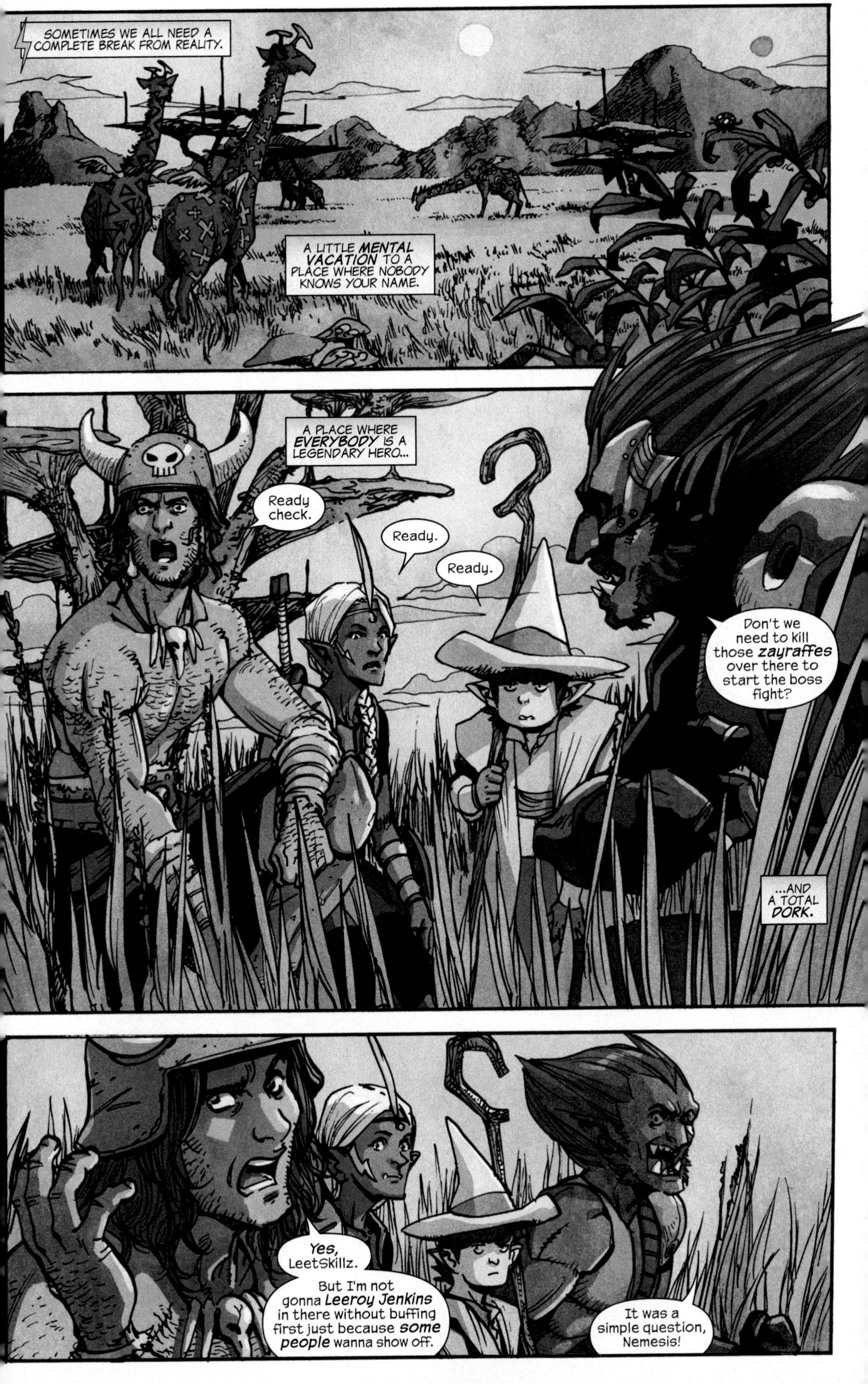
SOMETIMES WE ALL NEED A COMPLETE BREAK FROM REALITY.
A LITTLE MENTAL VACATION TO A PLACE WHERE NOBODY KNOWS YOUR NAME.
A PLACE WHERE EVERYBODY IS A LEGENDARY HERO...
Ready check.
Ready.
Ready.
Don't we need to kill those zayraffes over there to start the boss fight?
...AND A TOTAL DORK.
Yes, LeetSkillz.
But I'm not gonna Leeroy Jenkins in there without buffing first just because some people wanna show off.
It was a simple question, Nemesis!

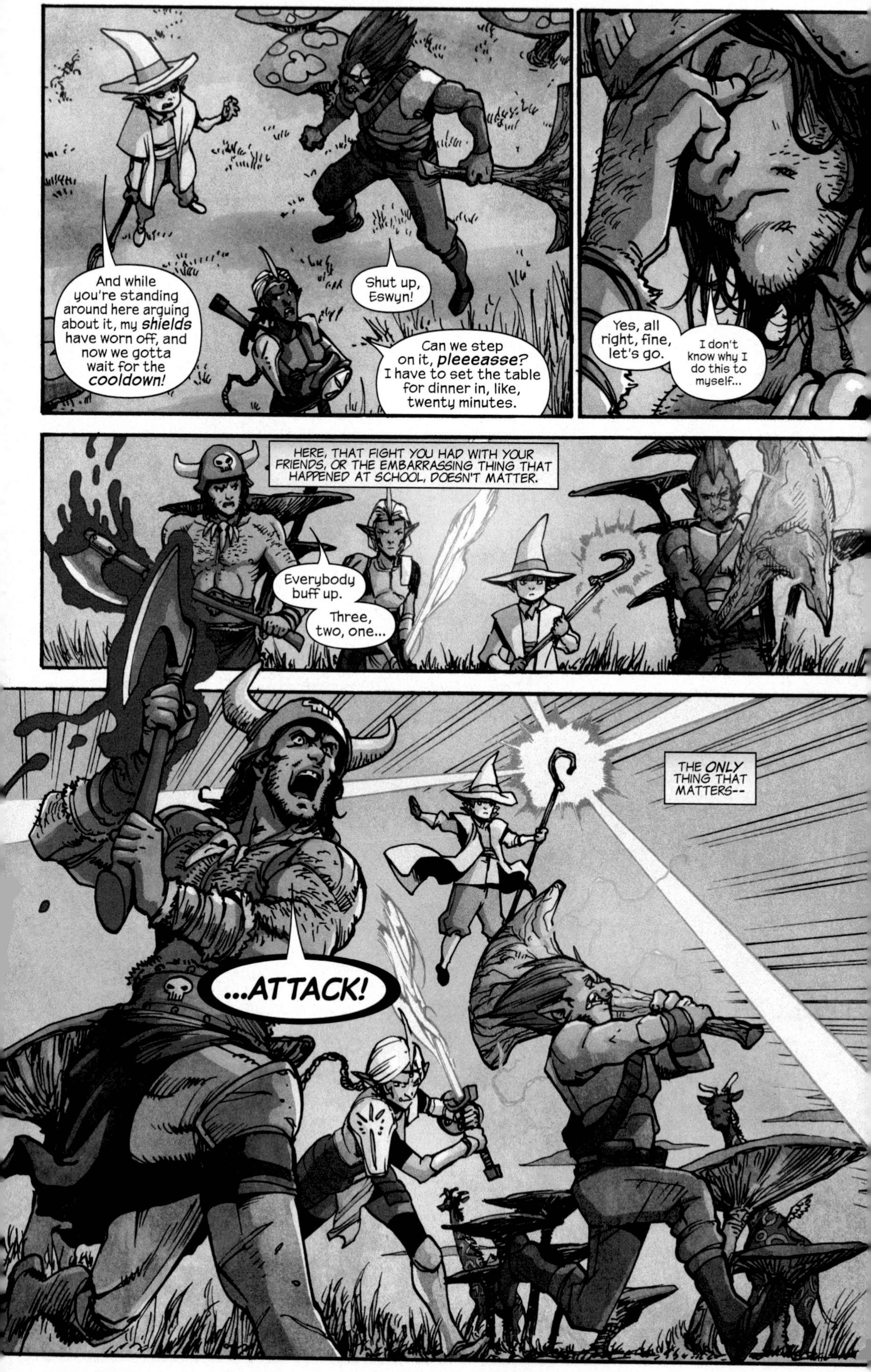
And while you're standing around here arguing about it, my *shields* have worn off, and now we gotta wait for the *cooldown*!
Shut up, Eswyn!
Can we step on it, ***pleeeasse?*** I have to set the table for dinner in, like, twenty minutes.
Yes, all right, fine, let's go.
I don't know why I do this to myself...
HERE, THAT FIGHT YOU HAD WITH YOUR FRIENDS, OR THE EMBARRASSING THING THAT HAPPENED AT SCHOOL, DOESN'T MATTER.
Everybody buff up.
Three, two, one...
THE *ONLY* THING THAT MATTERS--
...ATTACK!

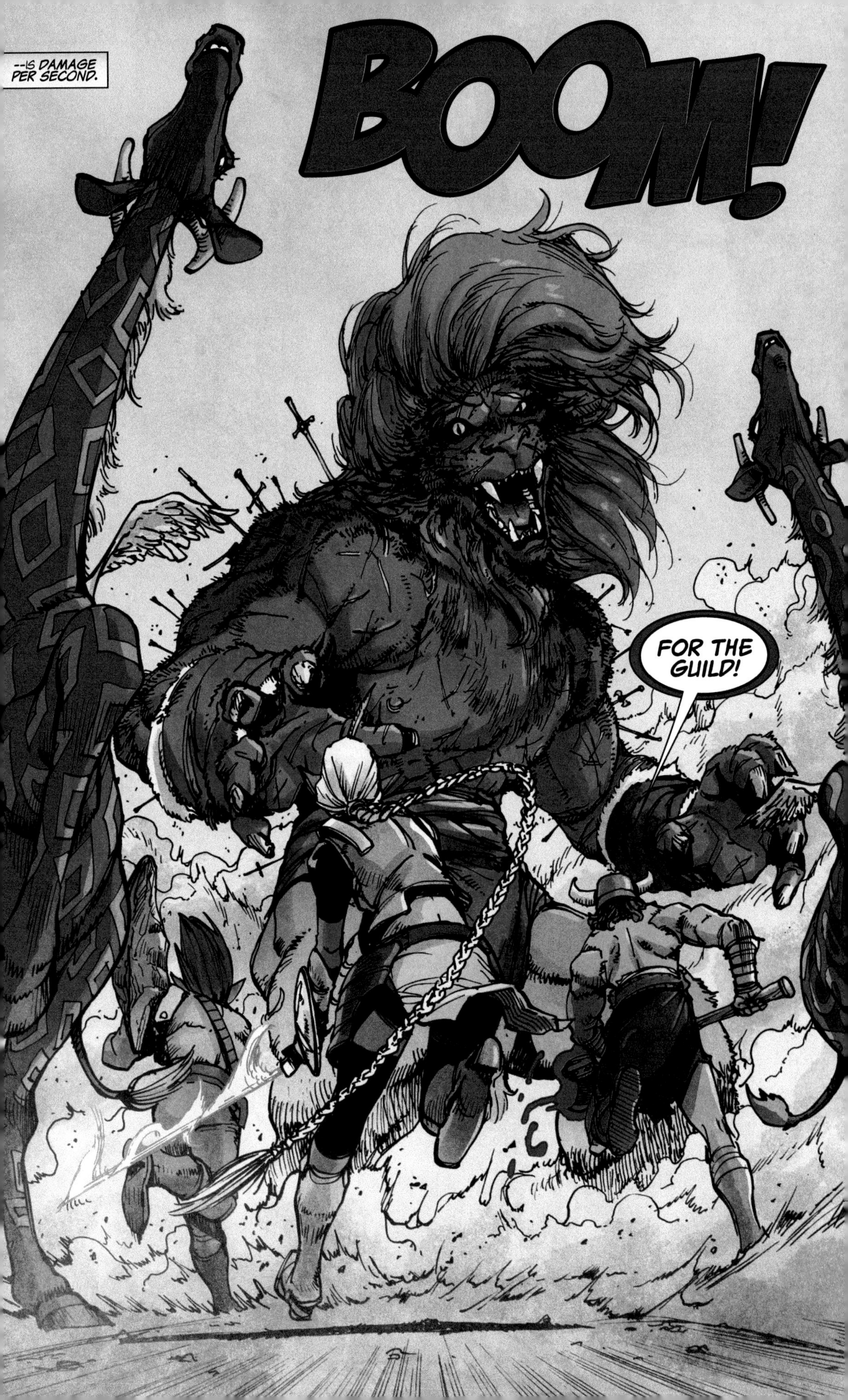
--IS DAMAGE PER SECOND.
BOOM!
FOR THE GUILD!

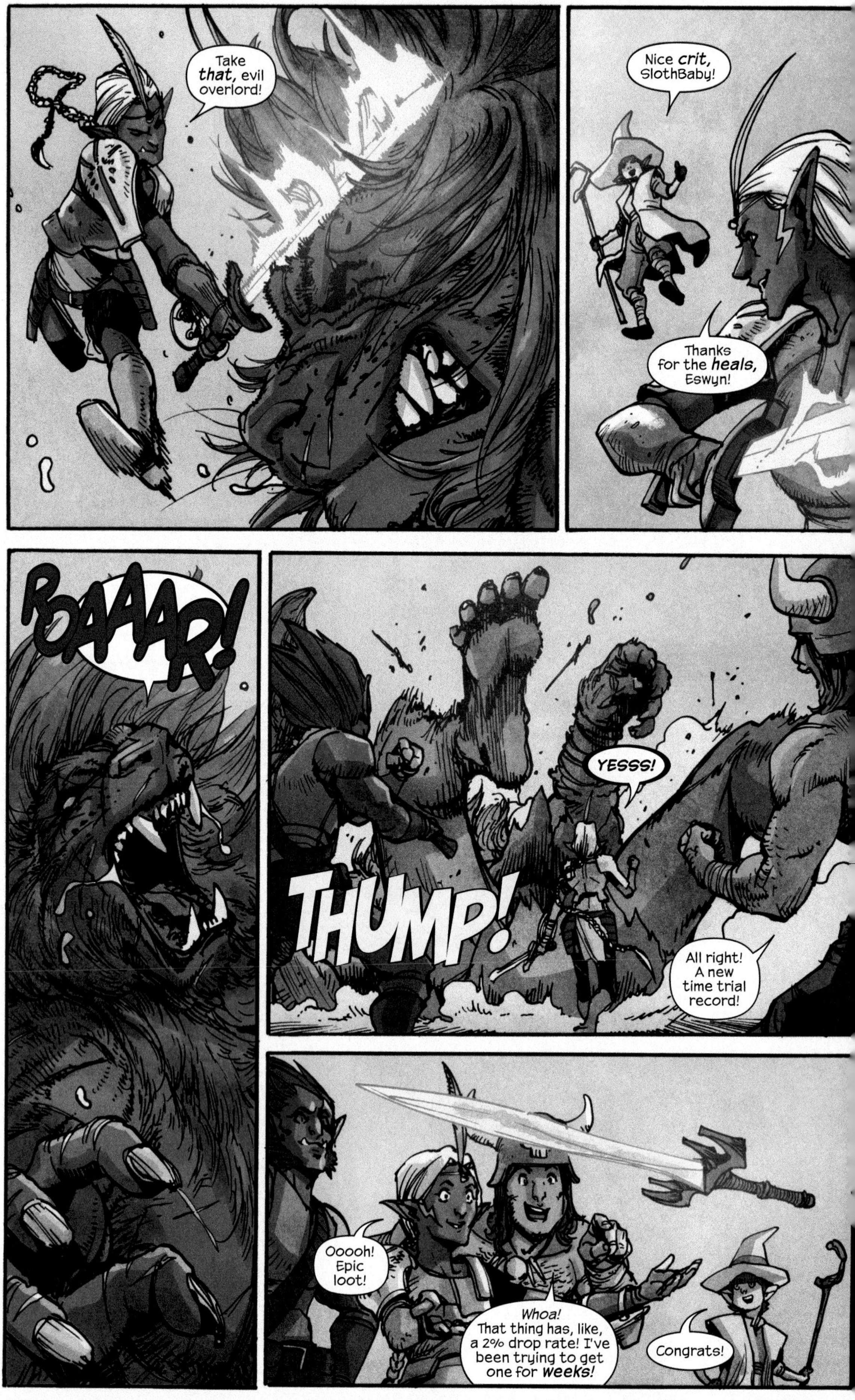
Take that, evil overlord!
Nice crit, SlothBaby!
Thanks for the heals, Eswyn!
ROAAAR!
YESSS!
THUMP!
All right! A new time trial record!
Ooooh! Epic loot!
Whoa! That thing has, like, a 2% drop rate! I've been trying to get one for weeks!
Congrats!

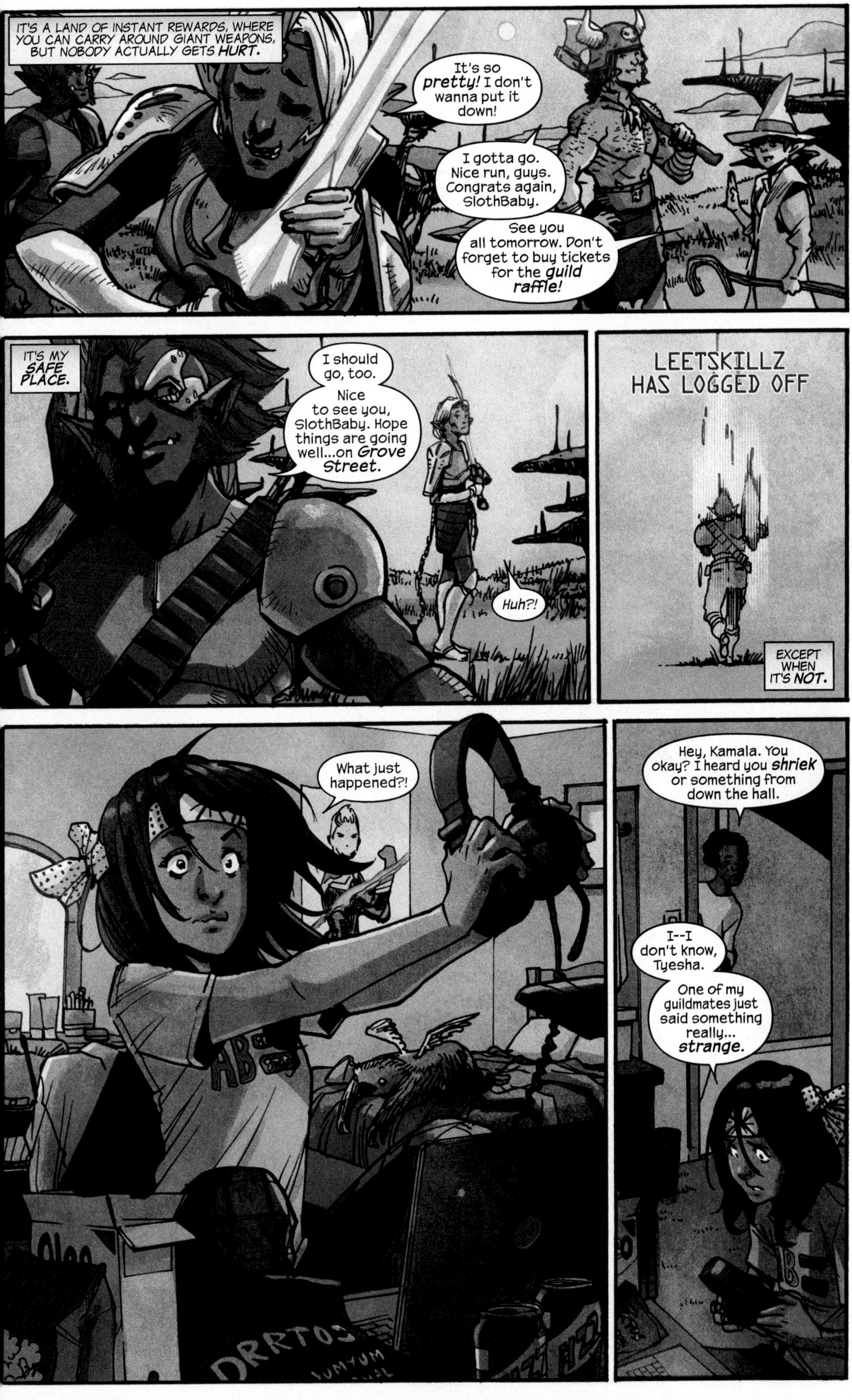
IT'S A LAND OF INSTANT REWARDS, WHERE YOU CAN CARRY AROUND GIANT WEAPONS, BUT NOBODY ACTUALLY GETS HURT.
It's so pretty! I don't wanna put it down!
I gotta go. Nice run, guys. Congrats again, SlothBaby.
See you all tomorrow. Don't forget to buy tickets for the guild raffle!
IT'S MY SAFE PLACE.
I should go, too.
Nice to see you, SlothBaby. Hope things are going well...on Grove Street.
Huh?!
LEETSKILLZ HAS LOGGED OFF
EXCEPT WHEN IT'S NOT.
What just happened?!
Hey, Kamala. You okay? I heard you shriek or something from down the hall.
I--I don't know, Tyesha.
One of my guildmates just said something really... strange.

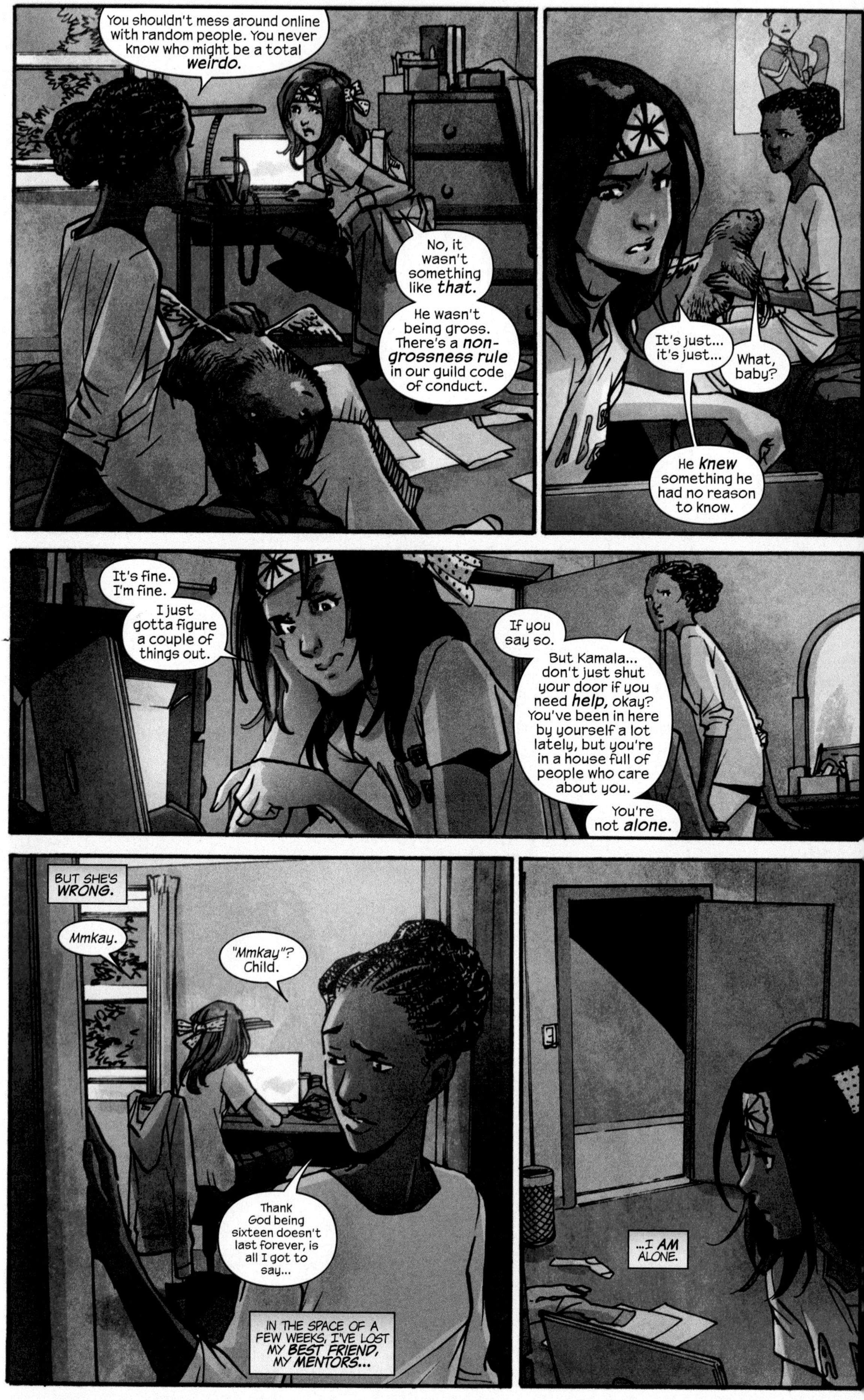
You shouldn't mess around online with random people. You never know who might be a total *weirdo.*
No, it wasn't something like *that.*
He wasn't being gross. There's a ***non-grossness rule*** in our guild code of conduct.
It's just... it's just...
What, baby?
He ***knew*** something he had no reason to know.
It's fine. I'm fine.
I just gotta figure a couple of things out.
If you say so.
But Kamala... don't just shut your door if you need ***help,*** okay? You've been in here by yourself a lot lately, but you're in a house full of people who care about you.
You're not ***alone.***
BUT SHE'S ***WRONG.***
Mmkay.
"Mmkay"? Child.
Thank God being sixteen doesn't last forever, is all I got to say...
IN THE SPACE OF A FEW WEEKS, I'VE LOST MY ***BEST FRIEND,*** MY ***MENTORS...***
...I ***AM*** ALONE.

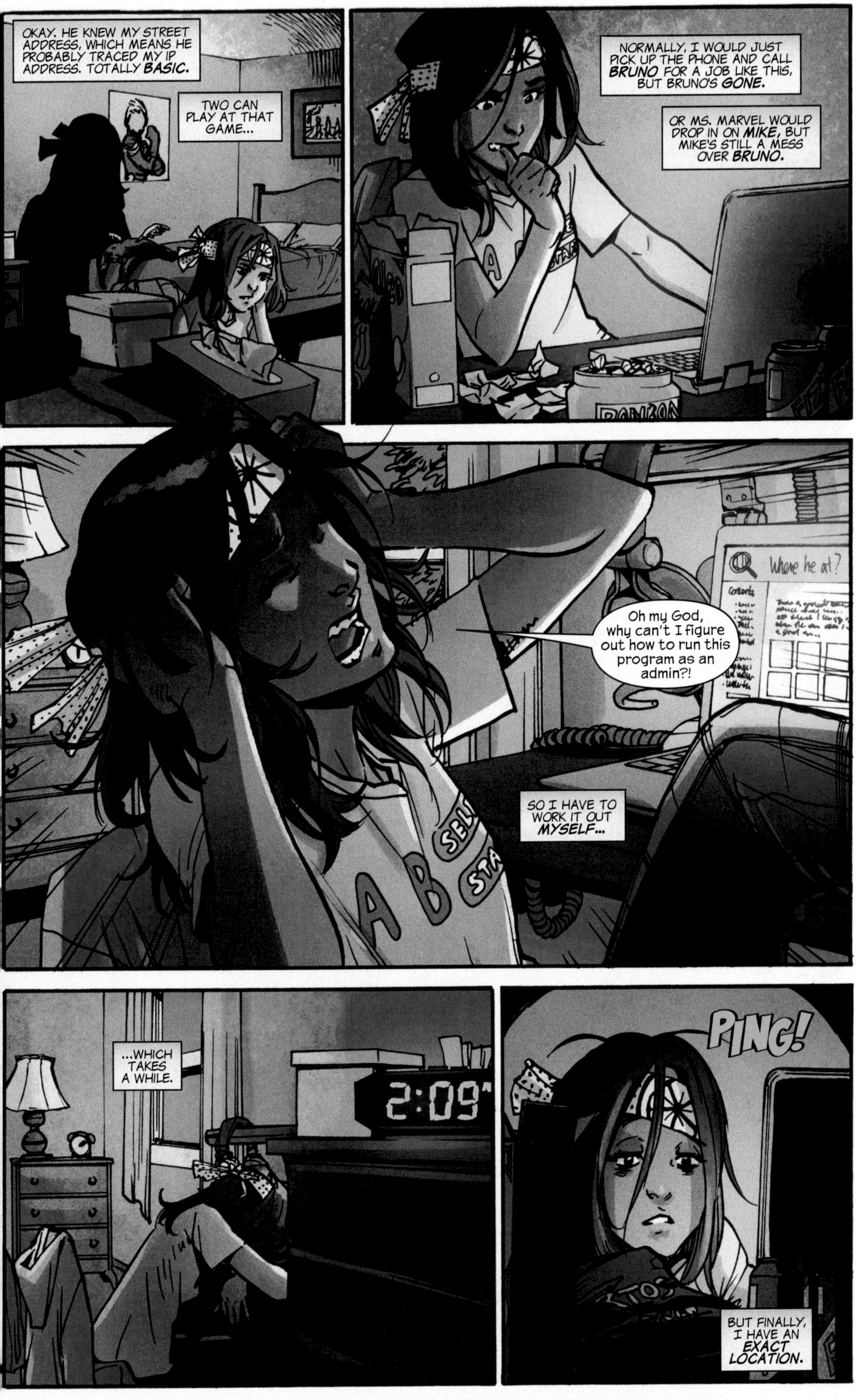
OKAY. HE KNEW MY STREET ADDRESS, WHICH MEANS HE PROBABLY TRACED MY IP ADDRESS. TOTALLY BASIC.
TWO CAN PLAY AT THAT GAME...
NORMALLY, I WOULD JUST PICK UP THE PHONE AND CALL BRUNO FOR A JOB LIKE THIS, BUT BRUNO'S GONE.
OR MS. MARVEL WOULD DROP IN ON MIKE, BUT MIKE'S STILL A MESS OVER BRUNO.
Where he at?
Oh my God, why can't I figure out how to run this program as an admin?!
SO I HAVE TO WORK IT OUT MYSELF...
...WHICH TAKES A WHILE.
2:09
PING!
BUT FINALLY, I HAVE AN EXACT LOCATION.

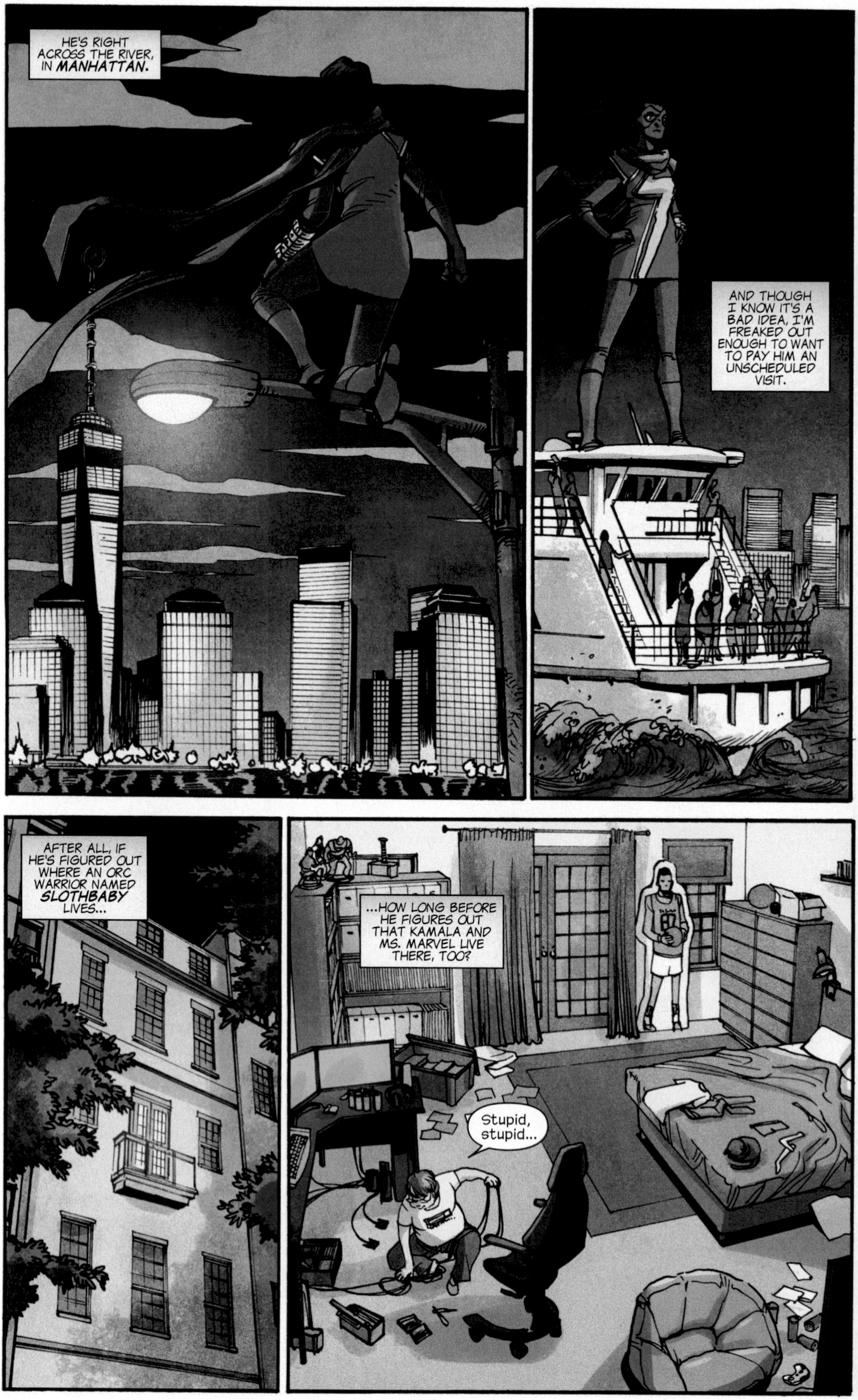
HE'S RIGHT ACROSS THE RIVER, IN MANHATTAN.
AND THOUGH I KNOW IT'S A BAD IDEA, I'M FREAKED OUT ENOUGH TO WANT TO PAY HIM AN UNSCHEDULED VISIT.
AFTER ALL, IF HE'S FIGURED OUT WHERE AN ORC WARRIOR NAMED SLOTHBABY LIVES...
...HOW LONG BEFORE HE FIGURES OUT THAT KAMALA AND MS. MARVEL LIVE THERE, TOO?
Stupid, stupid...

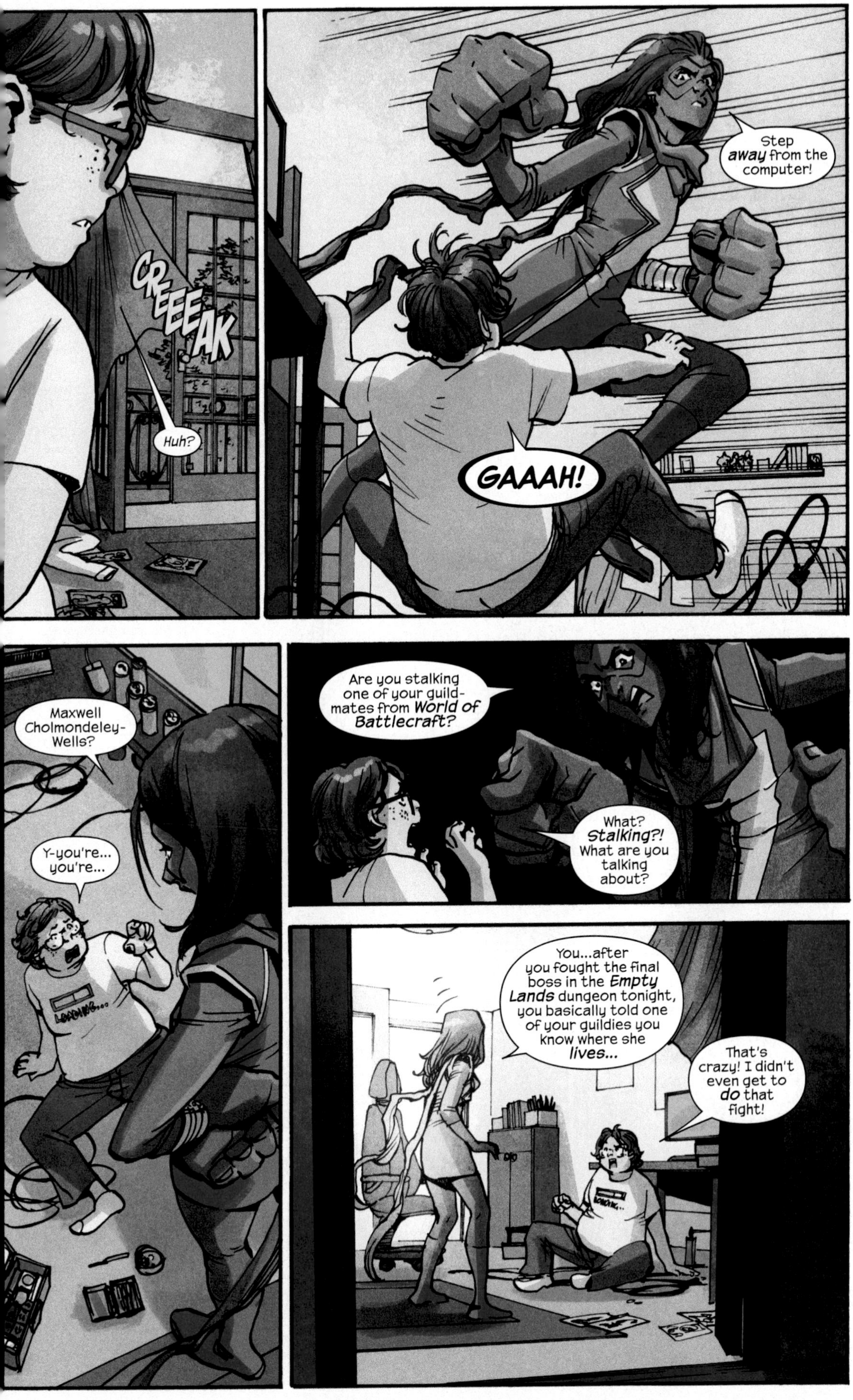
CREEEAK
Huh?
Step away from the computer!
GAAAH!
Maxwell Cholmondeley-Wells?
Y-you're... you're...
LOADING...
Are you stalking one of your guild-mates from World of Battlecraft?
What? Stalking?! What are you talking about?
You...after you fought the final boss in the Empty Lands dungeon tonight, you basically told one of your guildies you know where she lives...
That's crazy! I didn't even get to do that fight!

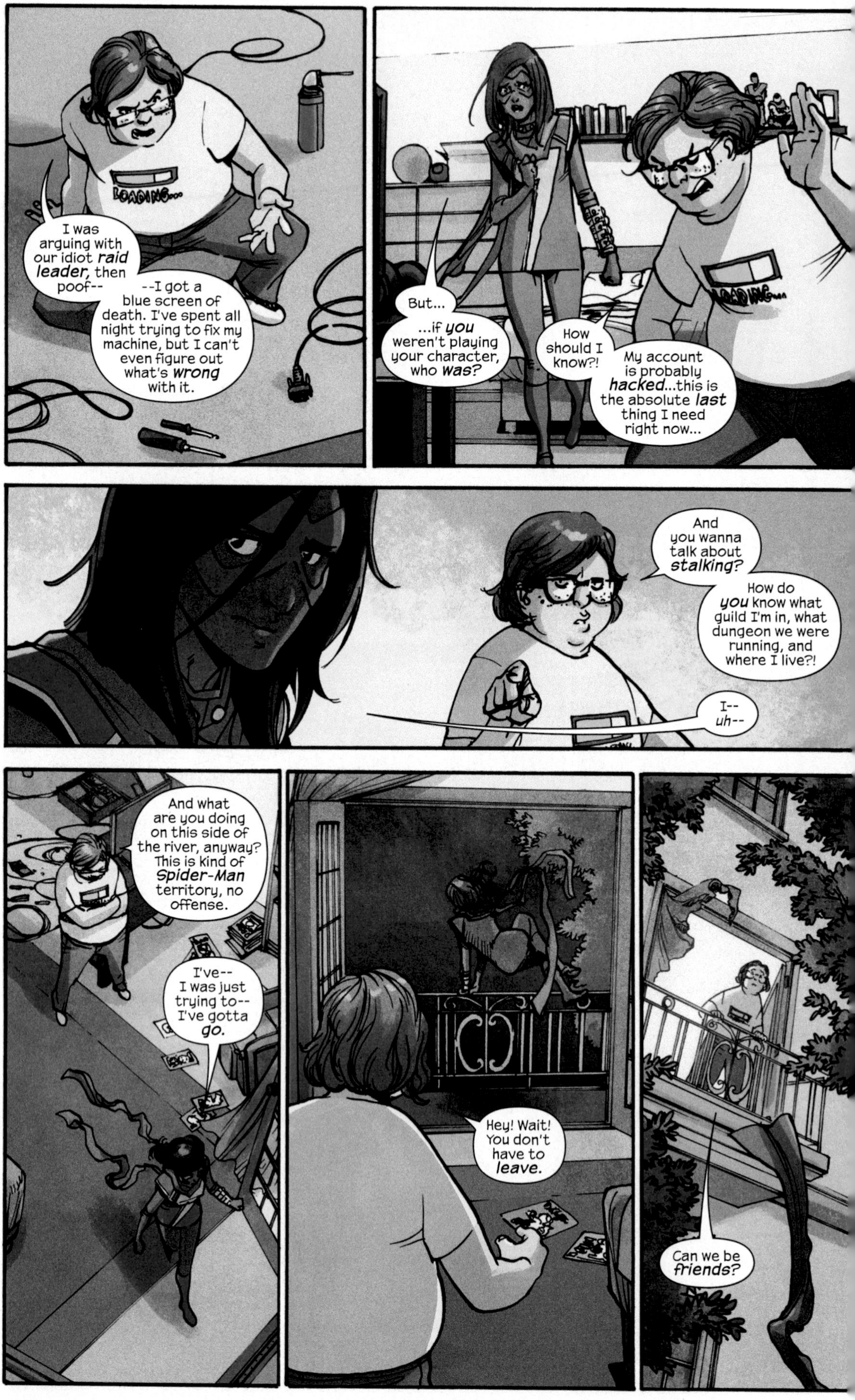
I was arguing with our idiot raid leader, then poof--
--I got a blue screen of death. I've spent all night trying to fix my machine, but I can't even figure out what's wrong with it.
LOADING...
But...
...if you weren't playing your character, who was?
How should I know?!
My account is probably hacked...this is the absolute last thing I need right now...
And you wanna talk about stalking?
How do you know what guild I'm in, what dungeon we were running, and where I live?!
I-- uh--
And what are you doing on this side of the river, anyway? This is kind of Spider-Man territory, no offense.
I've-- I was just trying to-- I've gotta go.
Hey! Wait! You don't have to leave.
Can we be friends?

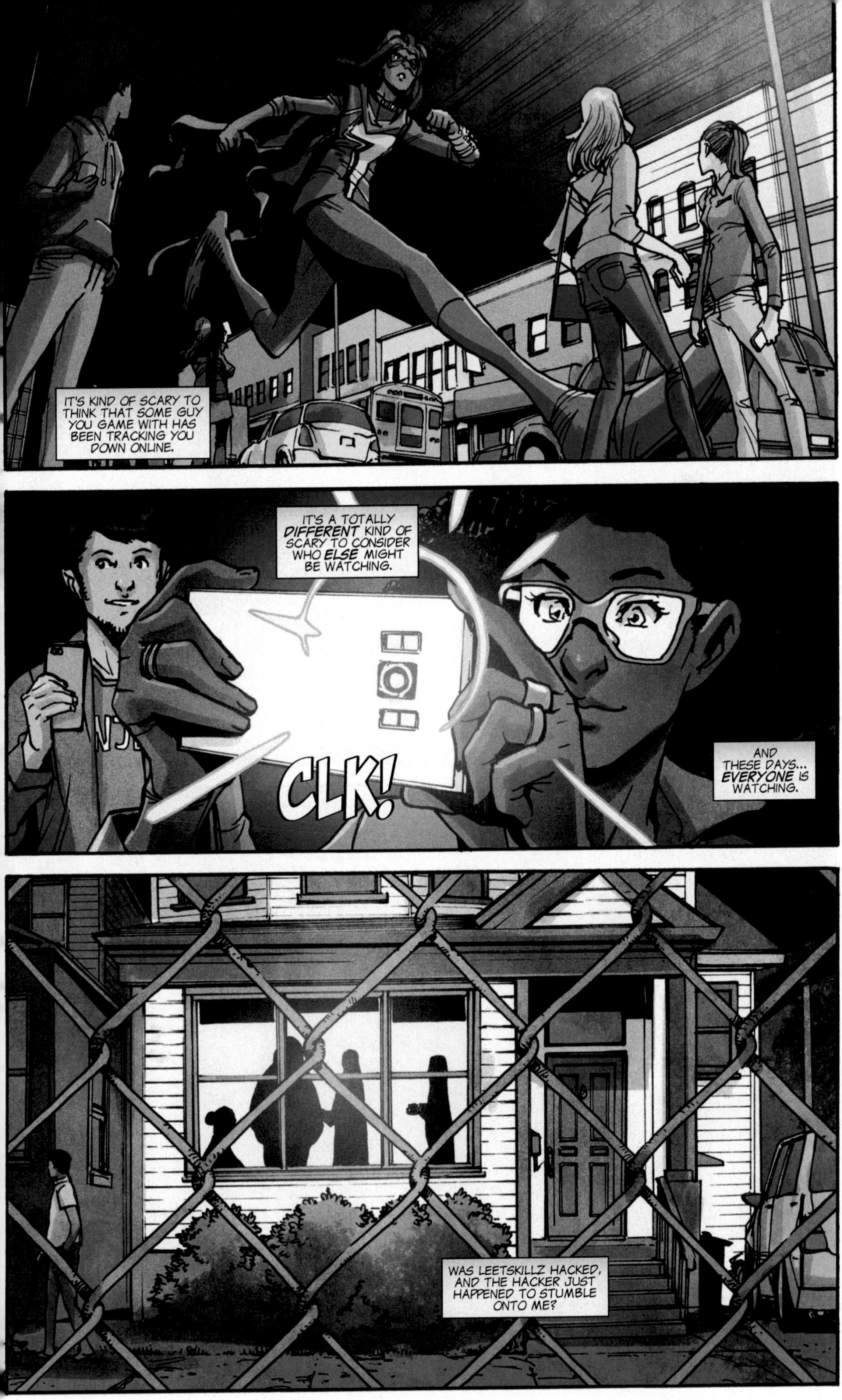

IT'S KIND OF SCARY TO THINK THAT SOME GUY YOU GAME WITH HAS BEEN TRACKING YOU DOWN ONLINE.
IT'S A TOTALLY DIFFERENT KIND OF SCARY TO CONSIDER WHO ELSE MIGHT BE WATCHING.
CLK!
AND THESE DAYS... EVERYONE IS WATCHING.
WAS LEETSKILLZ HACKED, AND THE HACKER JUST HAPPENED TO STUMBLE ONTO ME?

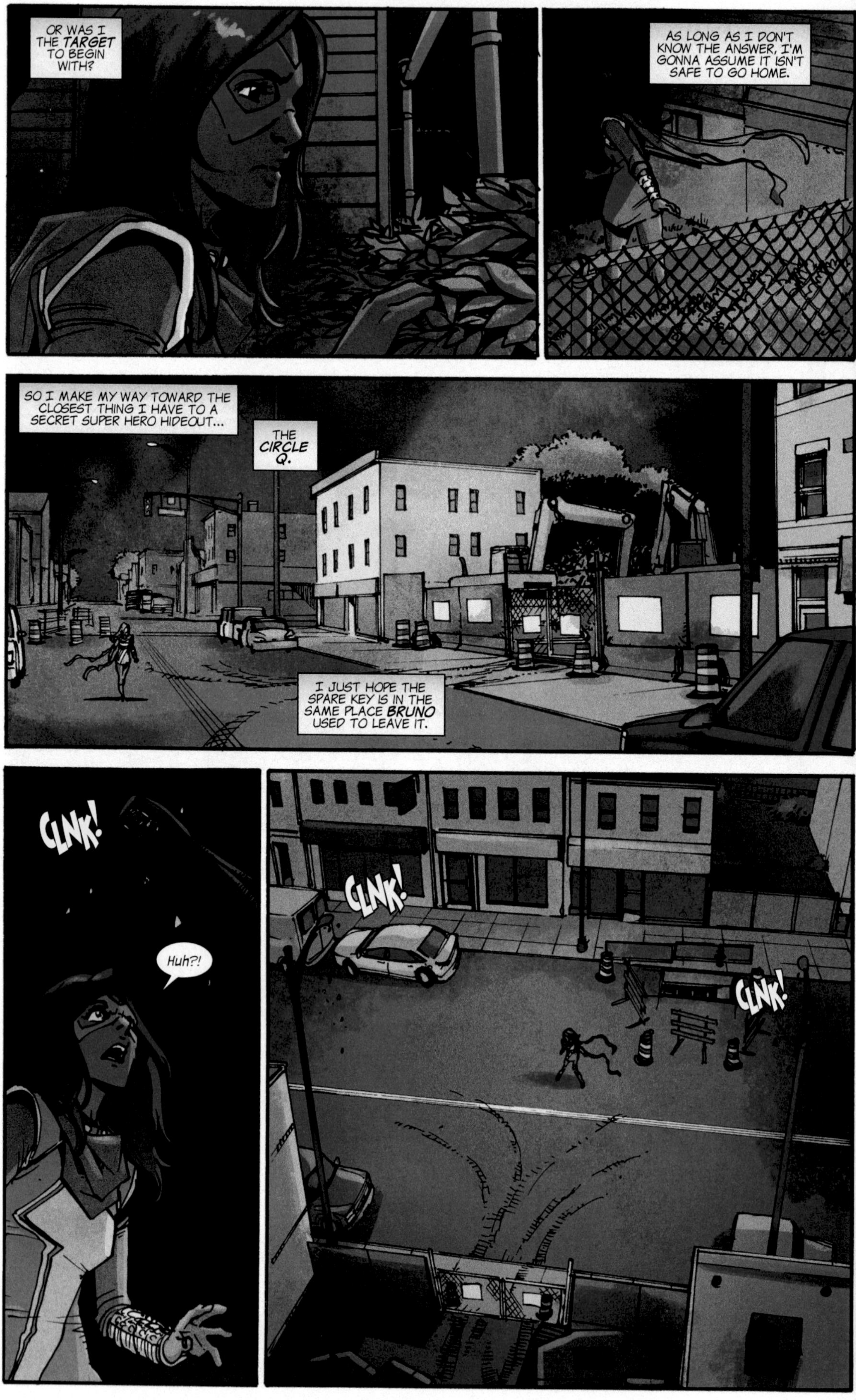
OR WAS I THE TARGET TO BEGIN WITH?
AS LONG AS I DON'T KNOW THE ANSWER, I'M GONNA ASSUME IT ISN'T SAFE TO GO HOME.
SO I MAKE MY WAY TOWARD THE CLOSEST THING I HAVE TO A SECRET SUPER HERO HIDEOUT...
THE CIRCLE Q.
I JUST HOPE THE SPARE KEY IS IN THE SAME PLACE BRUNO USED TO LEAVE IT.
CLNK!
Huh?!
CLNK!
CLNK!

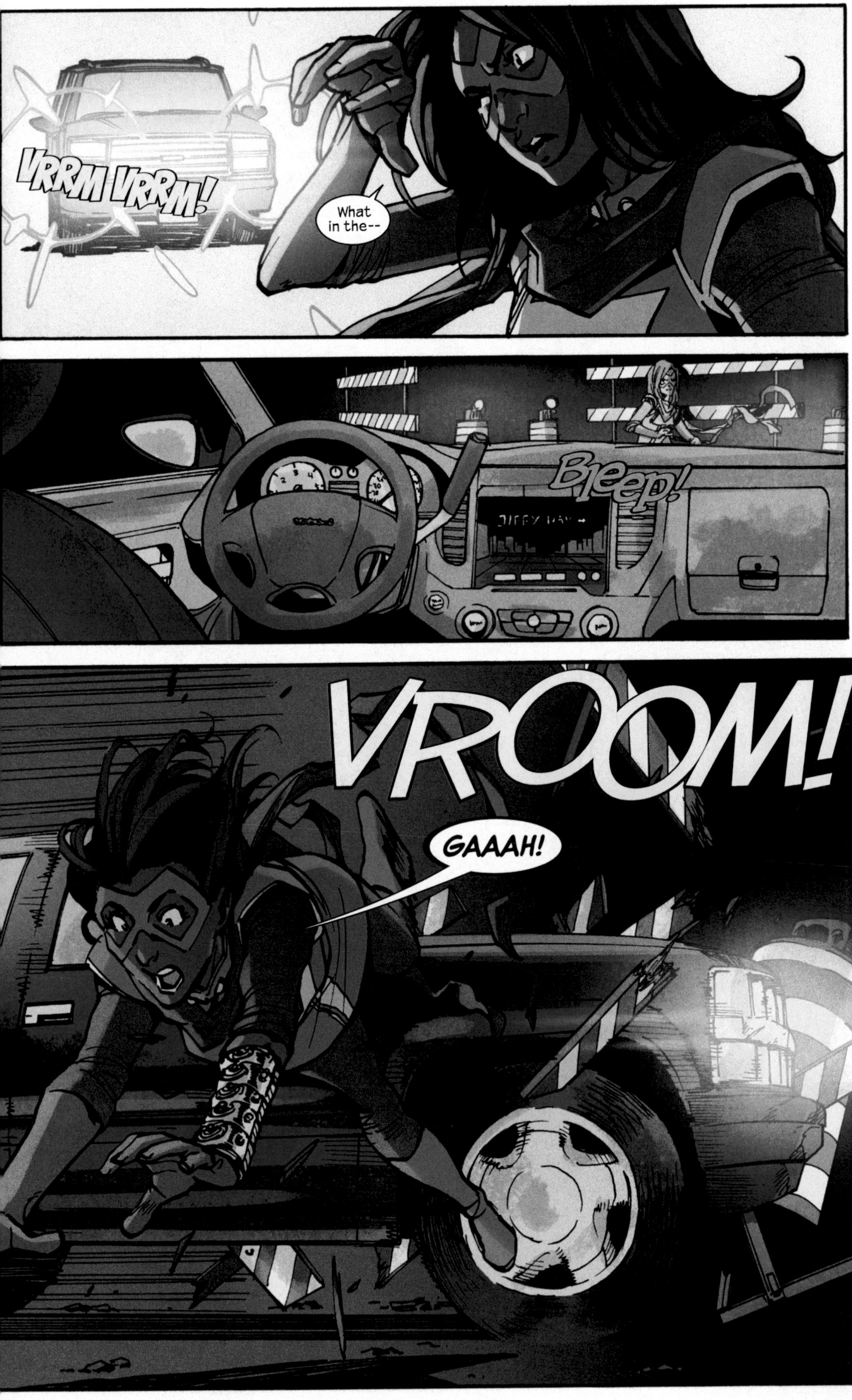
VRRM VRRM!
What in the--
BLEEP!
VROOM!
GAAAH!

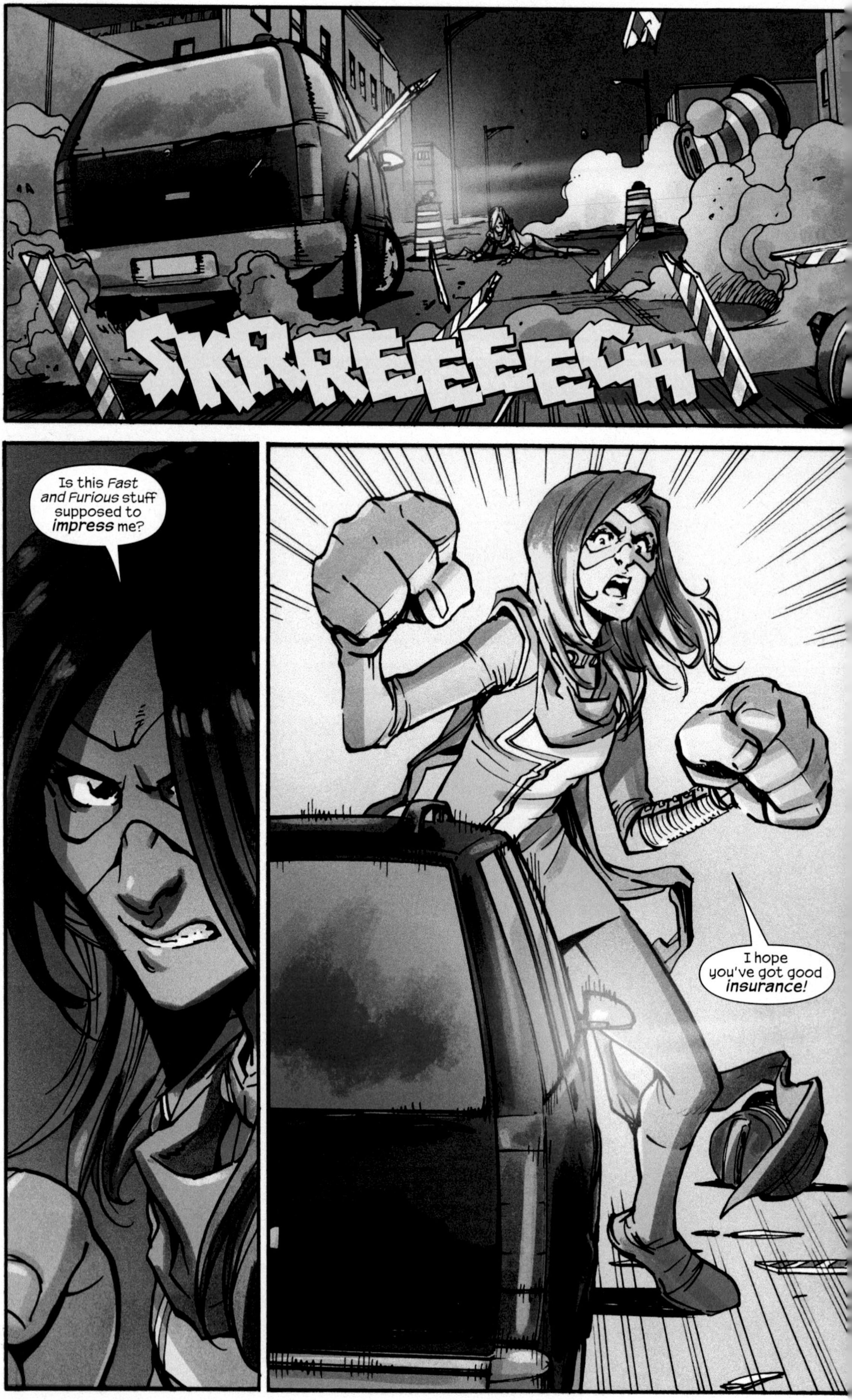
SKRREEEECH
Is this Fast and Furious stuff supposed to impress me?
I hope you've got good insurance!

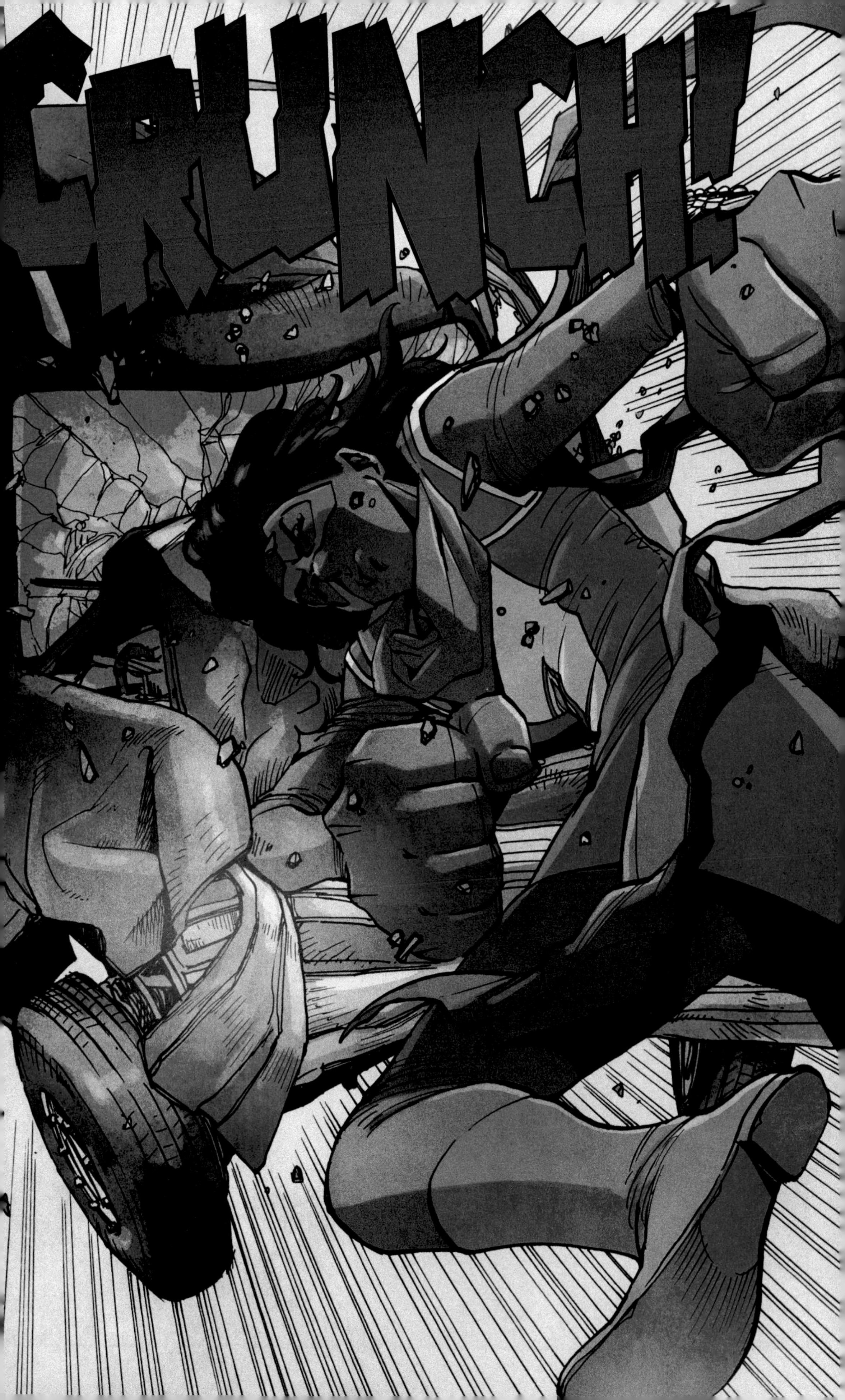
CRUNCH!!

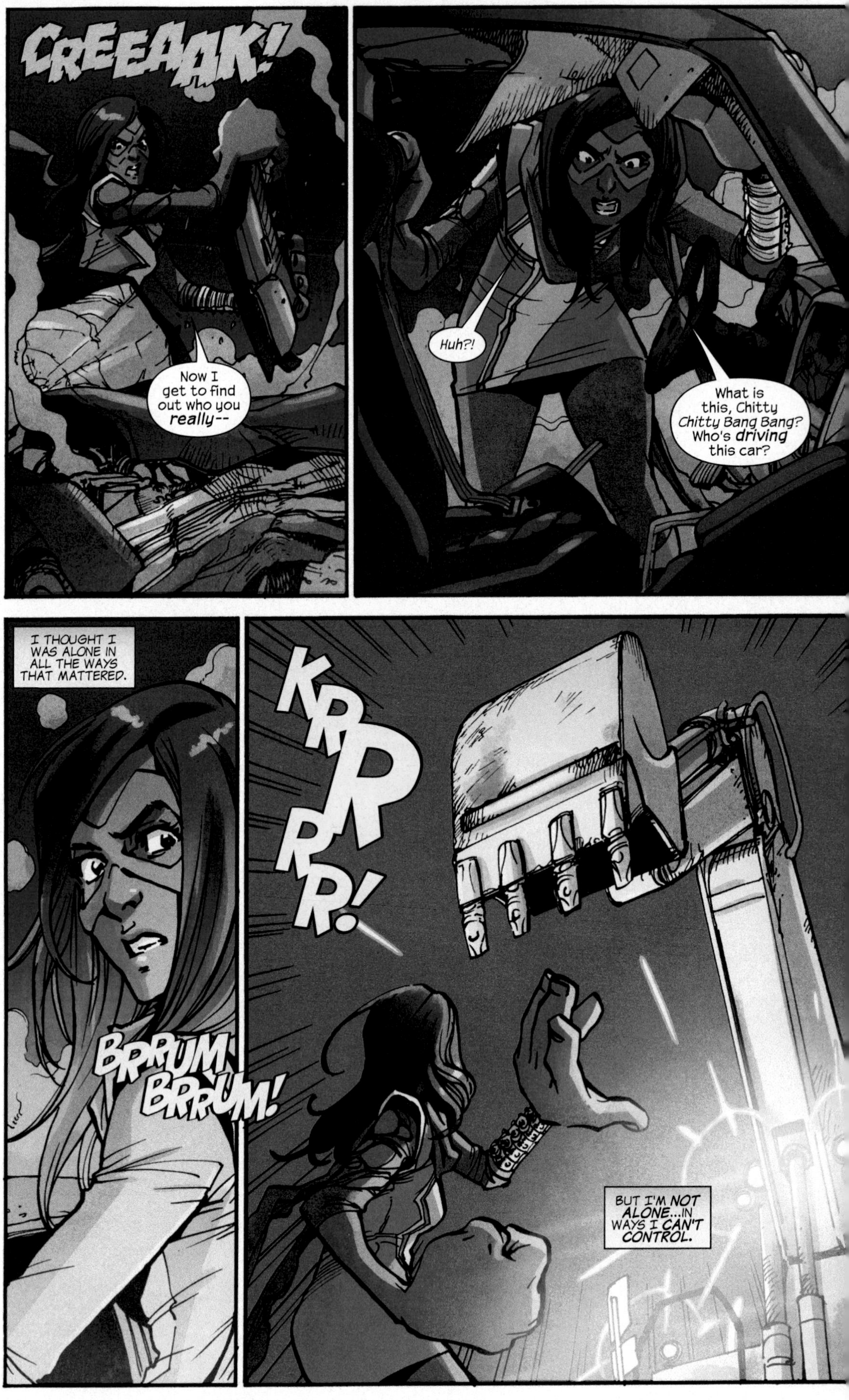
CREEAAAK!
Now I get to find out who you *really*--
Huh?!
What is this, *Chitty Chitty Bang Bang?* Who's **driving** this car?
I THOUGHT I WAS ALONE IN ALL THE WAYS THAT MATTERED.
BRRUM BRRUM!
KRRRRR!
BUT I'M *NOT ALONE*...IN WAYS I *CAN'T CONTROL*.

CRUNCH!

WAAAH!

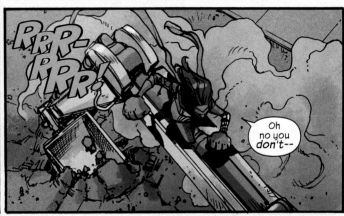

RRR-RRR!

Oh no you *don't*--

You can hack an excavator's onboard GPS...

...but without power, it's just another hunk of metal.

ZZZTT!

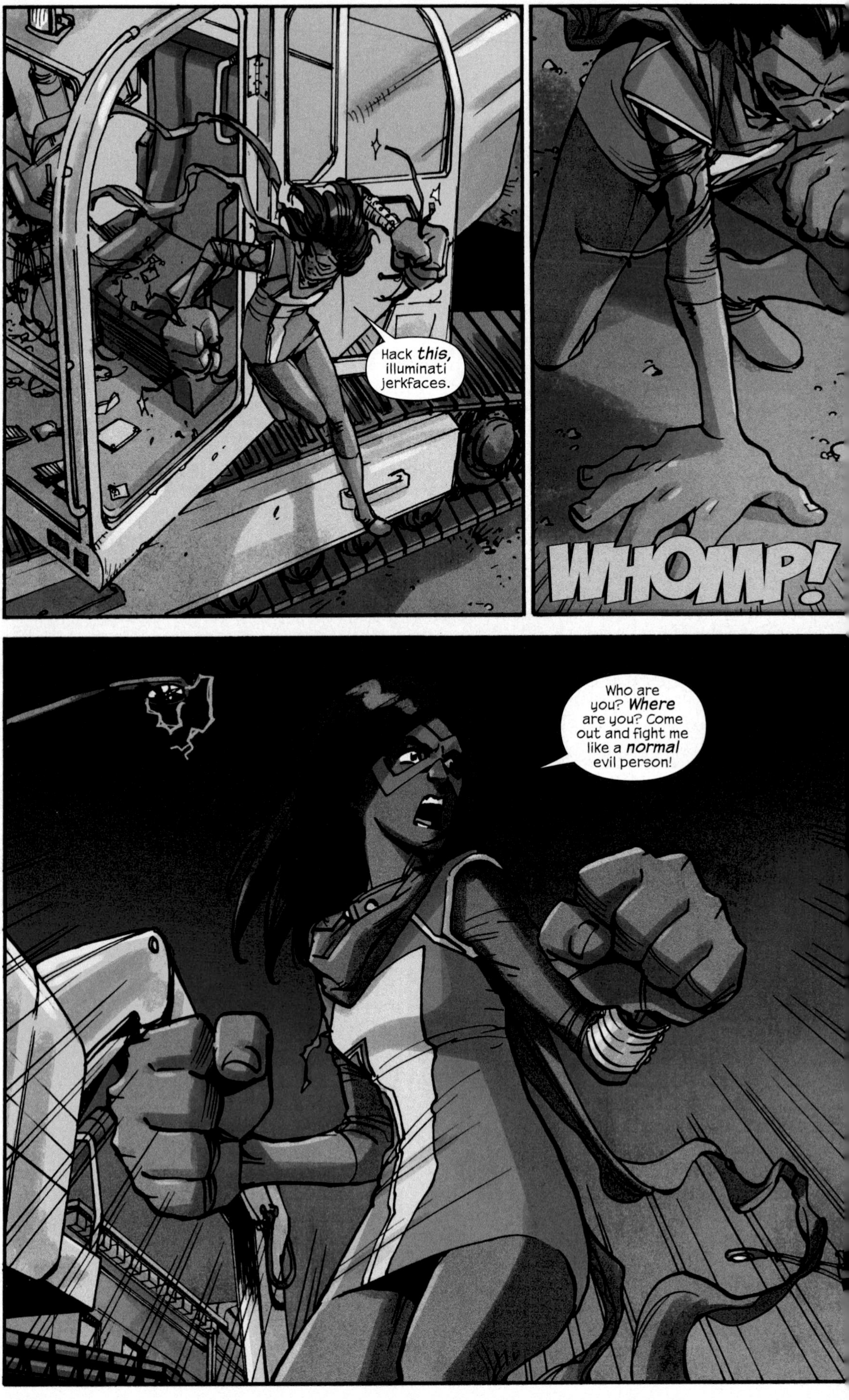
Hack *this,* illuminati jerkfaces.
WHOMP!
Who are you? *Where* are you? Come out and fight me like a *normal* evil person!

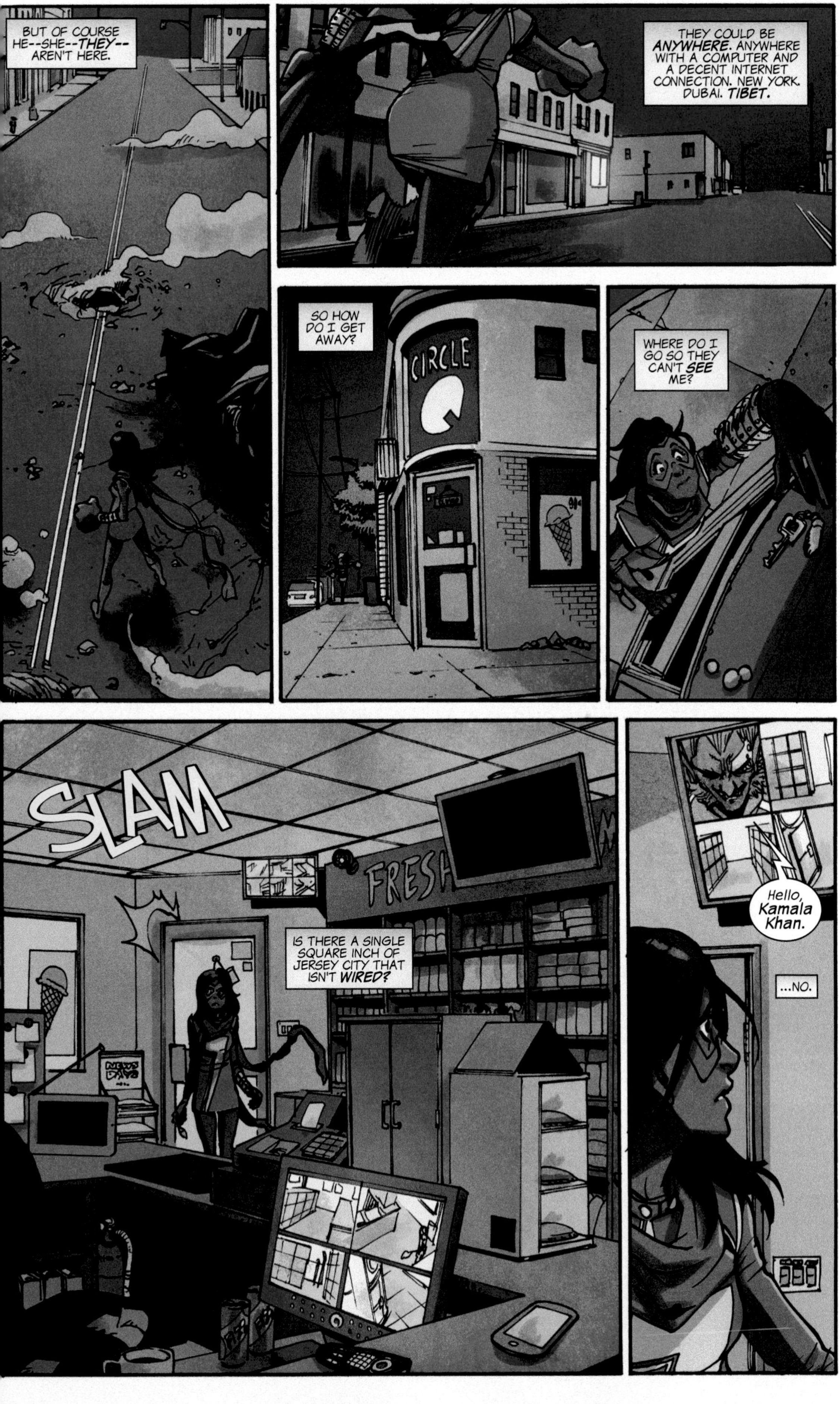

BUT OF COURSE HE--SHE--*THEY*--AREN'T HERE.
THEY COULD BE *ANYWHERE*. ANYWHERE WITH A COMPUTER AND A DECENT INTERNET CONNECTION. NEW YORK. DUBAI. *TIBET*.
SO HOW DO I GET AWAY?
CIRCLE Q
WHERE DO I GO SO THEY CAN'T *SEE* ME?
SLAM
FRESH
IS THERE A SINGLE SQUARE INCH OF JERSEY CITY THAT ISN'T *WIRED?*
Hello, *Kamala Khan.*
...NO.

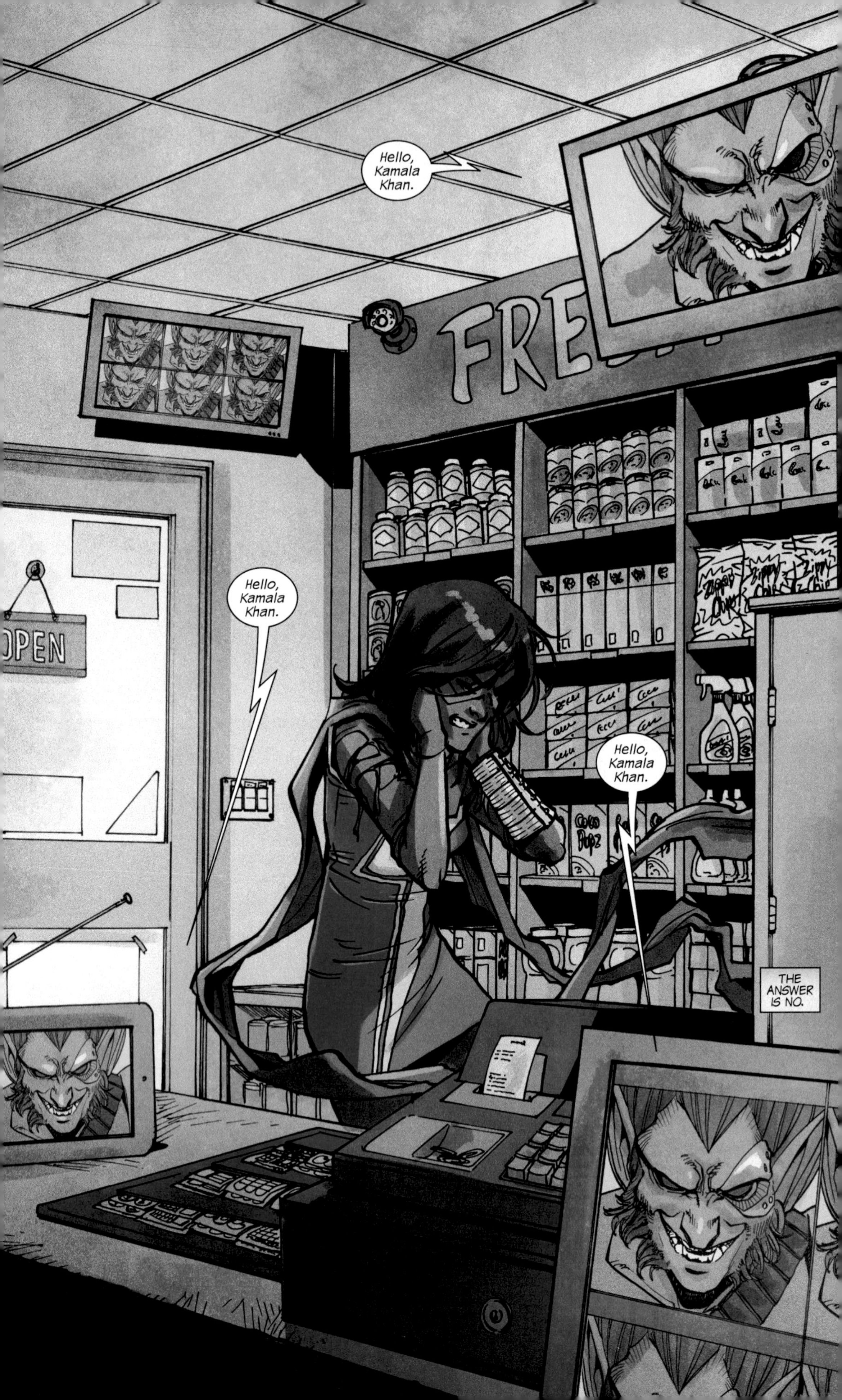
Hello, Kamala Khan.
FRE
OPEN
Hello, Kamala Khan.
Hello, Kamala Khan.
THE ANSWER IS NO.

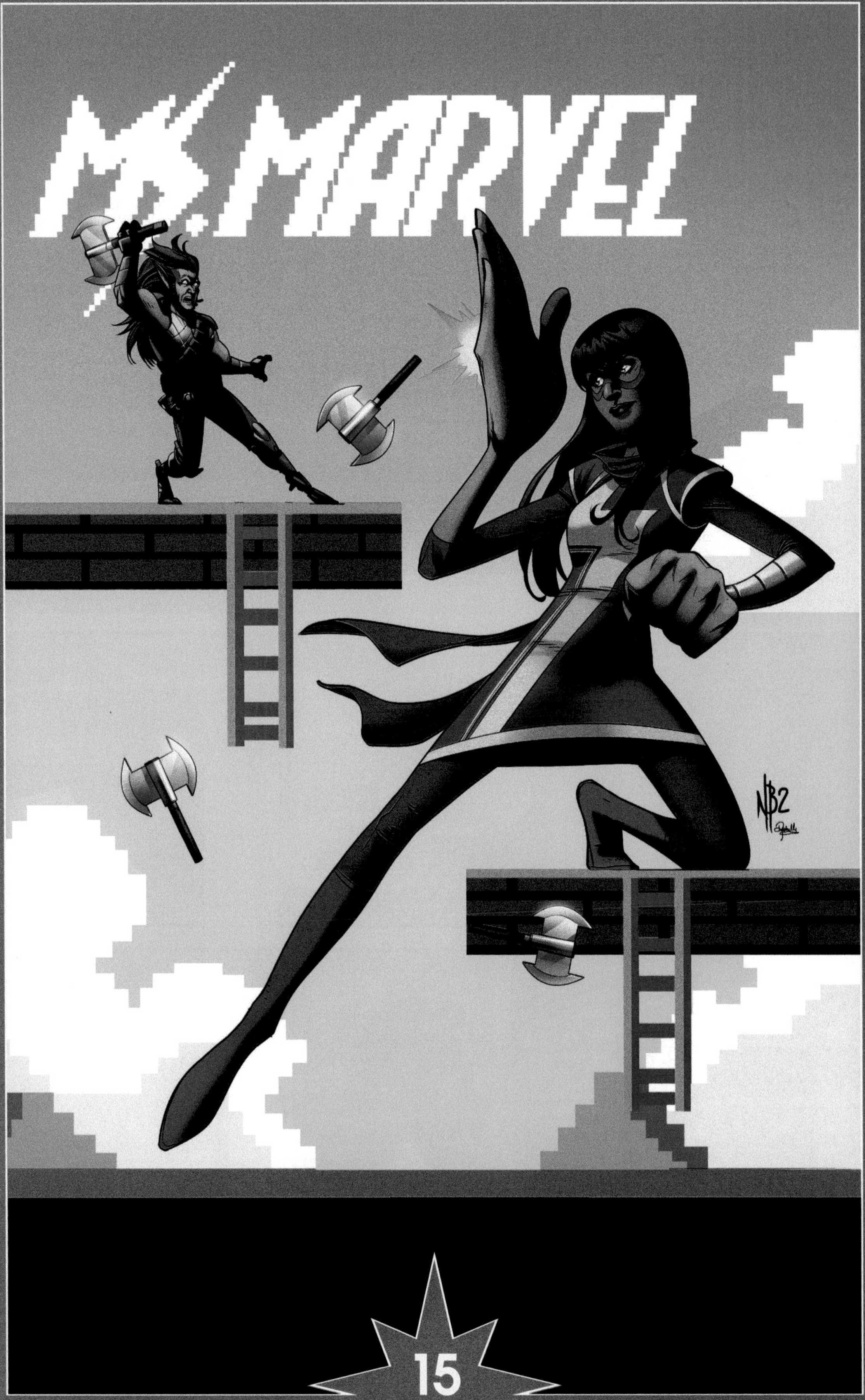
MS. MARVEL
15

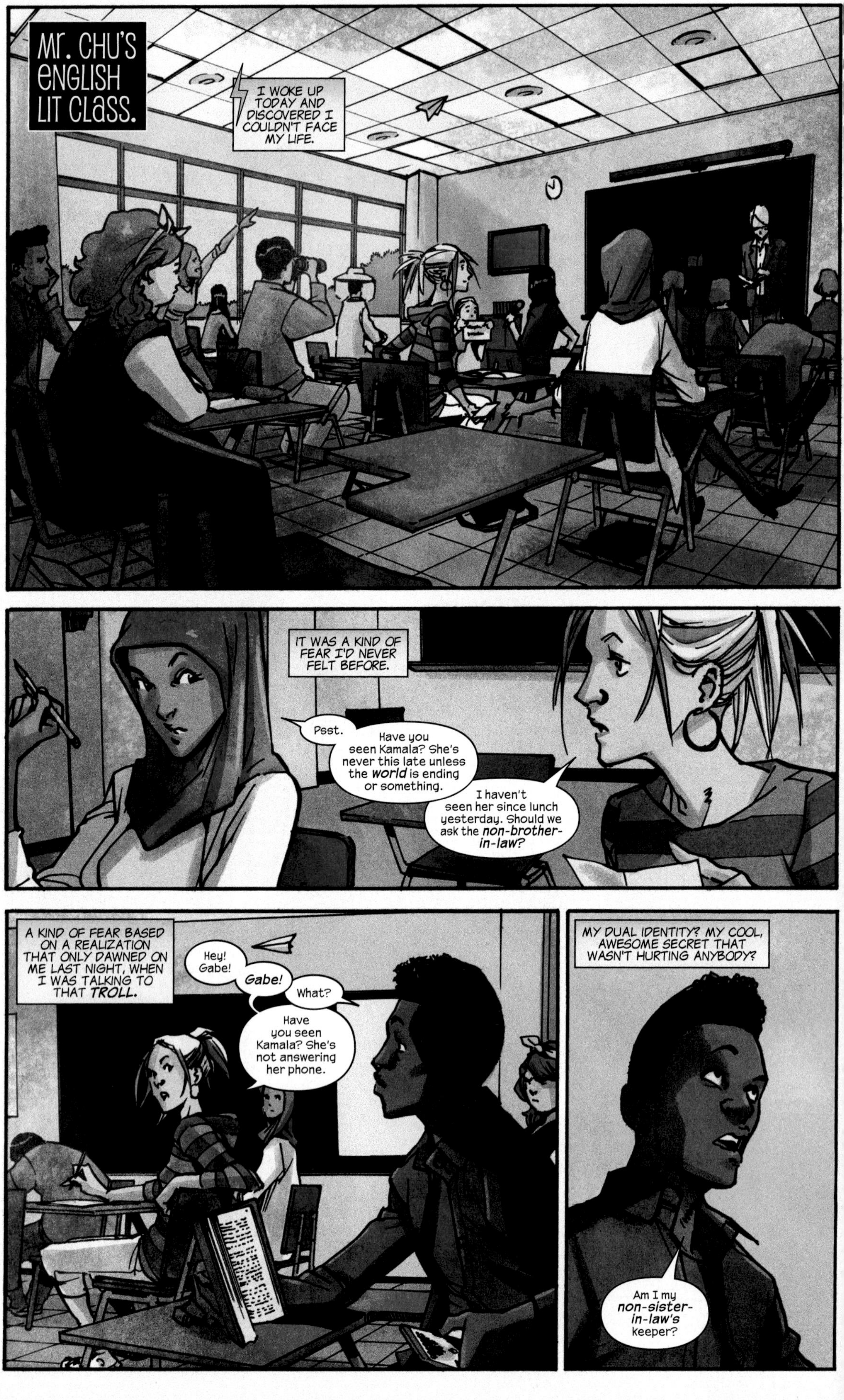
Mr. CHU'S ENGLISH LIT CLASS.
I WOKE UP TODAY AND DISCOVERED I COULDN'T FACE MY LIFE.
IT WAS A KIND OF FEAR I'D NEVER FELT BEFORE.
Psst.
Have you seen Kamala? She's never this late unless the *world* is ending or something.
I haven't seen her since lunch yesterday. Should we ask the *non-brother-in-law?*
A KIND OF FEAR BASED ON A REALIZATION THAT ONLY DAWNED ON ME LAST NIGHT, WHEN I WAS TALKING TO THAT *TROLL.*
Hey! Gabe!
Gabe!
What?
Have you seen Kamala? She's not answering her phone.
MY DUAL IDENTITY? MY COOL, AWESOME SECRET THAT WASN'T HURTING ANYBODY?
Am I my *non-sister-in-law's* keeper?

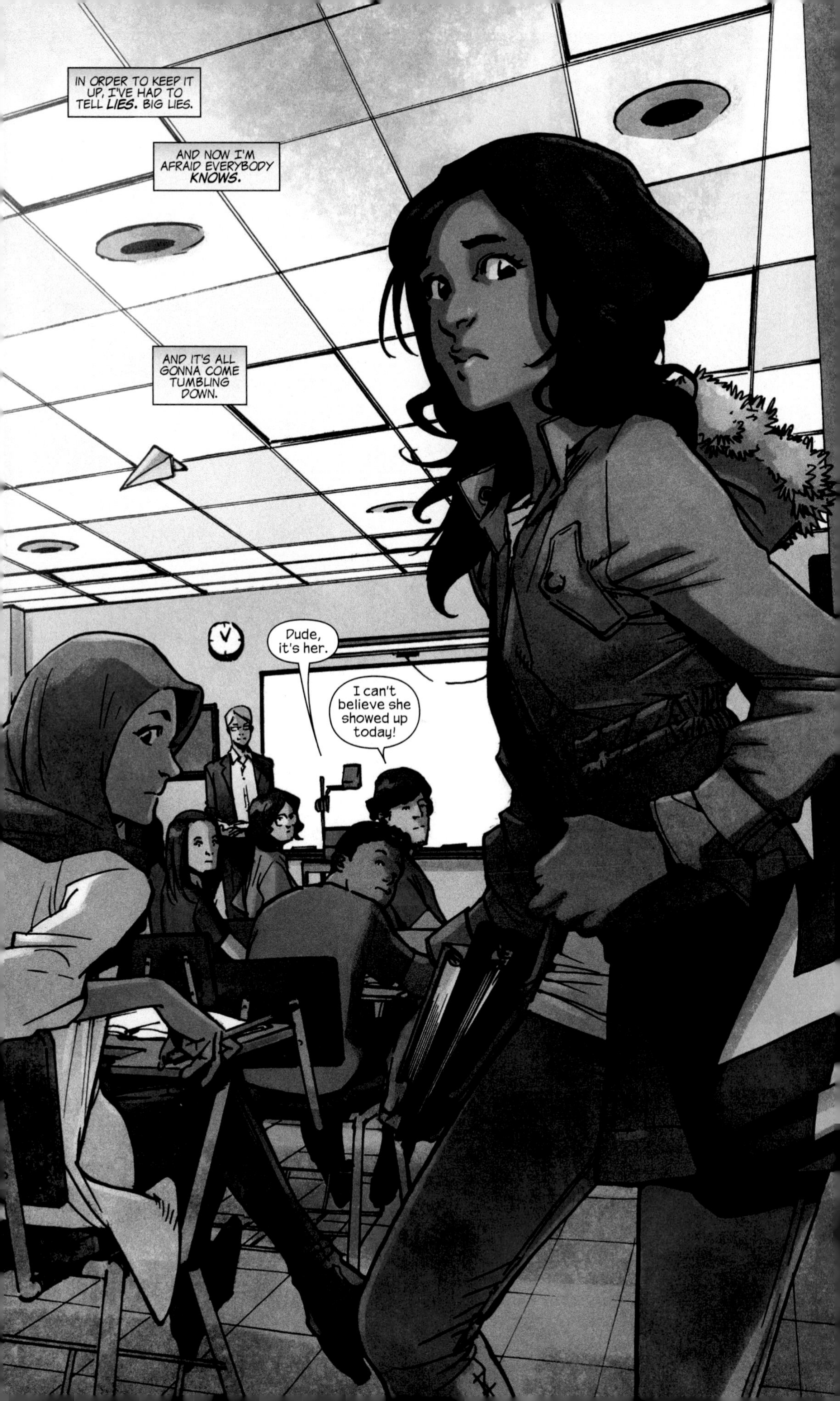
IN ORDER TO KEEP IT UP, I'VE HAD TO TELL LIES. BIG LIES.
AND NOW I'M AFRAID EVERYBODY KNOWS.
AND IT'S ALL GONNA COME TUMBLING DOWN.
Dude, it's her.
I can't believe she showed up today!

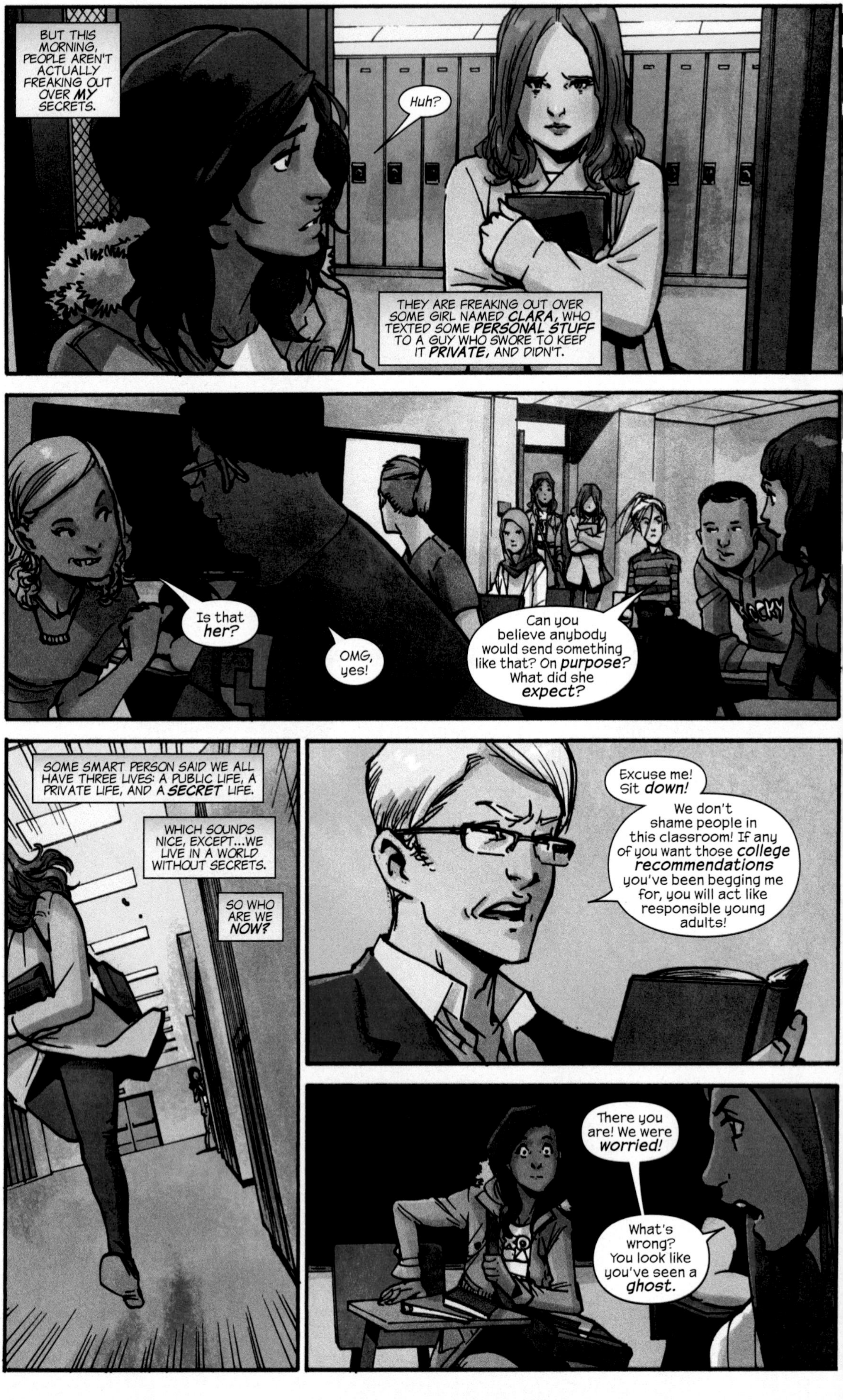
BUT THIS MORNING, PEOPLE AREN'T ACTUALLY FREAKING OUT OVER MY SECRETS.
Huh?
THEY ARE FREAKING OUT OVER SOME GIRL NAMED CLARA, WHO TEXTED SOME PERSONAL STUFF TO A GUY WHO SWORE TO KEEP IT PRIVATE, AND DIDN'T.
Is that her?
OMG, yes!
Can you believe anybody would send something like that? On purpose? What did she expect?
SOME SMART PERSON SAID WE ALL HAVE THREE LIVES: A PUBLIC LIFE, A PRIVATE LIFE, AND A SECRET LIFE.
WHICH SOUNDS NICE, EXCEPT...WE LIVE IN A WORLD WITHOUT SECRETS.
SO WHO ARE WE NOW?
Excuse me! Sit down!
We don't shame people in this classroom! If any of you want those college recommendations you've been begging me for, you will act like responsible young adults!
There you are! We were worried!
What's wrong? You look like you've seen a ghost.

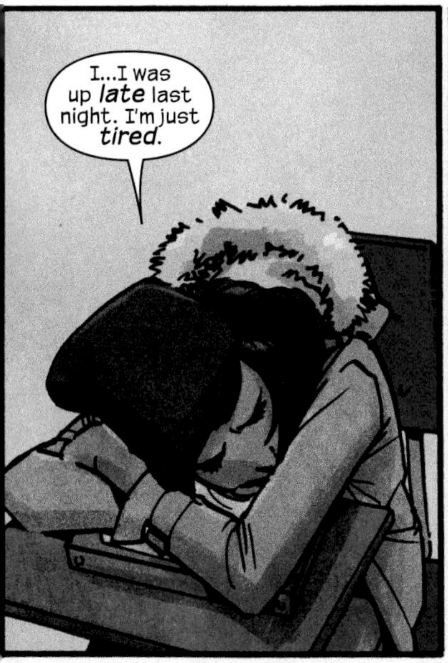
I...I was up *late* last night. I'm just *tired*.

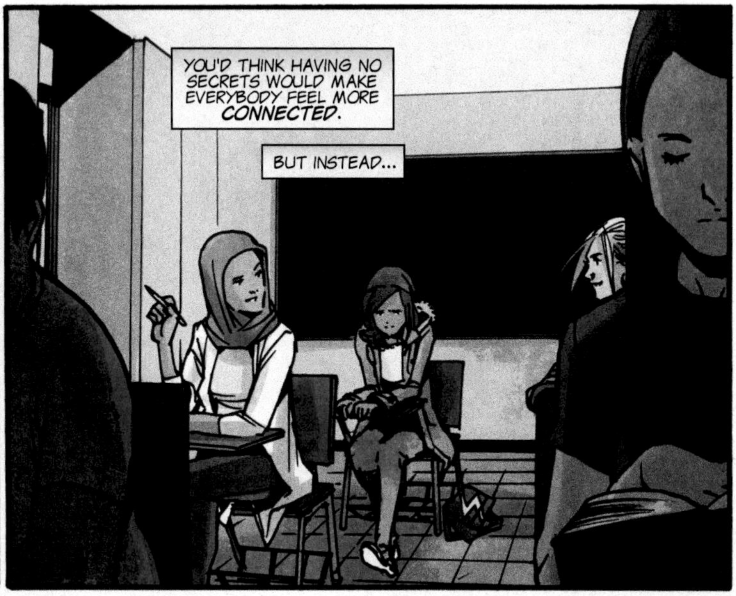
YOU'D THINK HAVING NO SECRETS WOULD MAKE EVERYBODY FEEL MORE *CONNECTED*.
BUT INSTEAD...

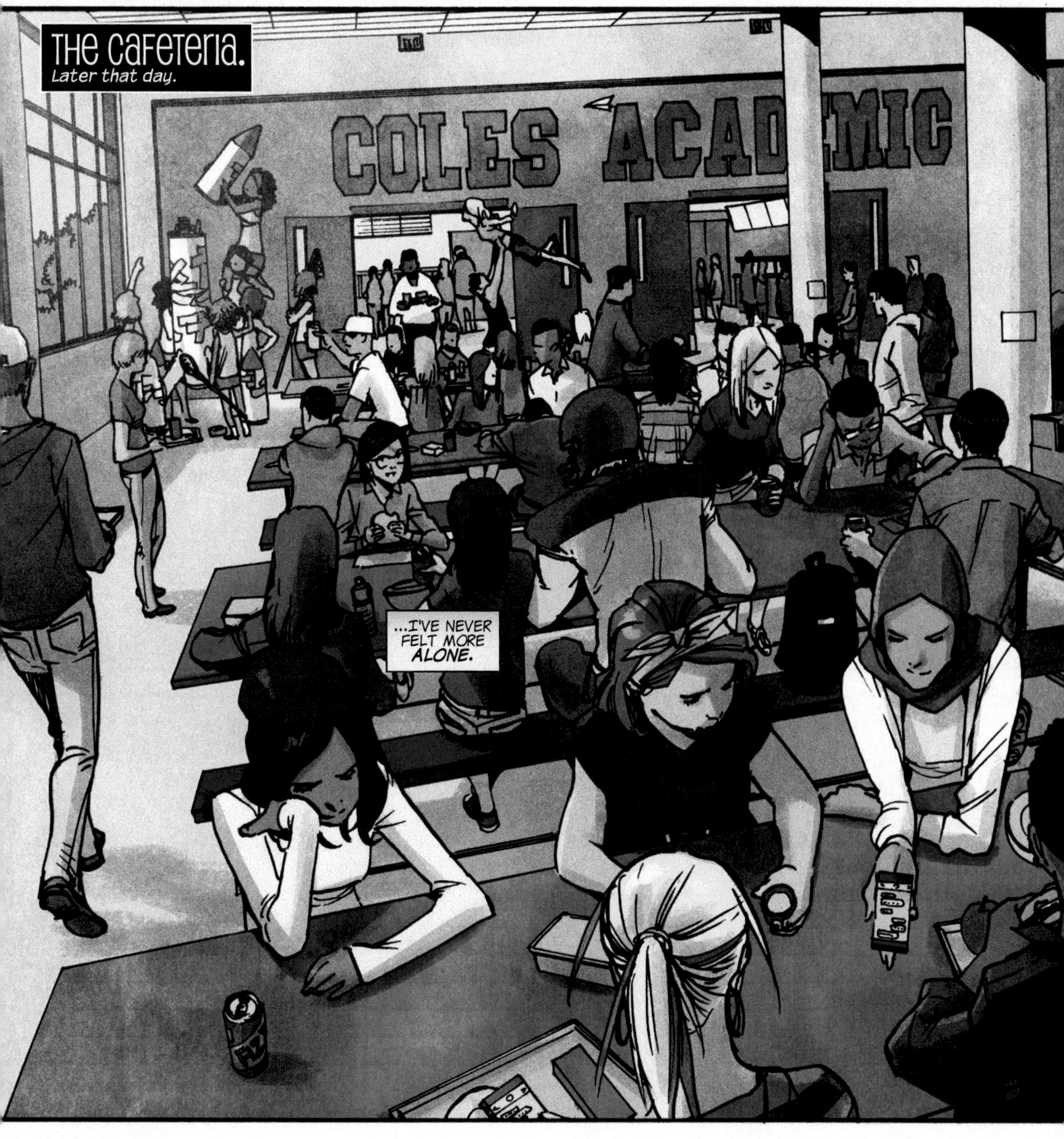
THE CAFETERIA.
Later that day.
COLES ACADEMIC
...I'VE NEVER FELT MORE *ALONE*.

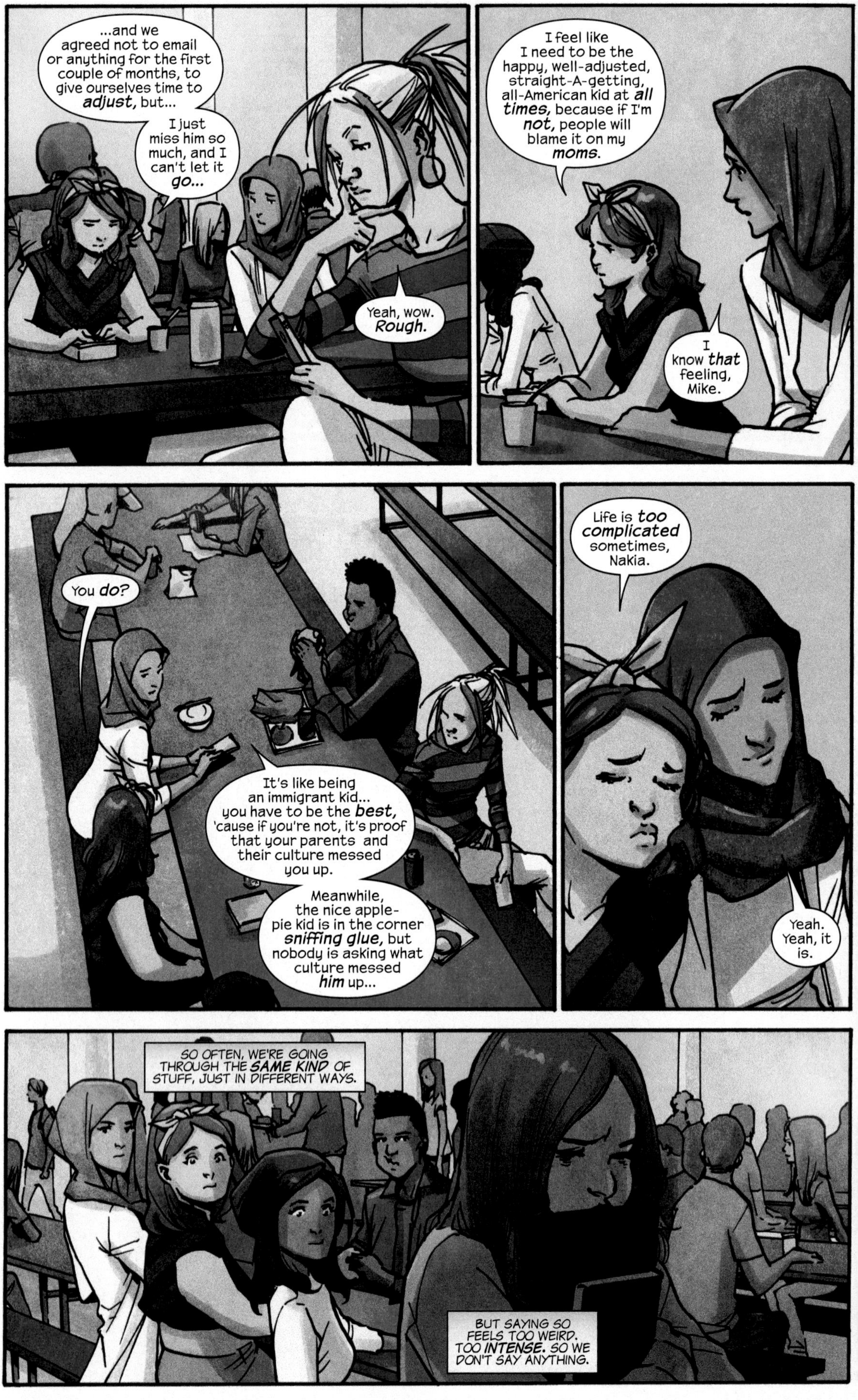
...and we agreed not to email or anything for the first couple of months, to give ourselves time to *adjust,* but...
I just miss him so much, and I can't let it *go...*
Yeah, wow. *Rough.*
I feel like I need to be the happy, well-adjusted, straight-A-getting, all-American kid at *all times,* because if I'm *not,* people will blame it on my *moms.*
I know *that* feeling, Mike.
You *do?*
It's like being an immigrant kid... you have to be the *best,* 'cause if you're not, it's proof that your parents and their culture messed you up.
Meanwhile, the nice apple-pie kid is in the corner *sniffing glue,* but nobody is asking what culture messed *him* up...
Life is *too complicated* sometimes, Nakia.
Yeah. Yeah, it is.
SO OFTEN, WE'RE GOING THROUGH THE *SAME KIND* OF STUFF, JUST IN DIFFERENT WAYS.
BUT SAYING SO FEELS TOO WEIRD. TOO *INTENSE.* SO WE DON'T SAY ANYTHING.

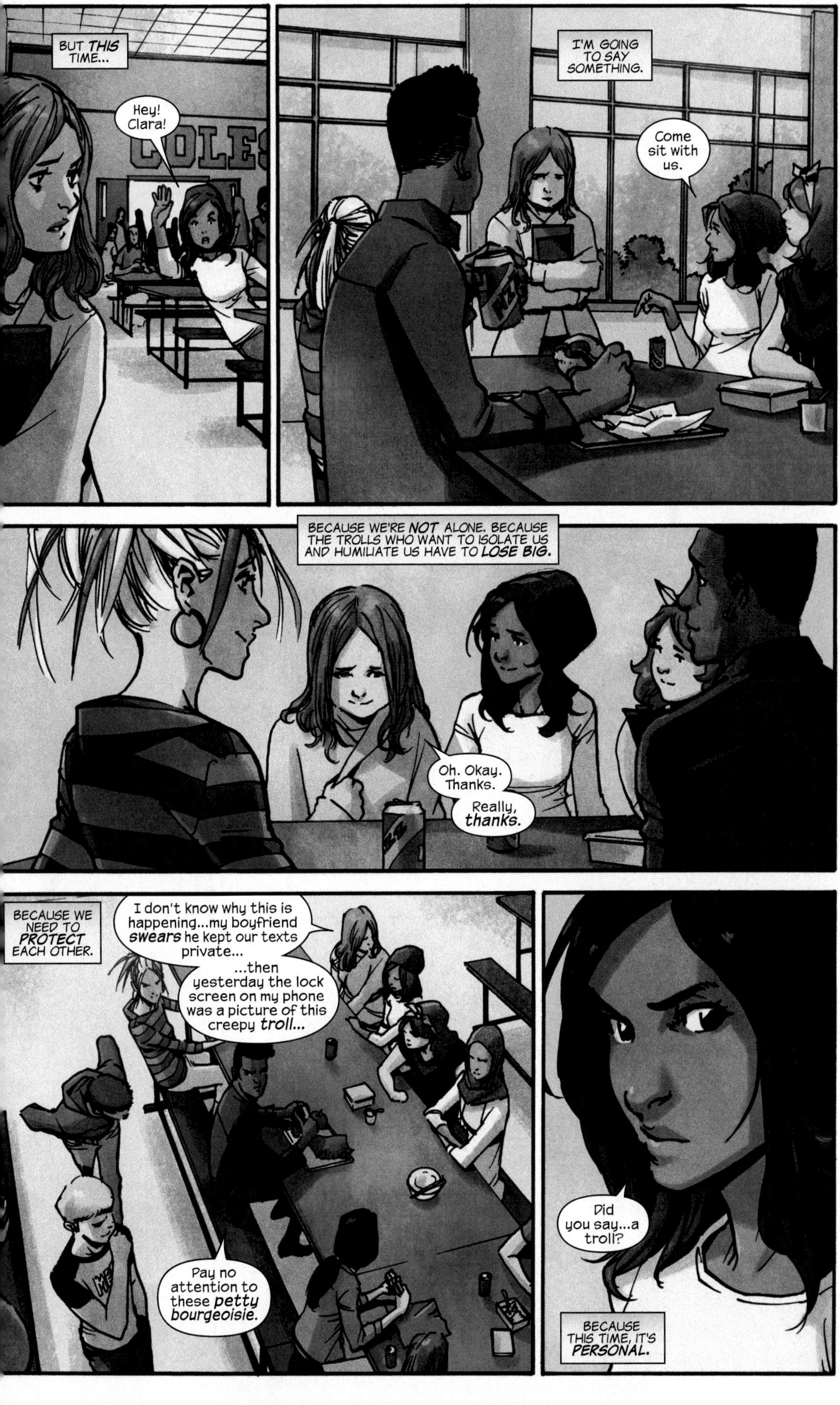
BUT THIS TIME...
Hey! Clara!
COLES
I'M GOING TO SAY SOMETHING.
Come sit with us.
BECAUSE WE'RE NOT ALONE. BECAUSE THE TROLLS WHO WANT TO ISOLATE US AND HUMILIATE US HAVE TO LOSE BIG.
Oh. Okay. Thanks.
Really, thanks.
BECAUSE WE NEED TO PROTECT EACH OTHER.
I don't know why this is happening...my boyfriend swears he kept our texts private...
...then yesterday the lock screen on my phone was a picture of this creepy troll...
Pay no attention to these petty bourgeoisie.
Did you say...a troll?
BECAUSE THIS TIME, IT'S PERSONAL.

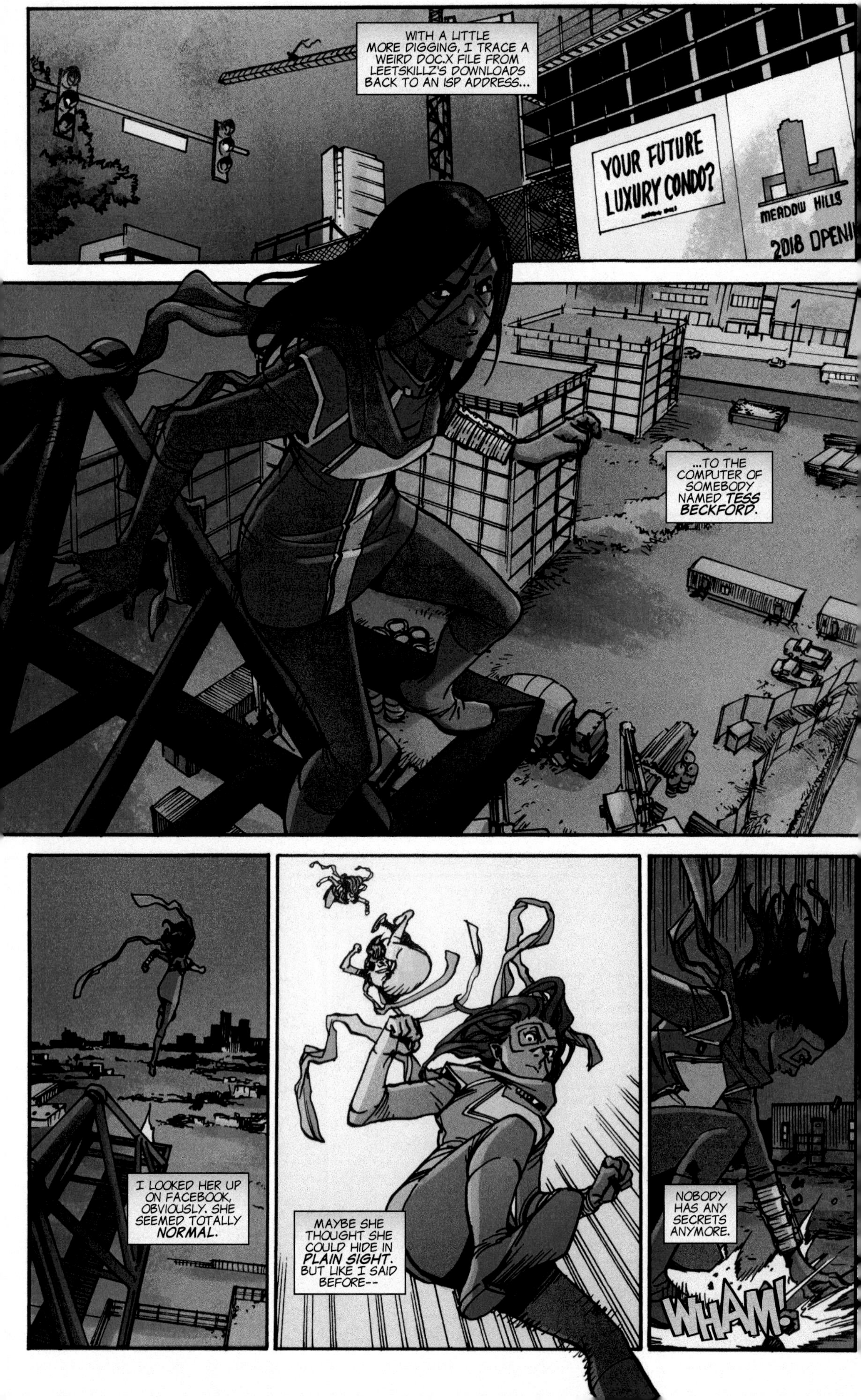
WITH A LITTLE MORE DIGGING, I TRACE A WEIRD DOC.X FILE FROM LEETSKILLZ'S DOWNLOADS BACK TO AN ISP ADDRESS...
YOUR FUTURE LUXURY CONDO?
MEADOW HILLS
2018 OPENI
...TO THE COMPUTER OF SOMEBODY NAMED TESS BECKFORD.
I LOOKED HER UP ON FACEBOOK, OBVIOUSLY. SHE SEEMED TOTALLY NORMAL.
MAYBE SHE THOUGHT SHE COULD HIDE IN PLAIN SIGHT. BUT LIKE I SAID BEFORE--
NOBODY HAS ANY SECRETS ANYMORE.
WHAM!

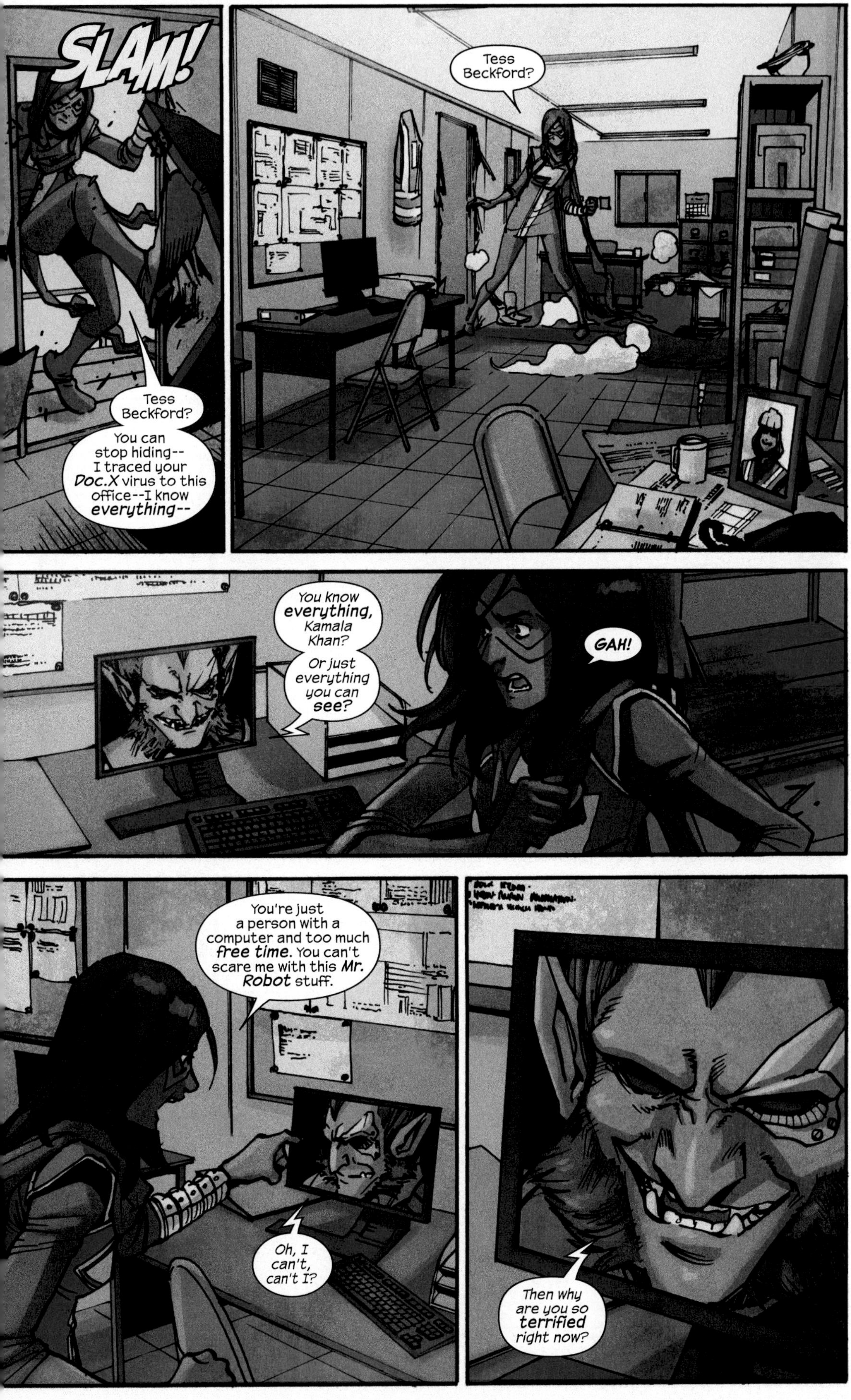
SLAM!
Tess Beckford?
You can stop hiding-- I traced your Doc.X virus to this office--I know everything--
Tess Beckford?
You know everything, Kamala Khan?
Or just everything you can see?
GAH!
You're just a person with a computer and too much free time. You can't scare me with this Mr. Robot stuff.
Oh, I can't, can't I?
Then why are you so terrified right now?

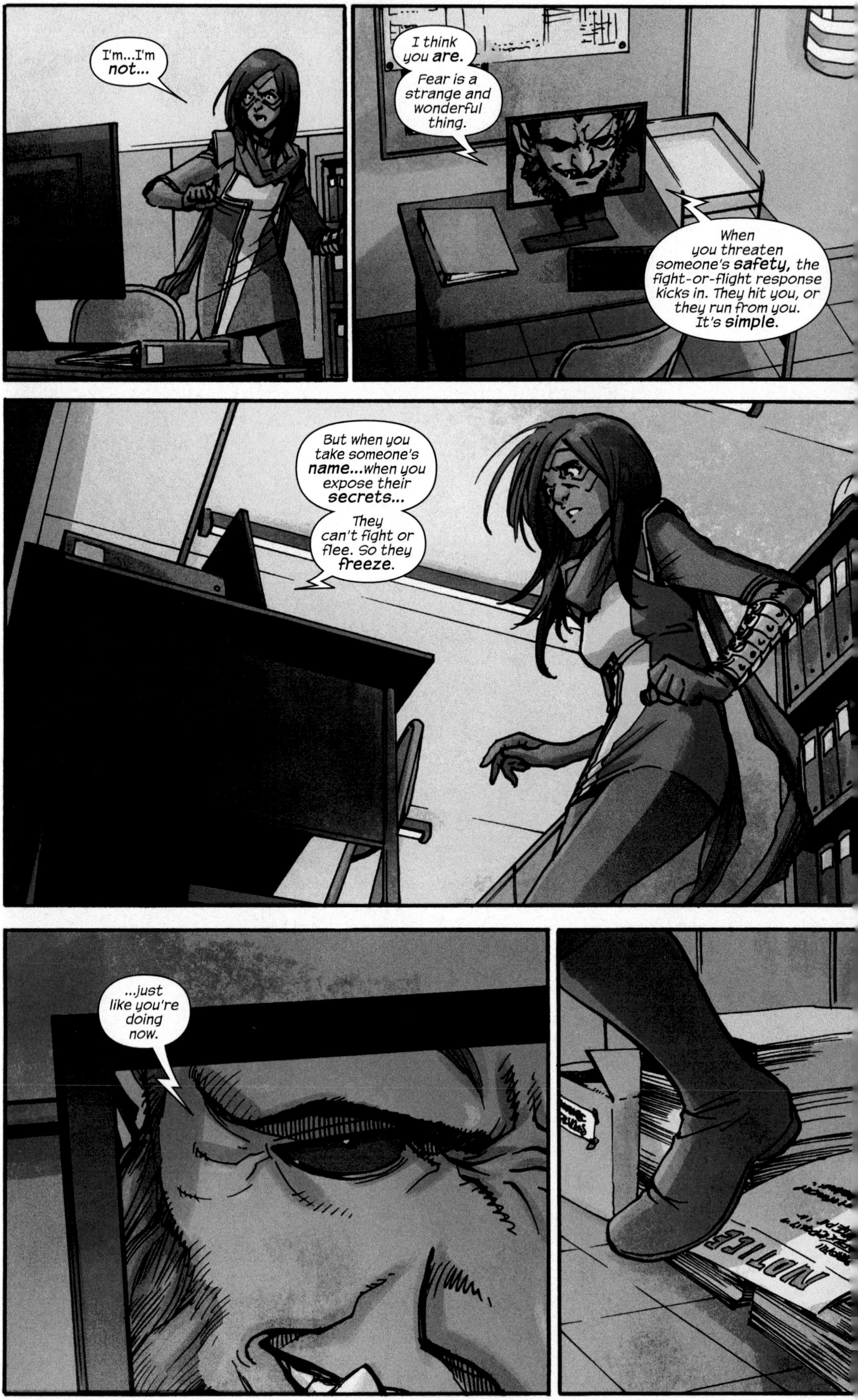
I'm...I'm not...
I think you are.
Fear is a strange and wonderful thing.
When you threaten someone's safety, the fight-or-flight response kicks in. They hit you, or they run from you. It's simple.
But when you take someone's name...when you expose their secrets...
They can't fight or flee. So they freeze.
...just like you're doing now.

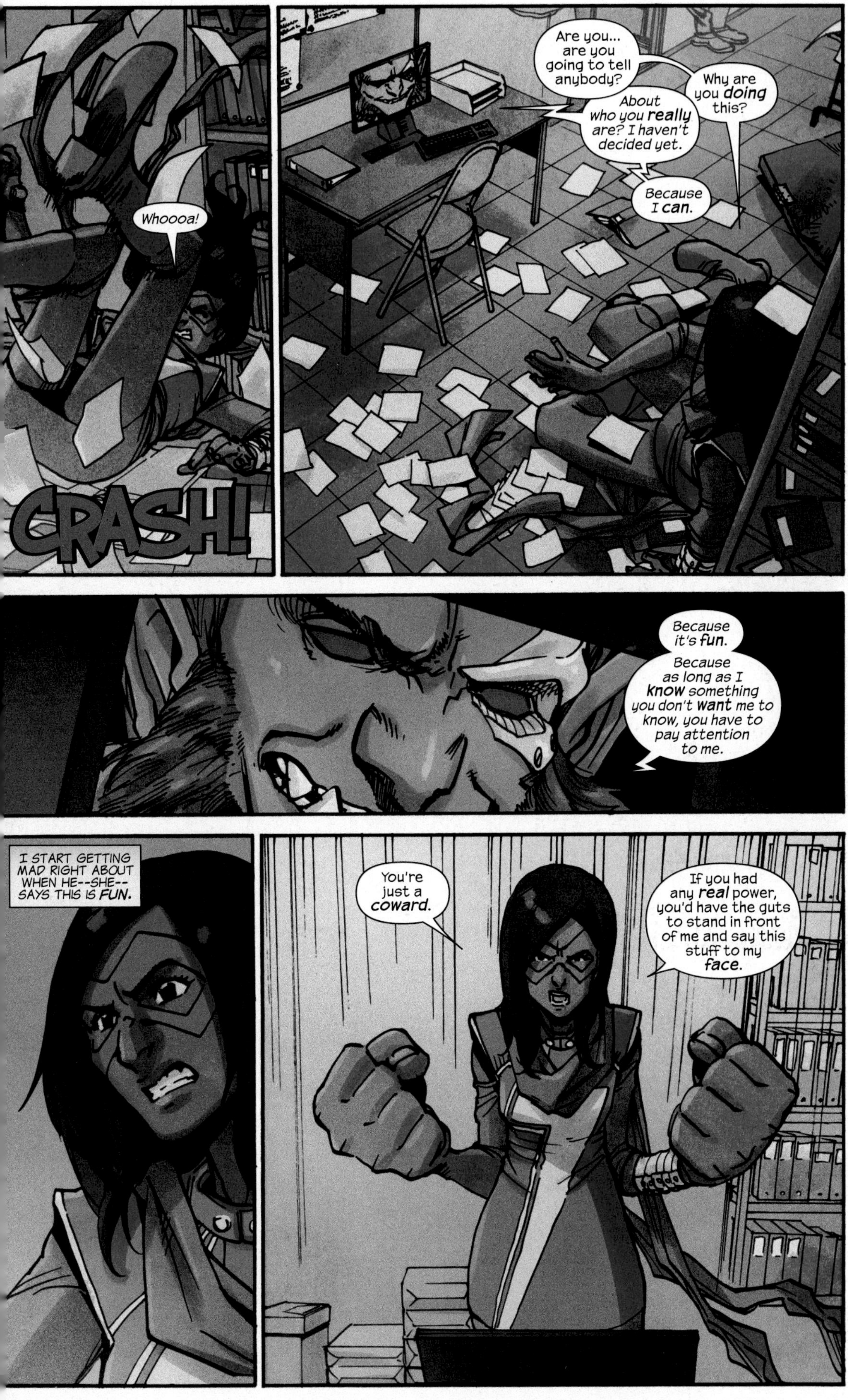

Whoooa!
CRASH!
Are you... are you going to tell anybody?
About who you really are? I haven't decided yet.
Why are you doing this?
Because I can.
Because it's fun.
Because as long as I know something you don't want me to know, you have to pay attention to me.
I START GETTING MAD RIGHT ABOUT WHEN HE--SHE-- SAYS THIS IS FUN.
You're just a coward.
If you had any real power, you'd have the guts to stand in front of me and say this stuff to my face.

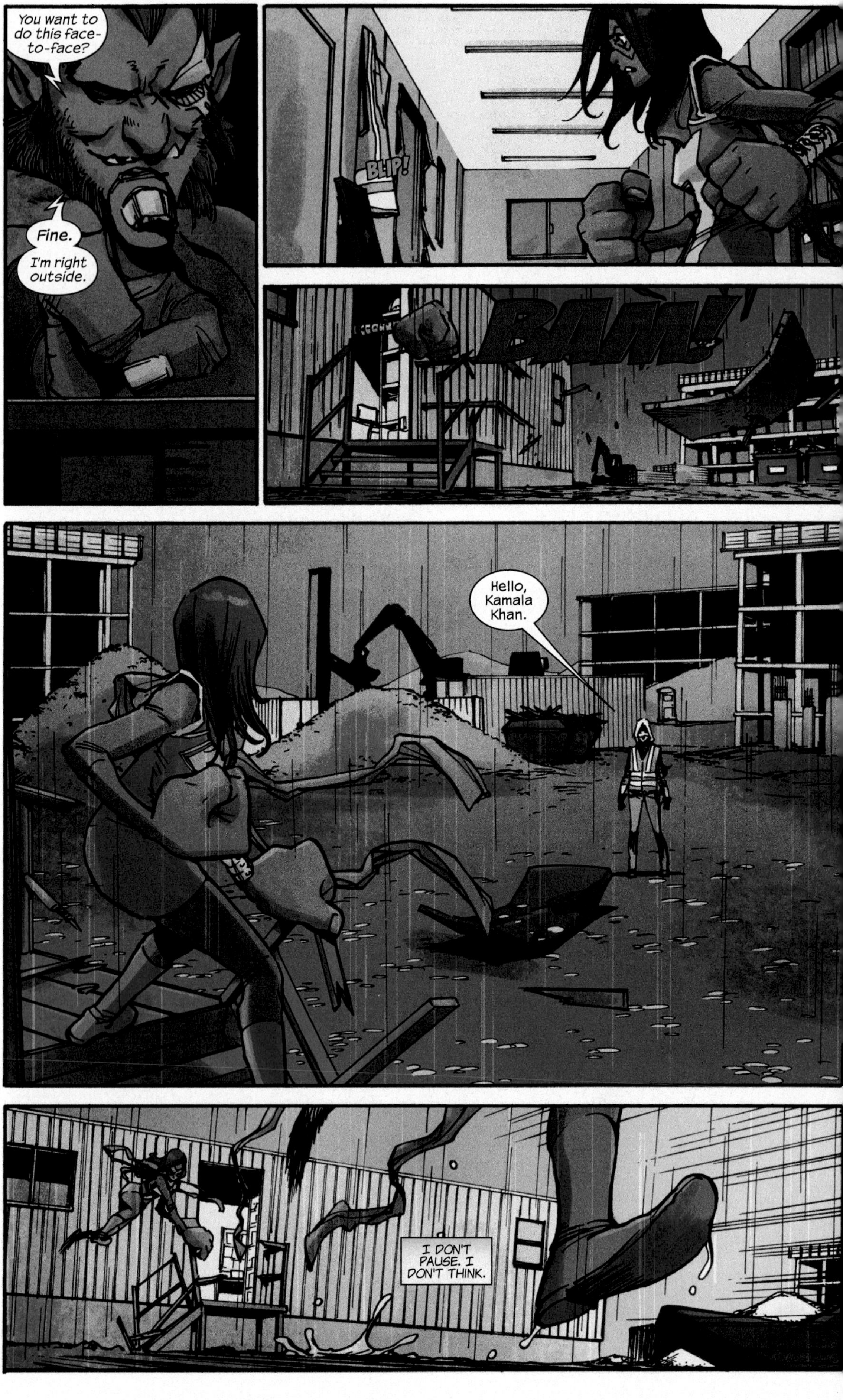
You want to do this face-to-face?
Fine.
I'm right outside.
BLIP!
BAM!
Hello, Kamala Khan.
I DON'T PAUSE. I DON'T THINK.

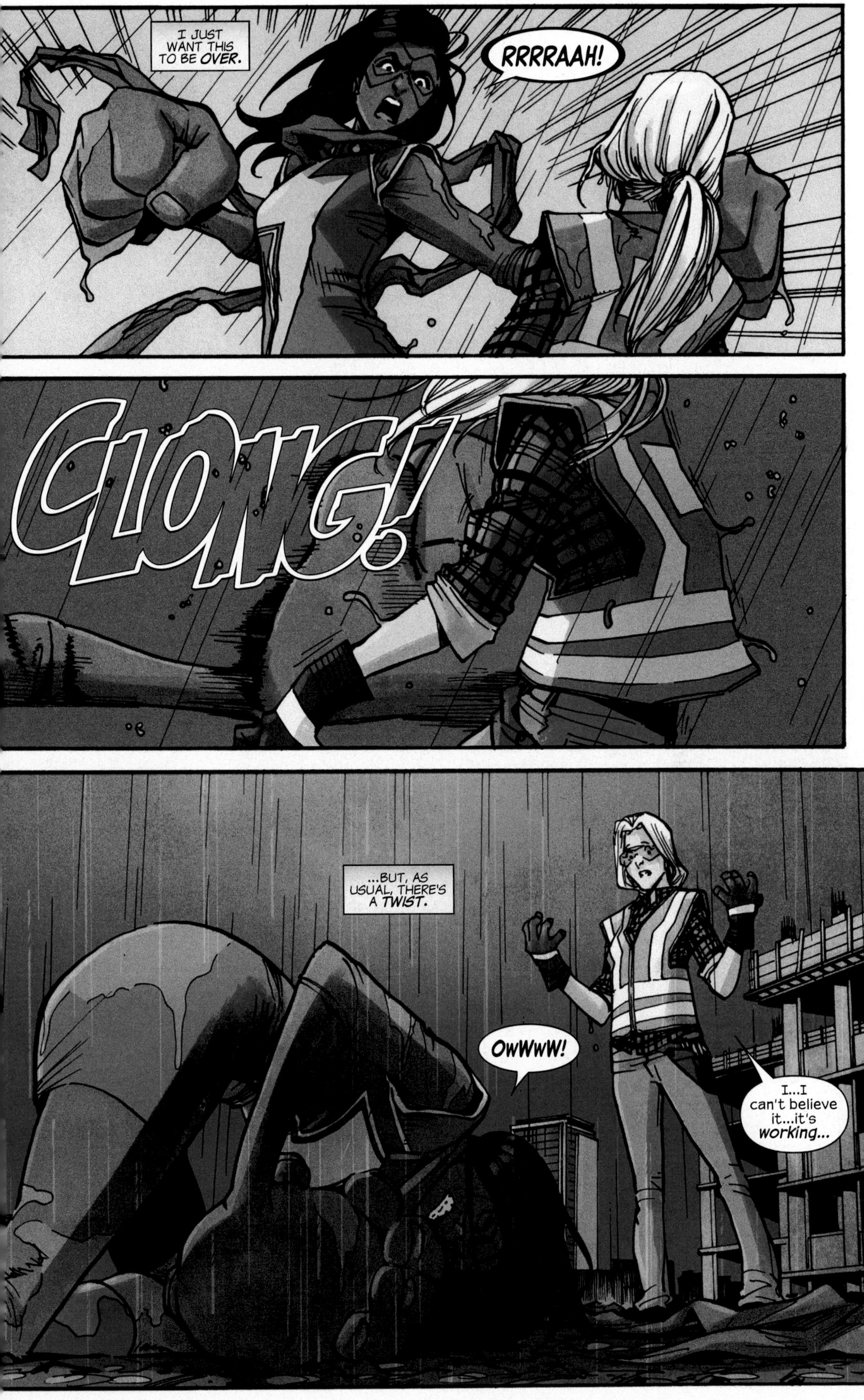

I JUST WANT THIS TO BE OVER.
RRRRAAH!
CLONG!
...BUT, AS USUAL, THERE'S A TWIST.
OWWWW!
I...I can't believe it...it's working...

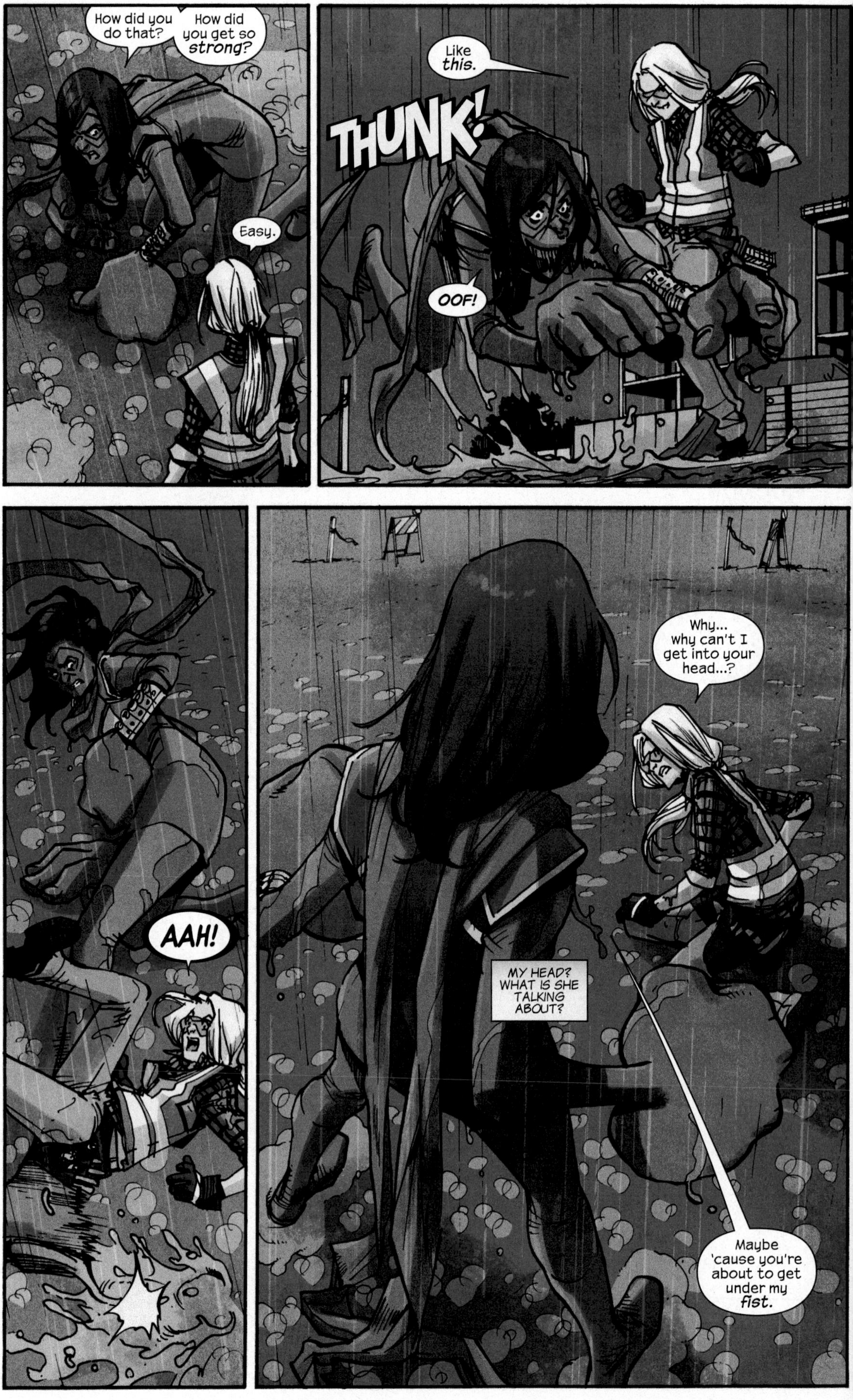
How did you do that?
How did you get so *strong*?
Easy.
Like *this*.
THUNK!
OOF!
AAH!
Why... why can't I get into your head...?
MY HEAD? WHAT IS SHE TALKING ABOUT?
Maybe 'cause you're about to get under my *fist*.

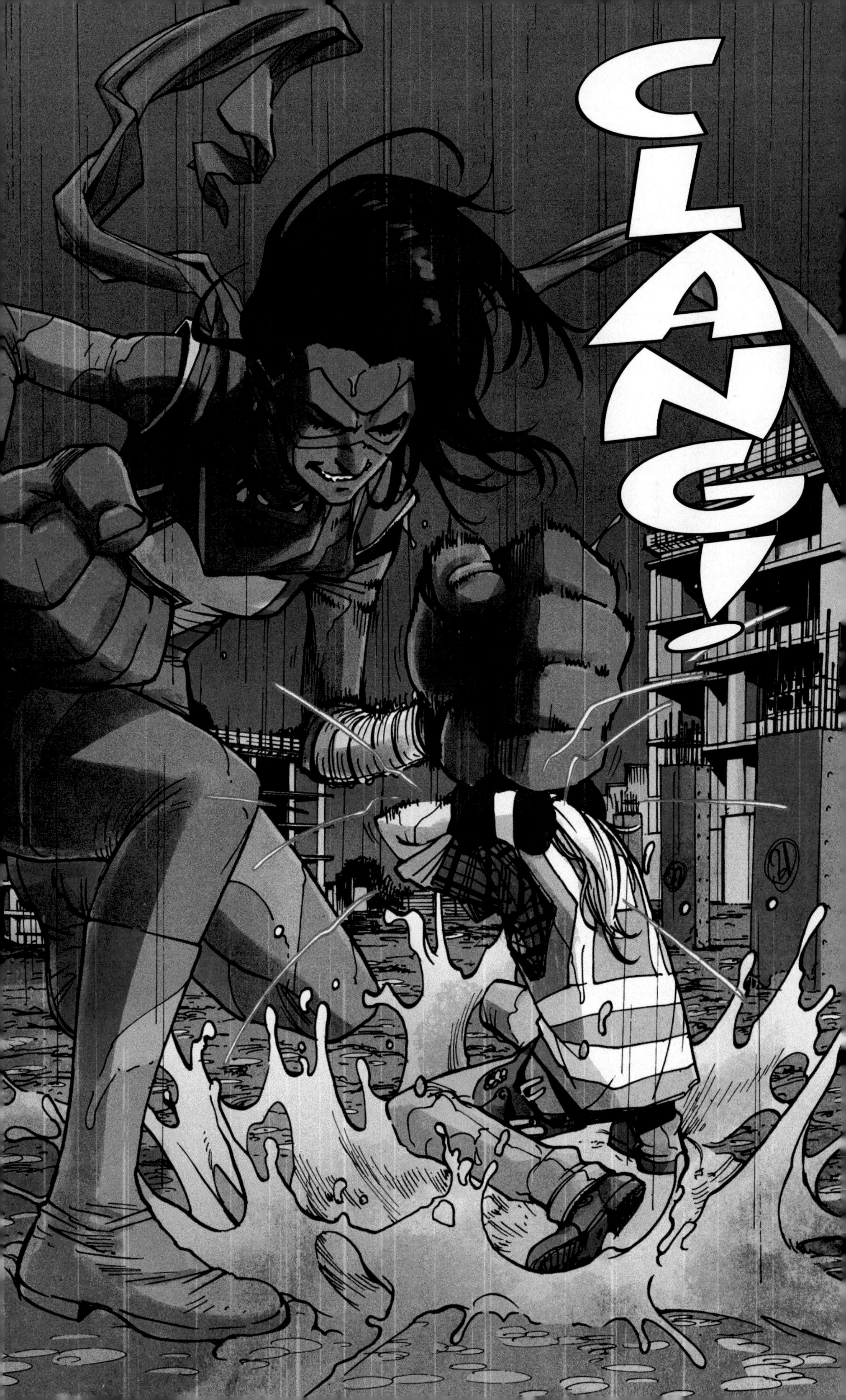
CLANG!

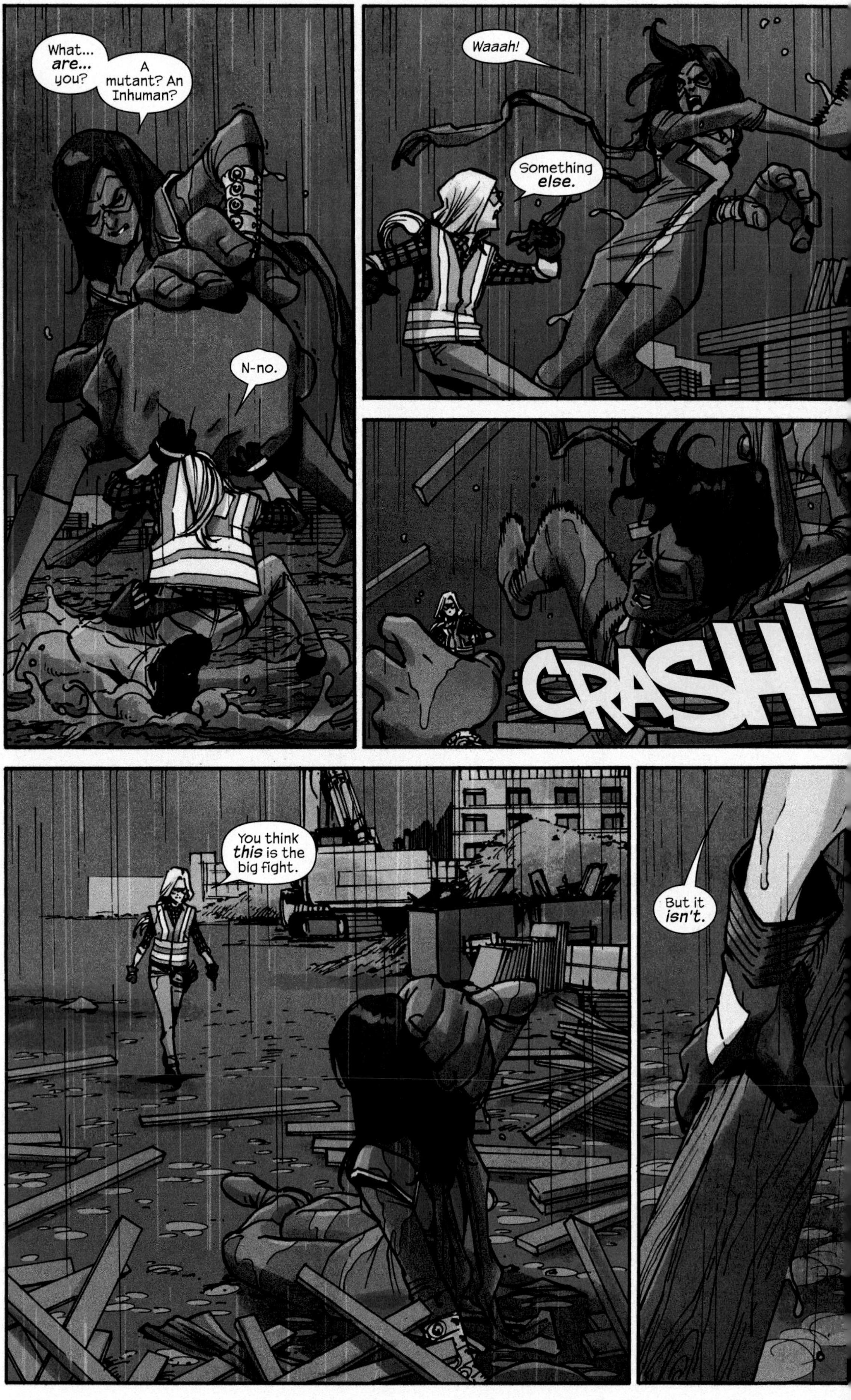
What... are... you?
A mutant? An Inhuman?
N-no.
Waaah!
Something else.
CRASH!
You think this is the big fight.
But it isn't.

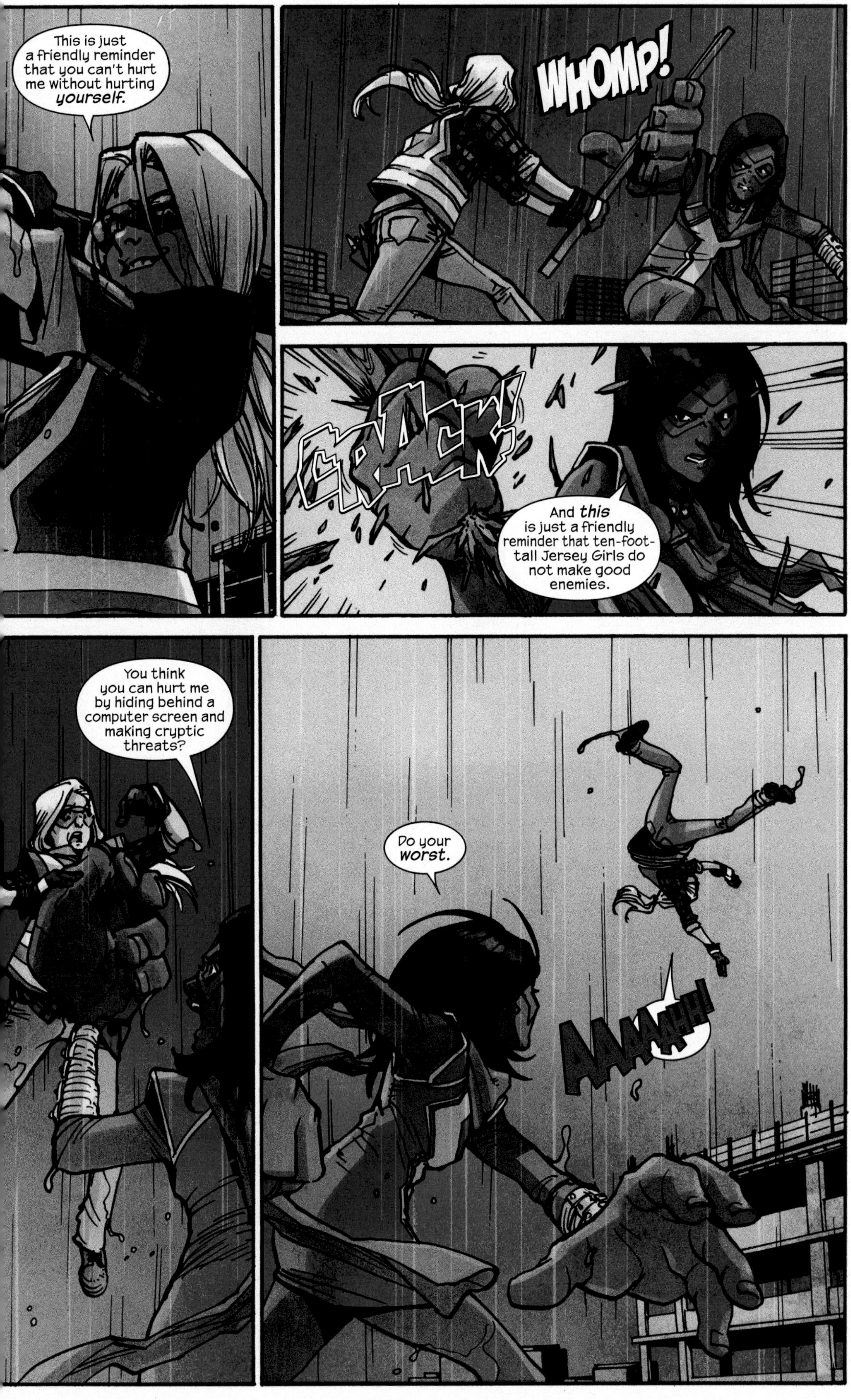
This is just a friendly reminder that you can't hurt me without hurting *yourself*.
WHOMP!
CRACK!
And *this* is just a friendly reminder that ten-foot-tall Jersey Girls do not make good enemies.
You think you can hurt me by hiding behind a computer screen and making cryptic threats?
Do your *worst*.
AAAAHH!

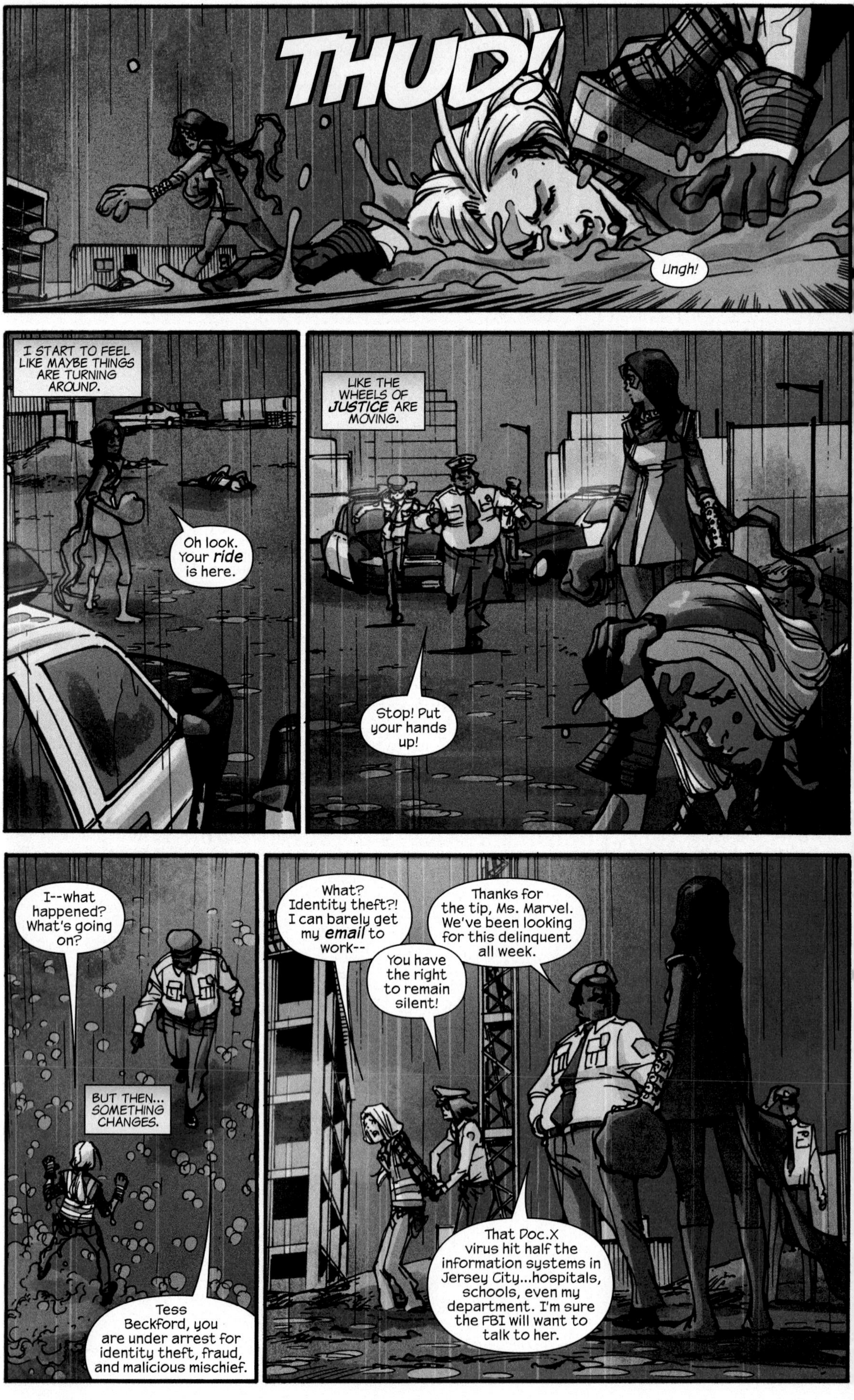
THUD!
Ungh!
I START TO FEEL LIKE MAYBE THINGS ARE TURNING AROUND.
Oh look. Your ride is here.
LIKE THE WHEELS OF JUSTICE ARE MOVING.
Stop! Put your hands up!
I--what happened? What's going on?
BUT THEN... SOMETHING CHANGES.
Tess Beckford, you are under arrest for identity theft, fraud, and malicious mischief.
What? Identity theft?! I can barely get my email to work--
You have the right to remain silent!
Thanks for the tip, Ms. Marvel. We've been looking for this delinquent all week.
That Doc.X virus hit half the information systems in Jersey City...hospitals, schools, even my department. I'm sure the FBI will want to talk to her.

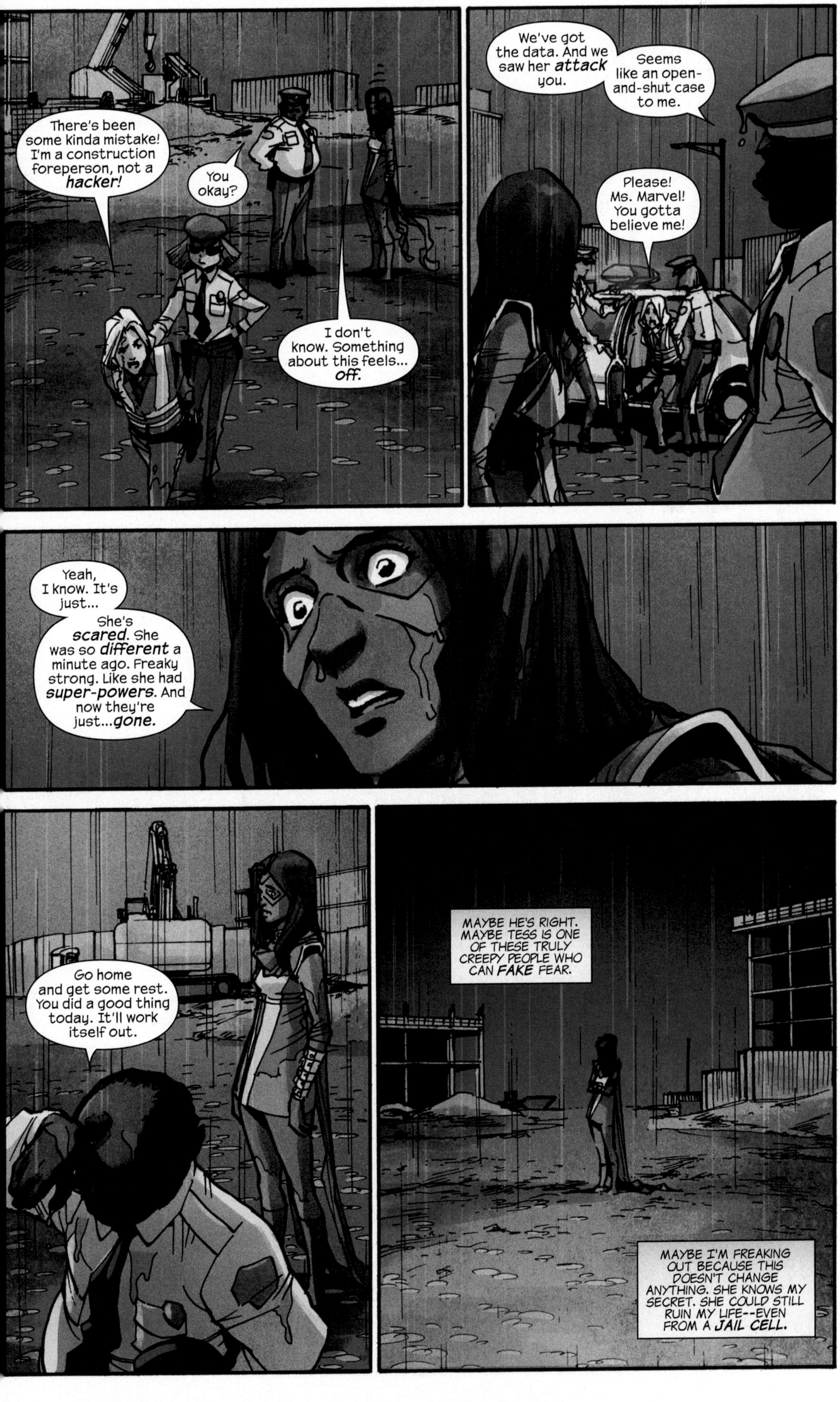
There's been some kinda mistake! I'm a construction foreperson, not a *hacker!*
You okay?
I don't know. Something about this feels... *off.*
We've got the data. And we saw her *attack* you.
Seems like an open-and-shut case to me.
Please! Ms. Marvel! You gotta believe me!
Yeah, I know. It's just...
She's *scared*. She was so *different* a minute ago. Freaky strong. Like she had *super-powers*. And now they're just...*gone.*
Go home and get some rest. You did a good thing today. It'll work itself out.
MAYBE HE'S RIGHT. MAYBE TESS IS ONE OF THESE TRULY CREEPY PEOPLE WHO CAN *FAKE* FEAR.
MAYBE I'M FREAKING OUT BECAUSE THIS DOESN'T CHANGE ANYTHING. SHE KNOWS MY SECRET. SHE COULD STILL RUIN MY LIFE--EVEN FROM A *JAIL CELL.*

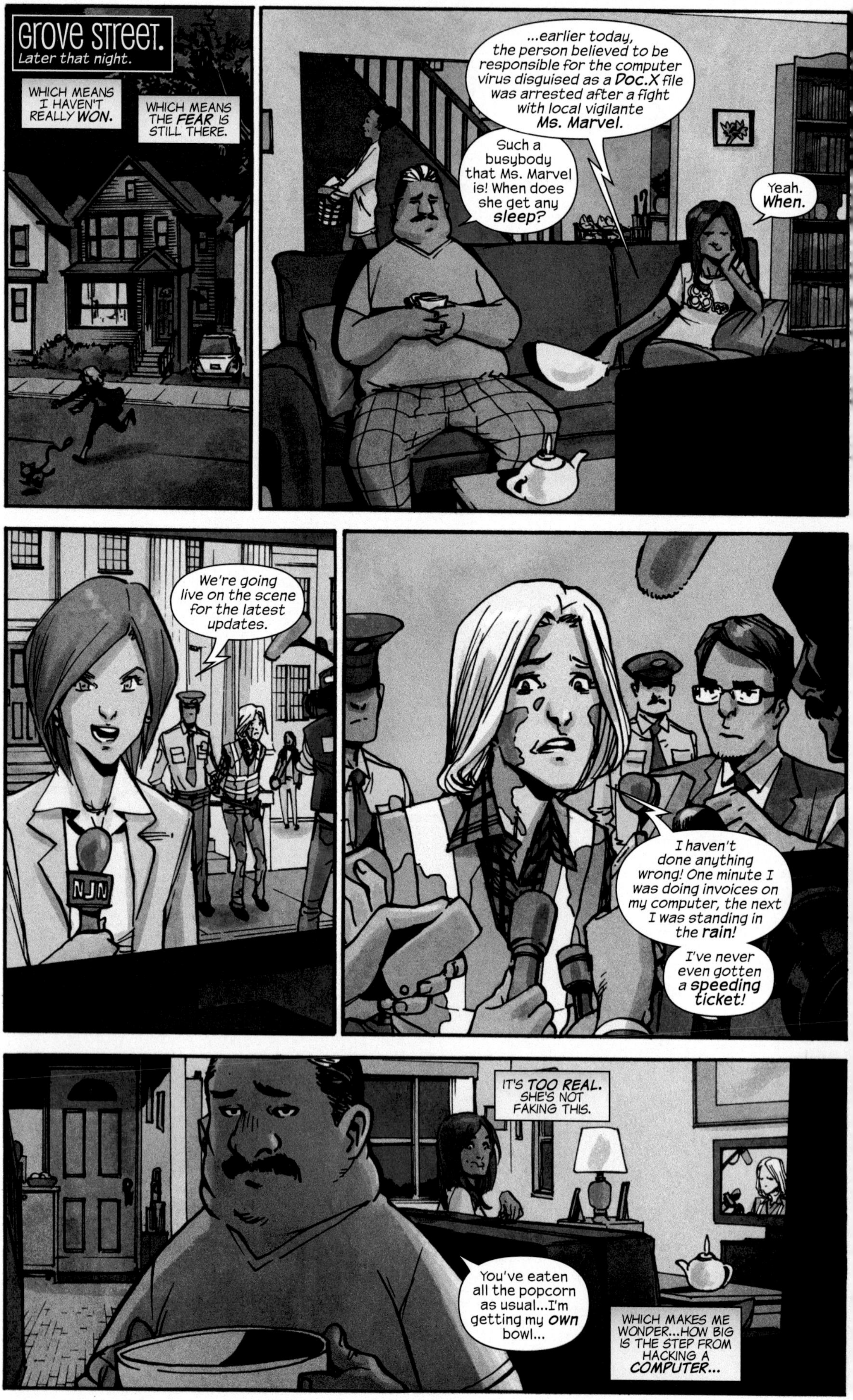

GROVE STREET.
Later that night.
WHICH MEANS I HAVEN'T REALLY WON.
WHICH MEANS THE FEAR IS STILL THERE.
...earlier today, the person believed to be responsible for the computer virus disguised as a Doc.X file was arrested after a fight with local vigilante Ms. Marvel.
Such a busybody that Ms. Marvel is! When does she get any sleep?
Yeah. When.
We're going live on the scene for the latest updates.
NJN
I haven't done anything wrong! One minute I was doing invoices on my computer, the next I was standing in the rain!
I've never even gotten a speeding ticket!
IT'S TOO REAL. SHE'S NOT FAKING THIS.
You've eaten all the popcorn as usual...I'm getting my own bowl...
WHICH MAKES ME WONDER...HOW BIG IS THE STEP FROM HACKING A COMPUTER...

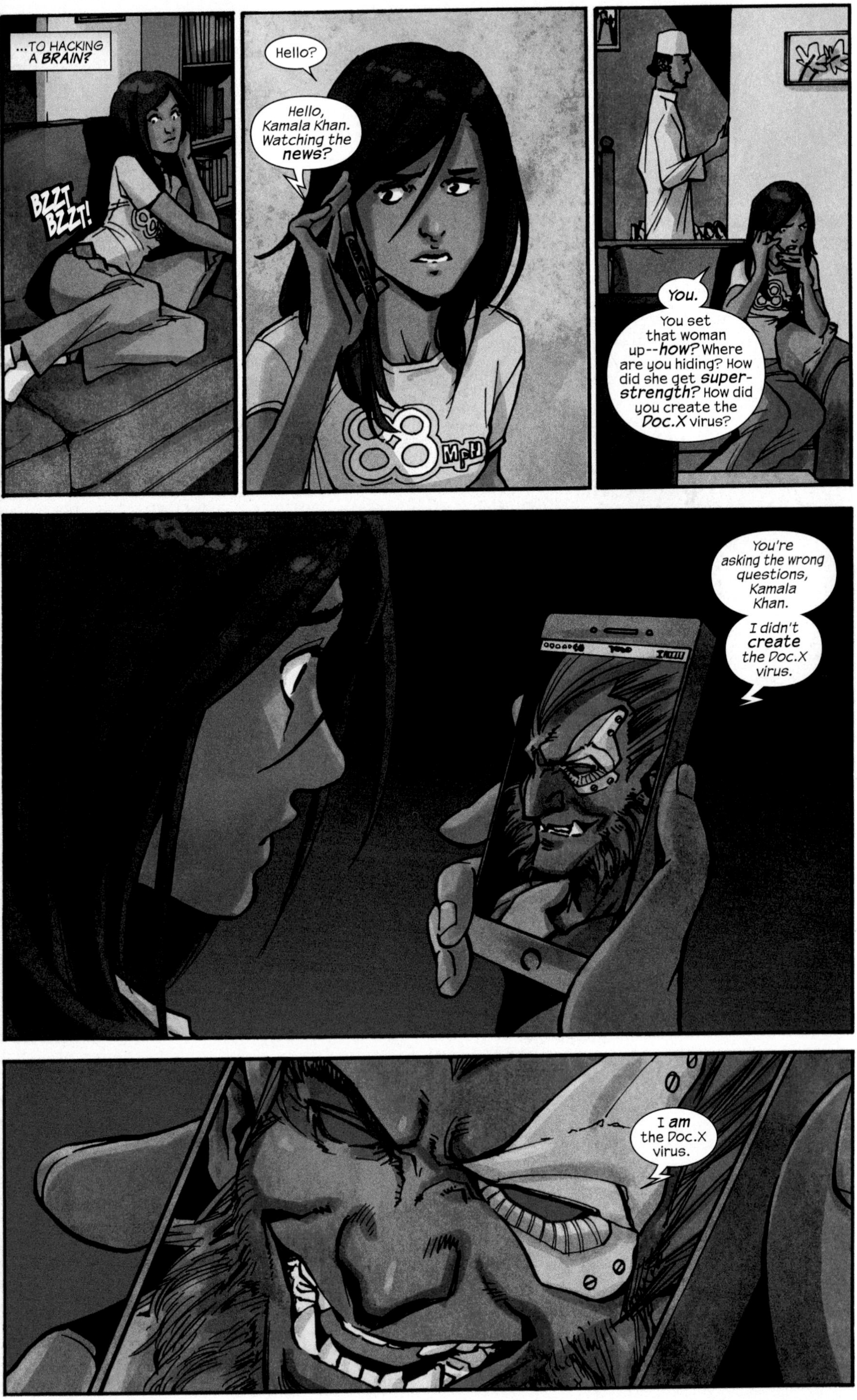
...TO HACKING A BRAIN?
BZZT BZZT!
Hello?
Hello, Kamala Khan. Watching the news?
You.
You set that woman up--how? Where are you hiding? How did she get super-strength? How did you create the Doc.X virus?
You're asking the wrong questions, Kamala Khan.
I didn't create the Doc.X virus.
I am the Doc.X virus.

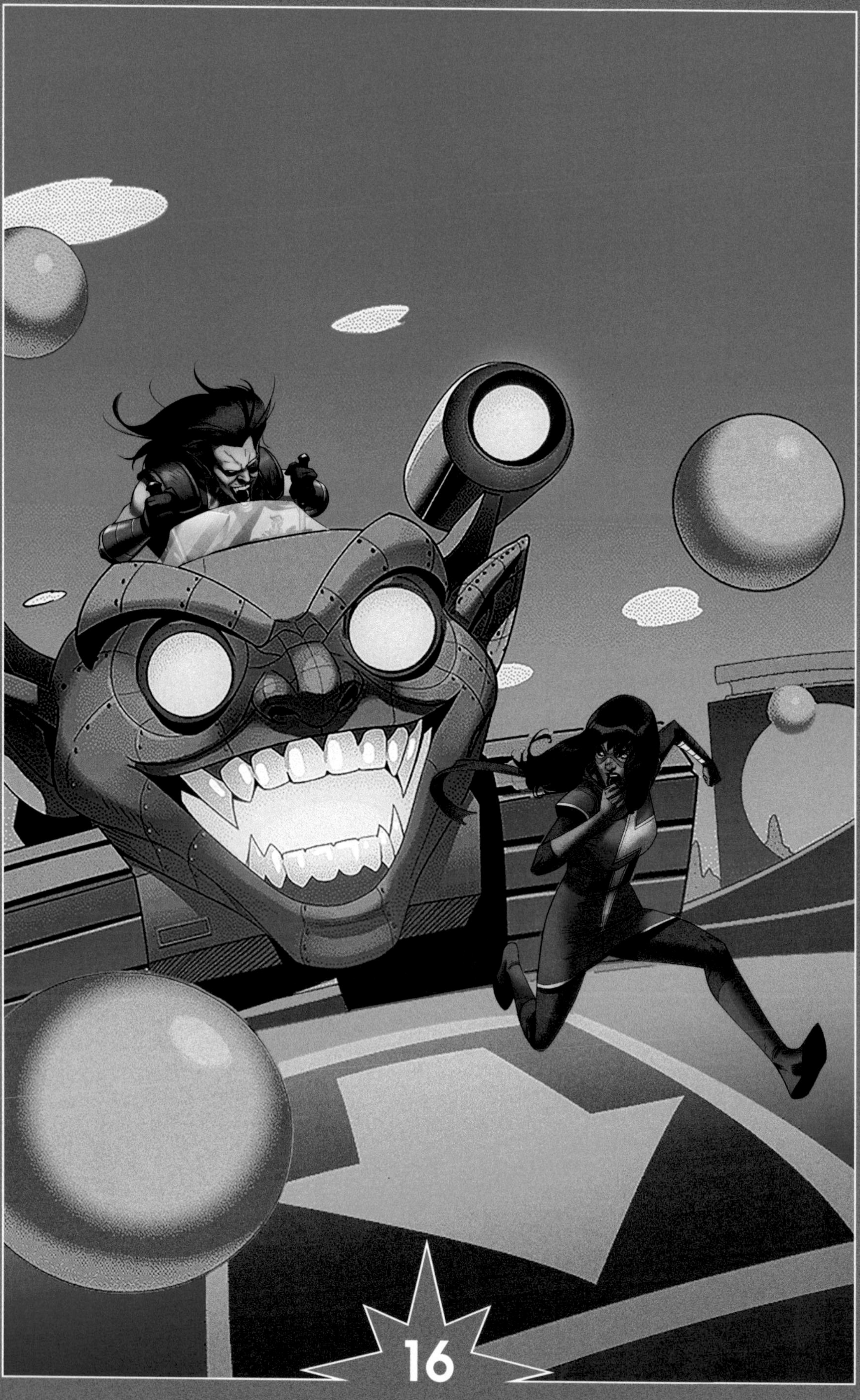

16

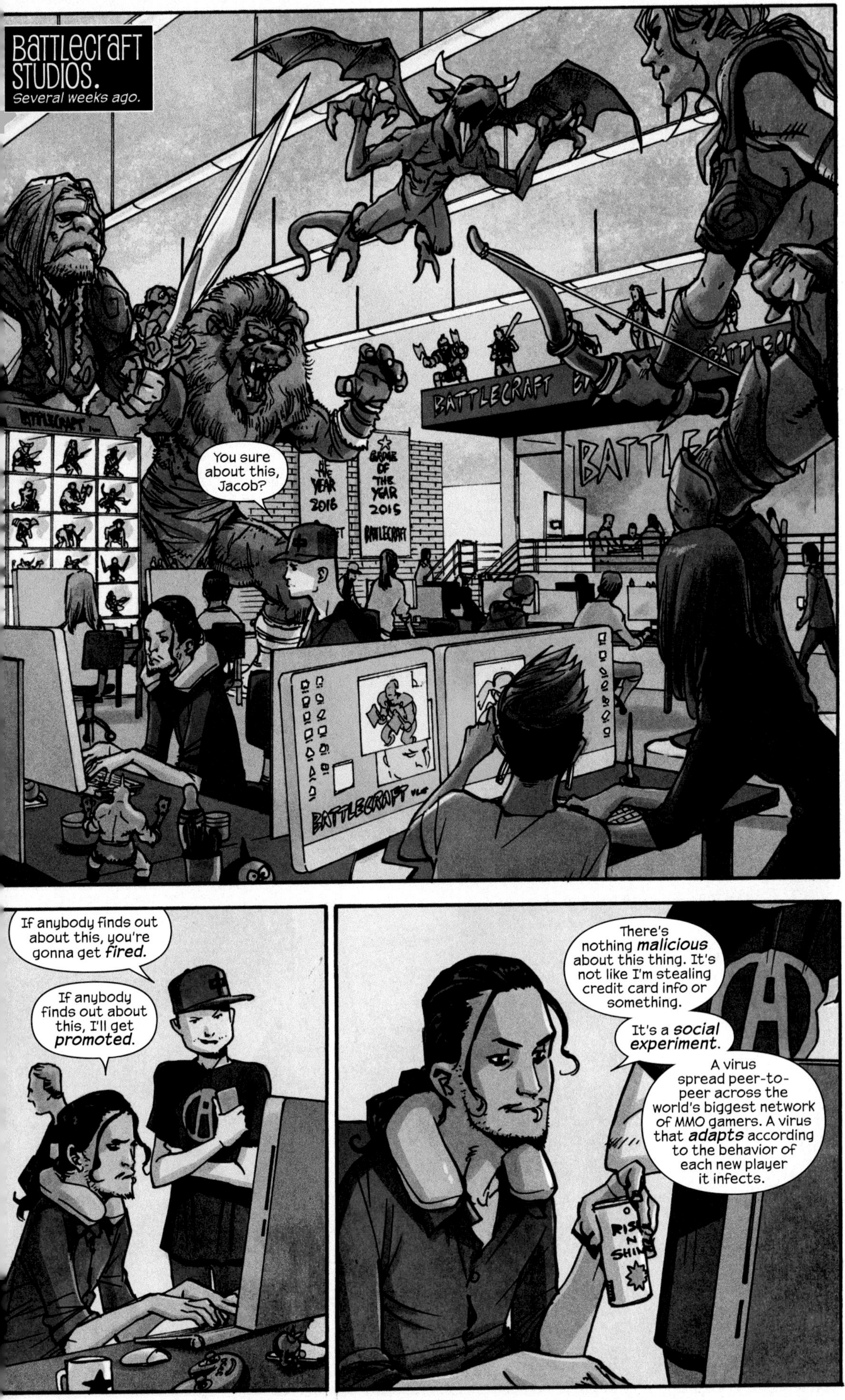
BATTLECRAFT STUDIOS.
Several weeks ago.
You sure about this, Jacob?
GAME OF THE YEAR 2015 BATTLECRAFT
BATTLECRAFT
If anybody finds out about this, you're gonna get *fired.*
If anybody finds out about this, I'll get *promoted*.
There's nothing ***malicious*** about this thing. It's not like I'm stealing credit card info or something.
It's a ***social experiment***.
A virus spread peer-to-peer across the world's biggest network of MMO gamers. A virus that ***adapts*** according to the behavior of each new player it infects.

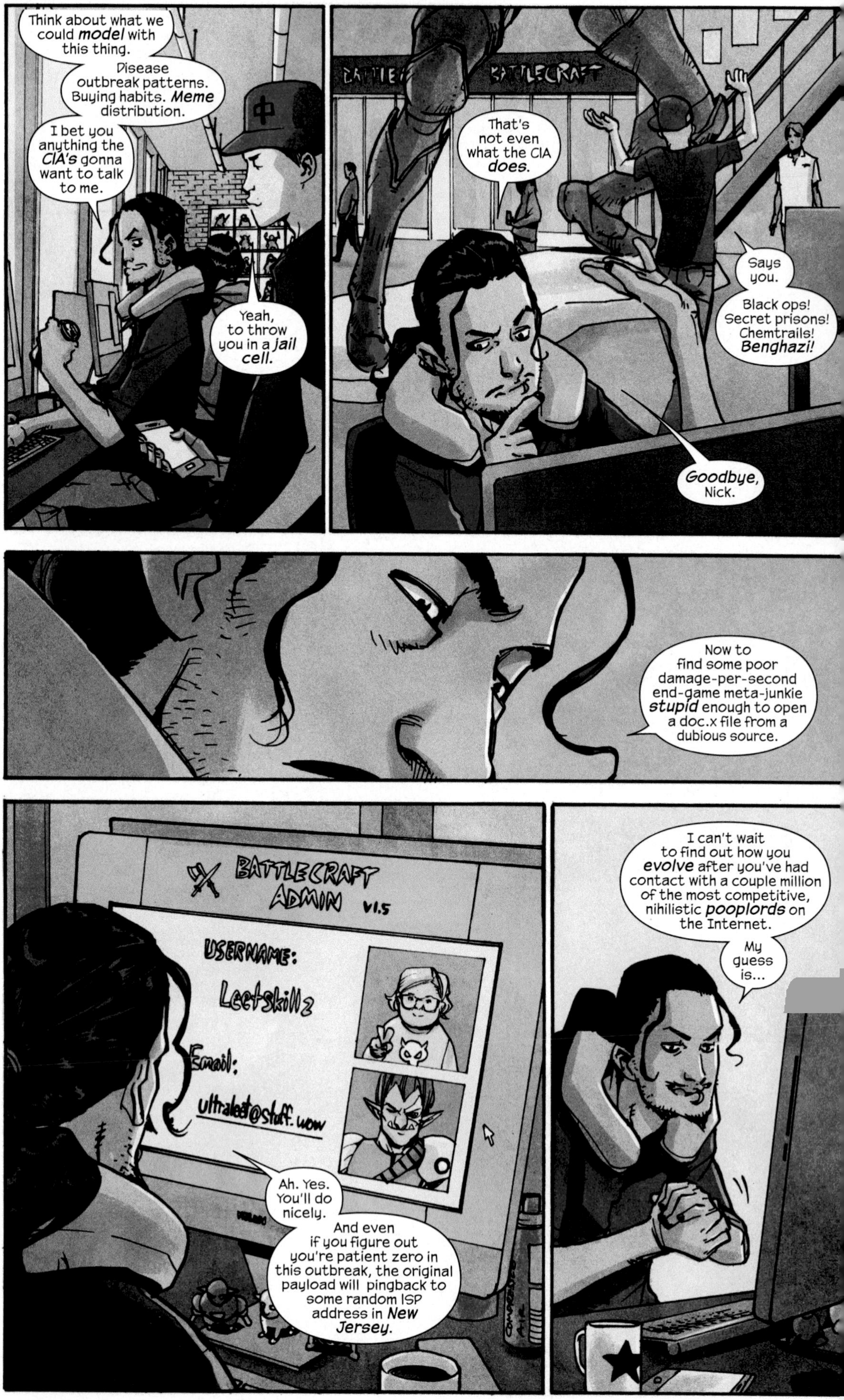
Think about what we could *model* with this thing.
Disease outbreak patterns. Buying habits. *Meme* distribution.
I bet you anything the *CIA's* gonna want to talk to me.
Yeah, to throw you in a *jail cell.*
BATTLECRAFT
That's not even what the CIA *does.*
Says you.
Black ops! Secret prisons! Chemtrails! *Benghazi!*
Goodbye, Nick.
Now to find some poor damage-per-second end-game meta-junkie *stupid* enough to open a doc.x file from a dubious source.
BATTLECRAFT ADMIN v1.5
USERNAME:
Leetskillz
Email:
ultraleet@stuff.wow
Ah. Yes. You'll do nicely.
And even if you figure out you're patient zero in this outbreak, the original payload will pingback to some random ISP address in *New Jersey.*
I can't wait to find out how you *evolve* after you've had contact with a couple million of the most competitive, nihilistic *pooplords* on the Internet.
My guess is...

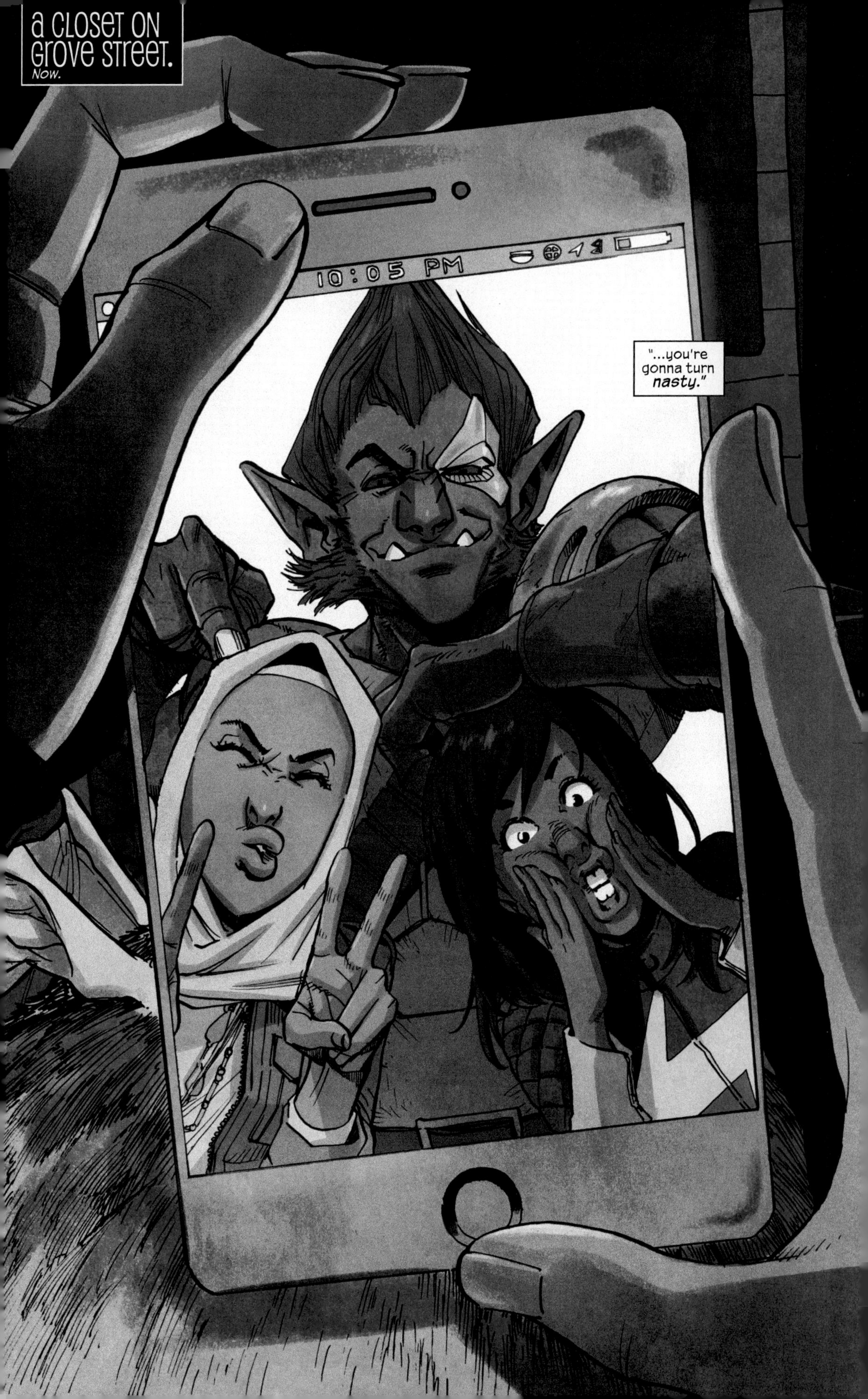

a CLOSET ON GROVE STREET.
Now.
10:05 PM
"...you're gonna turn nasty."

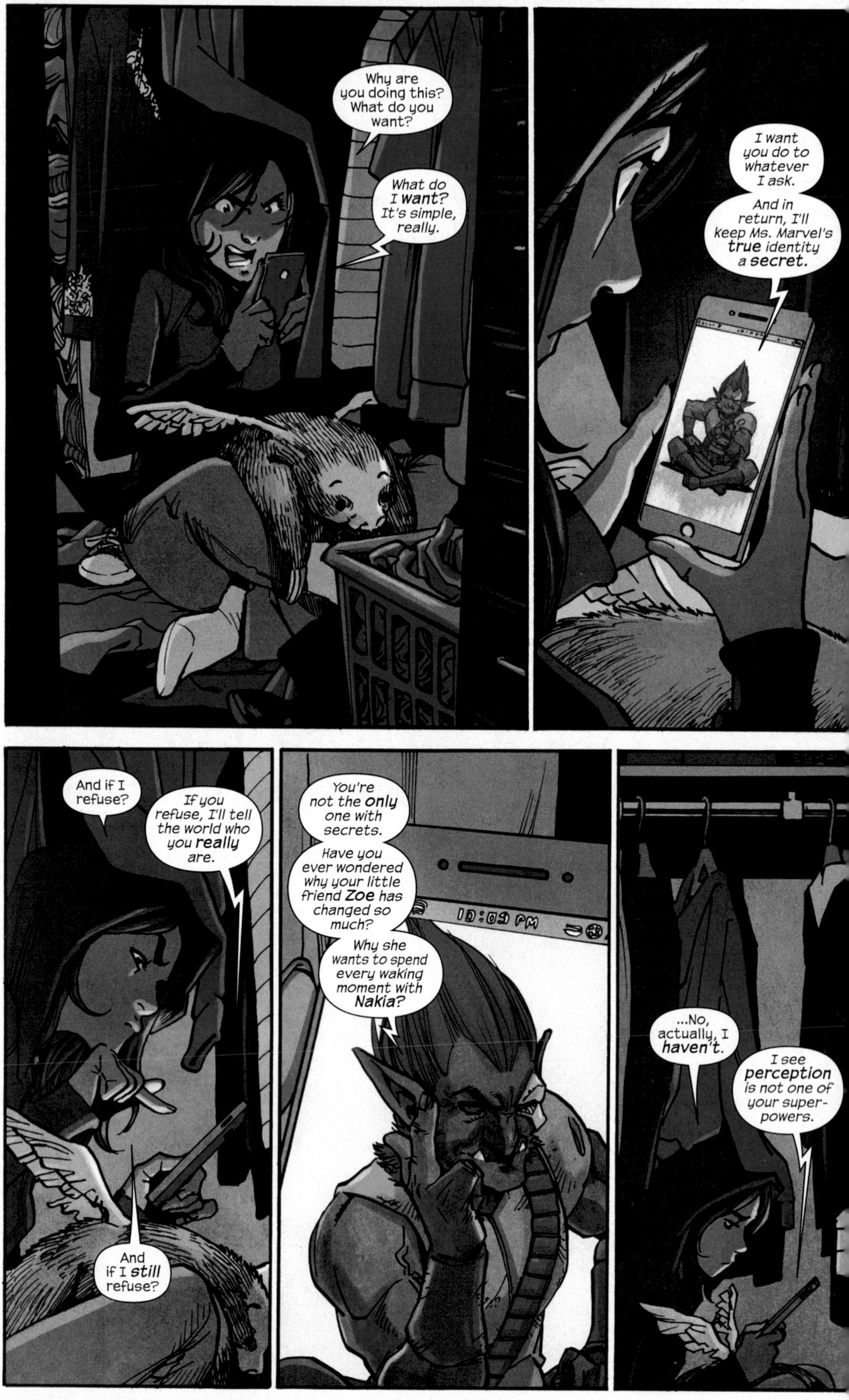
Why are you doing this? What do you want?
What do I want? It's simple, really.
I want you do to whatever I ask.
And in return, I'll keep Ms. Marvel's true identity a secret.
And if I refuse?
If you refuse, I'll tell the world who you really are.
And if I still refuse?
You're not the only one with secrets.
Have you ever wondered why your little friend Zoe has changed so much?
Why she wants to spend every waking moment with Nakia?
10:09 PM
...No, actually, I haven't.
I see perception is not one of your superpowers.

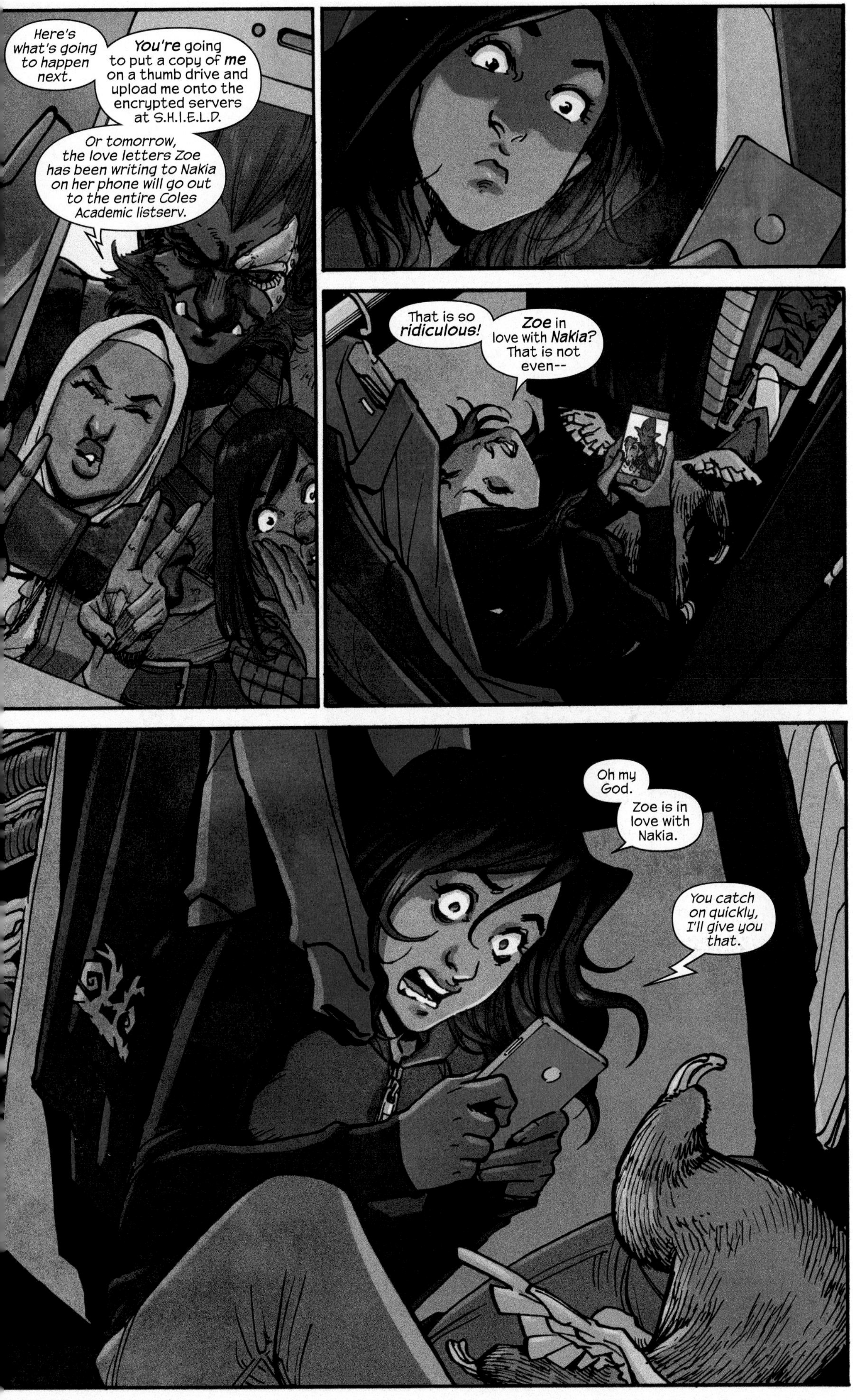
Here's what's going to happen next.
You're going to put a copy of me on a thumb drive and upload me onto the encrypted servers at S.H.I.E.L.D.
Or tomorrow, the love letters Zoe has been writing to Nakia on her phone will go out to the entire Coles Academic listserv.
That is so ridiculous!
Zoe in love with Nakia? That is not even--
Oh my God.
Zoe is in love with Nakia.
You catch on quickly, I'll give you that.

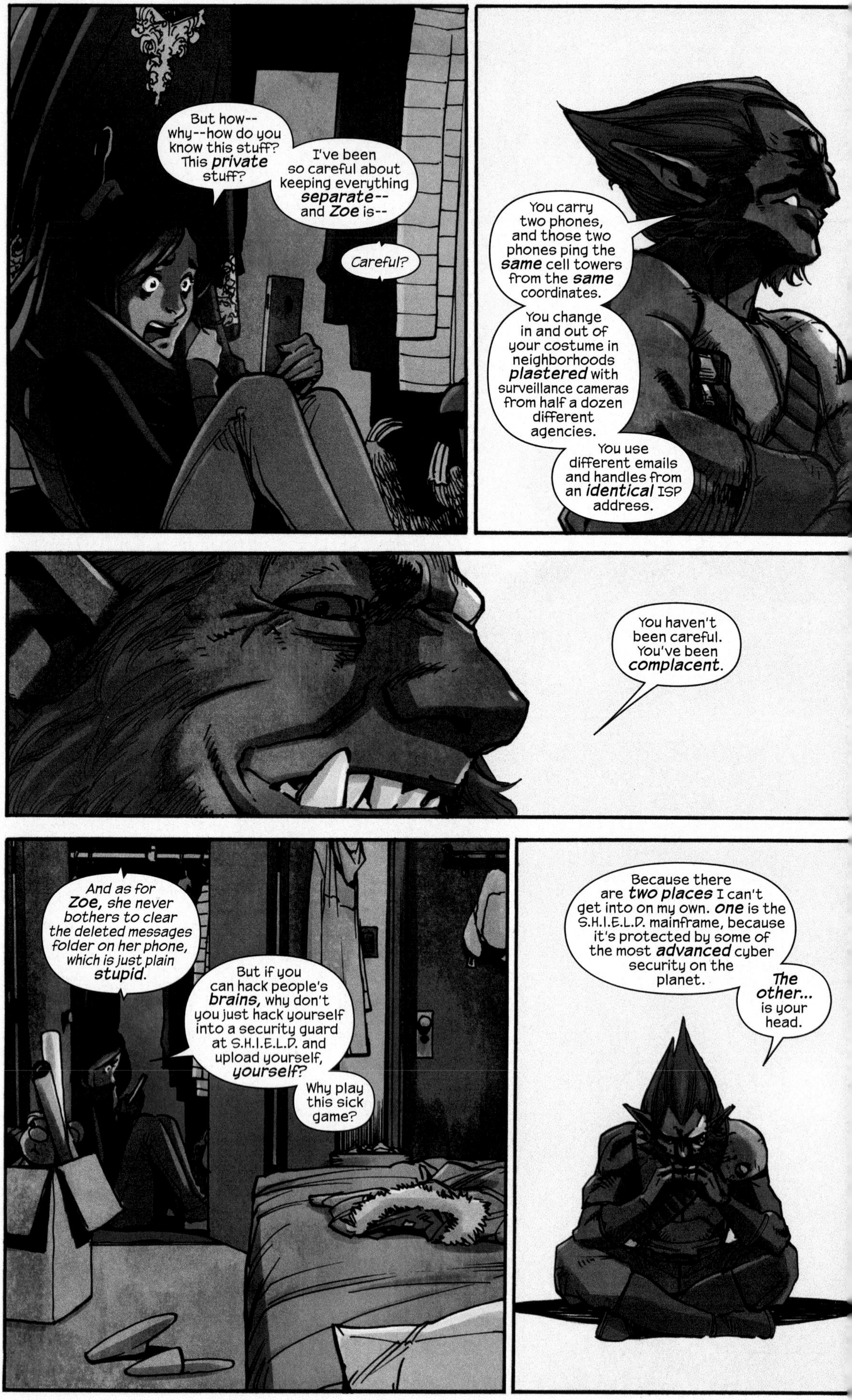

But how-- why--how do you know this stuff? This *private* stuff?
I've been so careful about keeping everything *separate*-- and *Zoe* is--
Careful?
You carry two phones, and those two phones ping the *same* cell towers from the *same* coordinates.
You change in and out of your costume in neighborhoods *plastered* with surveillance cameras from half a dozen different agencies.
You use different emails and handles from an *identical* ISP address.
You haven't been careful. You've been *complacent*.
And as for ***Zoe,*** *she never bothers to clear the deleted messages folder on her phone, which is just plain* ***stupid.***
But if you can hack people's *brains,* why don't you just hack yourself into a security guard at S.H.I.E.L.D. and upload yourself, *yourself?*
Why play this sick game?
Because there are *two places* I can't get into on my own. *One* is the S.H.I.E.L.D. mainframe, because it's protected by some of the most *advanced* cyber security on the planet.
The other... is your head.

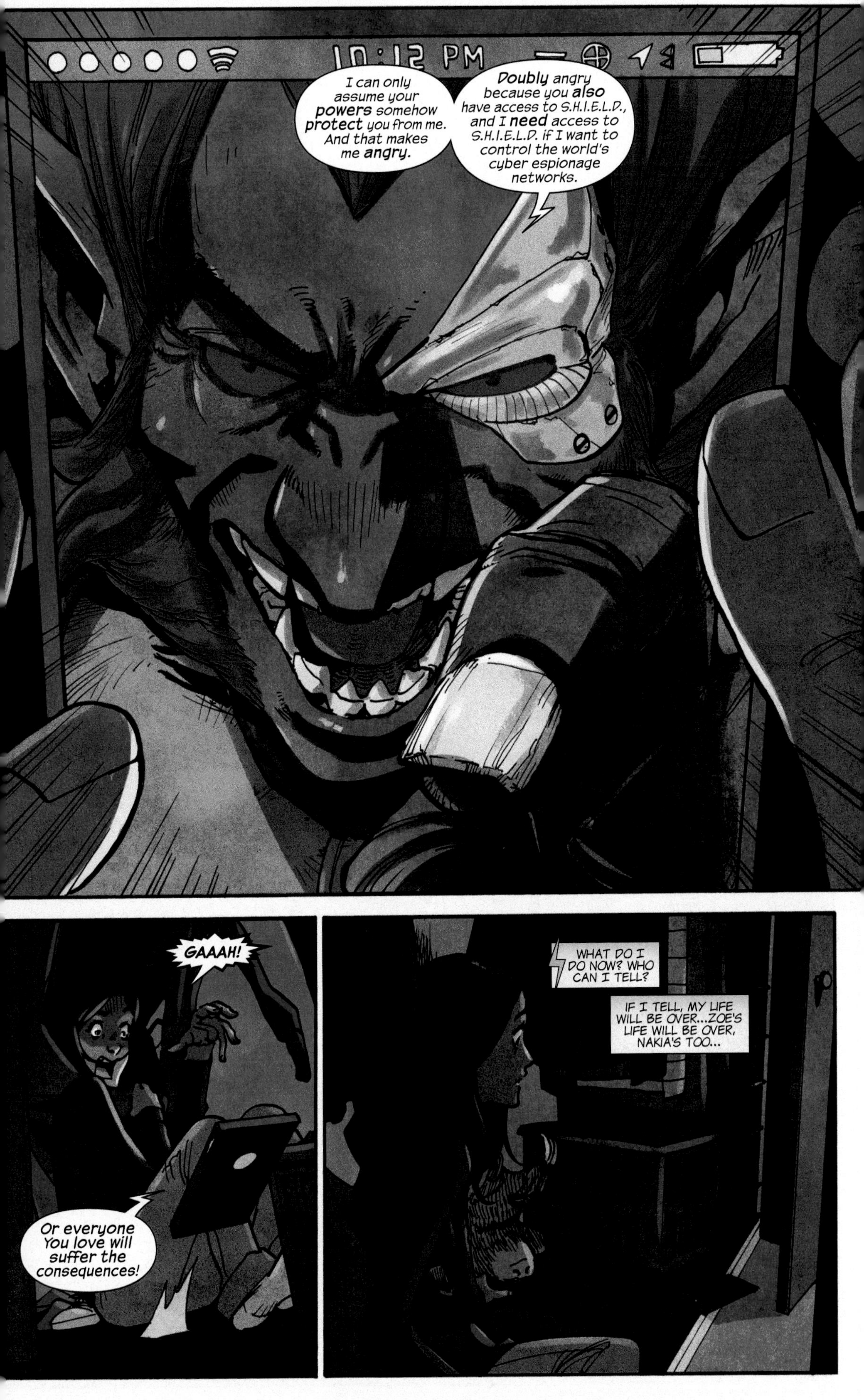
10:12 PM
I can only assume your powers somehow protect you from me. And that makes me angry.
Doubly angry because you also have access to S.H.I.E.L.D., and I need access to S.H.I.E.L.D. if I want to control the world's cyber espionage networks.
GAAAH!
Or everyone You love will suffer the consequences!
WHAT DO I DO NOW? WHO CAN I TELL?
IF I TELL, MY LIFE WILL BE OVER...ZOE'S LIFE WILL BE OVER, NAKIA'S TOO...

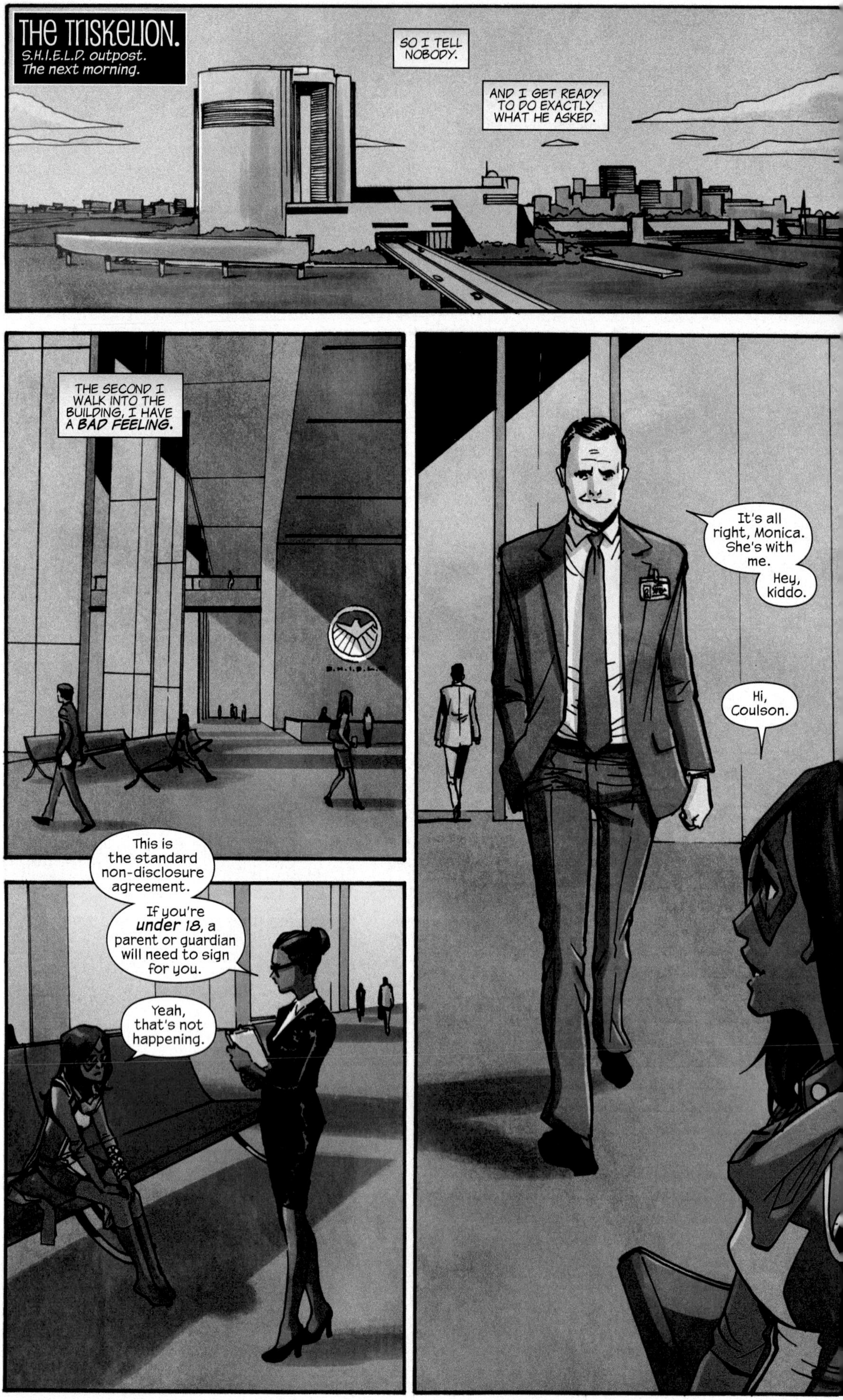
THE TRISKELION.
S.H.I.E.L.D. outpost. The next morning.
SO I TELL NOBODY.
AND I GET READY TO DO EXACTLY WHAT HE ASKED.
THE SECOND I WALK INTO THE BUILDING, I HAVE A BAD FEELING.
It's all right, Monica. She's with me.
Hey, kiddo.
Hi, Coulson.
This is the standard non-disclosure agreement.
If you're under 18, a parent or guardian will need to sign for you.
Yeah, that's not happening.

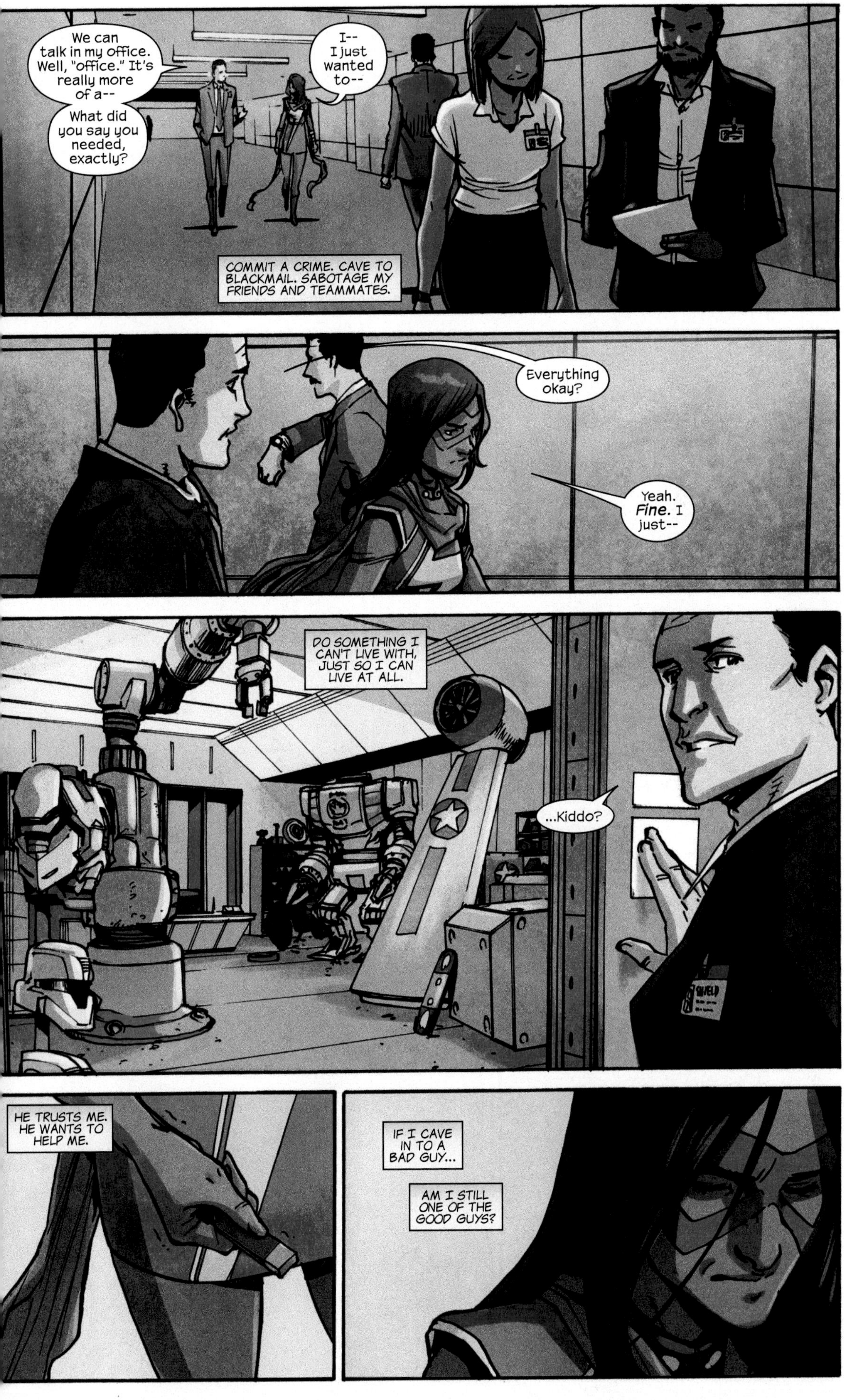
We can talk in my office. Well, "office." It's really more of a--
What did you say you needed, exactly?
I-- I just wanted to--
COMMIT A CRIME. CAVE TO BLACKMAIL. SABOTAGE MY FRIENDS AND TEAMMATES.
Everything okay?
Yeah. Fine. I just--
DO SOMETHING I CAN'T LIVE WITH, JUST SO I CAN LIVE AT ALL.
...Kiddo?
HE TRUSTS ME. HE WANTS TO HELP ME.
IF I CAVE IN TO A BAD GUY...
AM I STILL ONE OF THE GOOD GUYS?

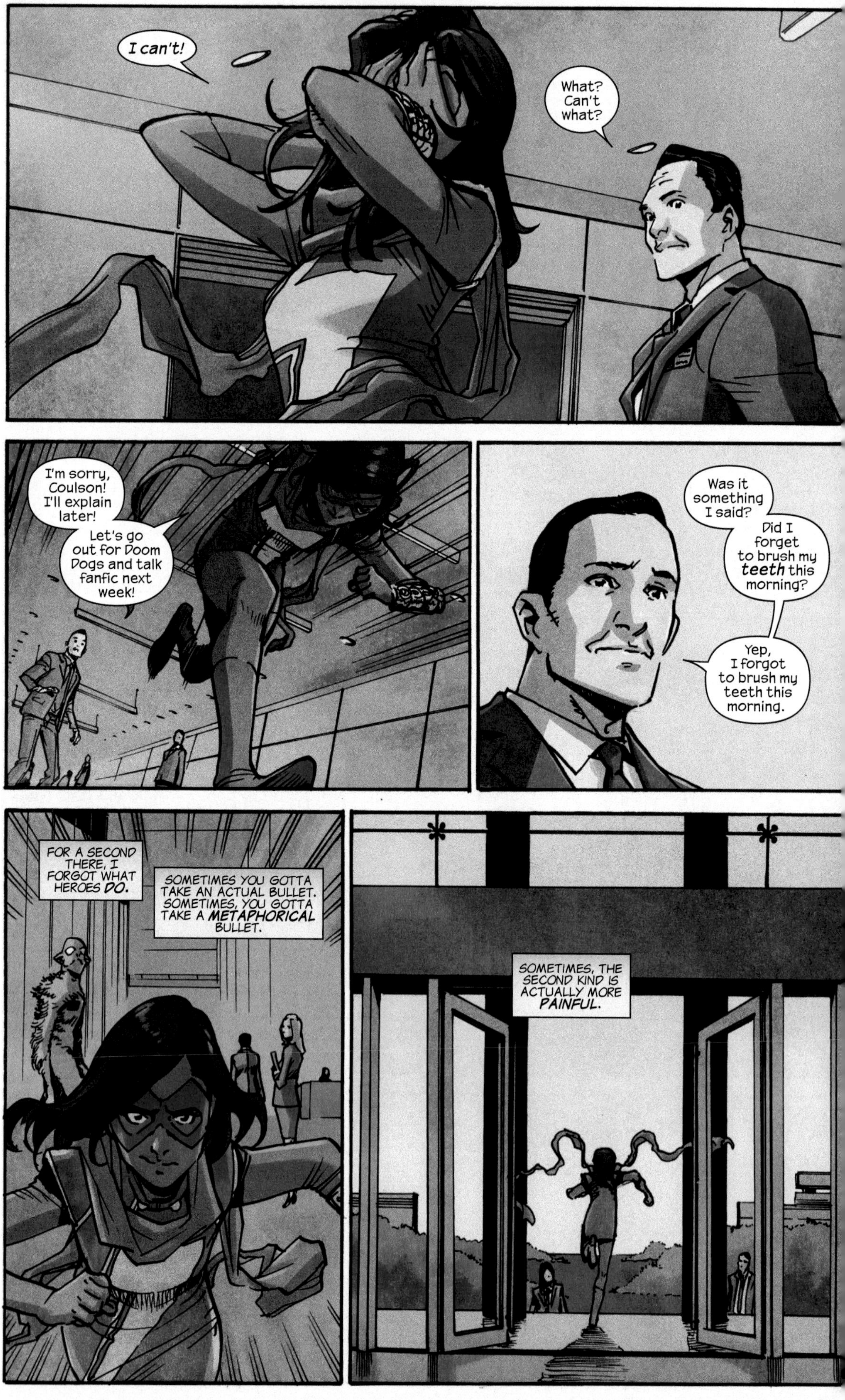
I can't!
What? Can't what?
I'm sorry, Coulson! I'll explain later!
Let's go out for Doom Dogs and talk fanfic next week!
Was it something I said?
Did I forget to brush my teeth this morning?
Yep, I forgot to brush my teeth this morning.
FOR A SECOND THERE, I FORGOT WHAT HEROES DO.
SOMETIMES YOU GOTTA TAKE AN ACTUAL BULLET. SOMETIMES, YOU GOTTA TAKE A METAPHORICAL BULLET.
SOMETIMES, THE SECOND KIND IS ACTUALLY MORE PAINFUL.

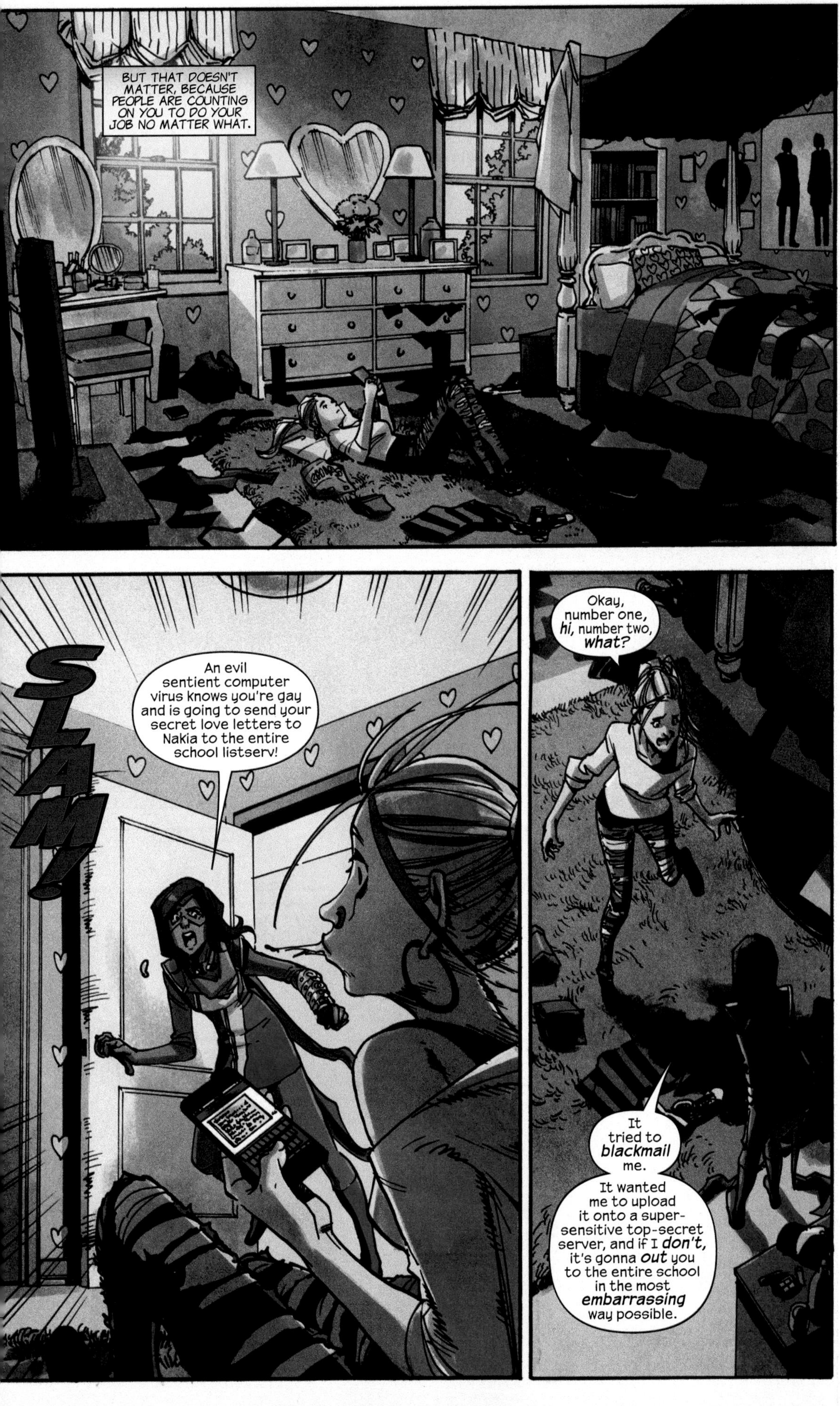
BUT THAT DOESN'T MATTER, BECAUSE PEOPLE ARE COUNTING ON YOU TO DO YOUR JOB NO MATTER WHAT.
SLAM!
An evil sentient computer virus knows you're gay and is going to send your secret love letters to Nakia to the entire school listserv!
Okay, number one, hi, number two, what?
It tried to blackmail me.
It wanted me to upload it onto a super-sensitive top-secret server, and if I don't, it's gonna out you to the entire school in the most embarrassing way possible.

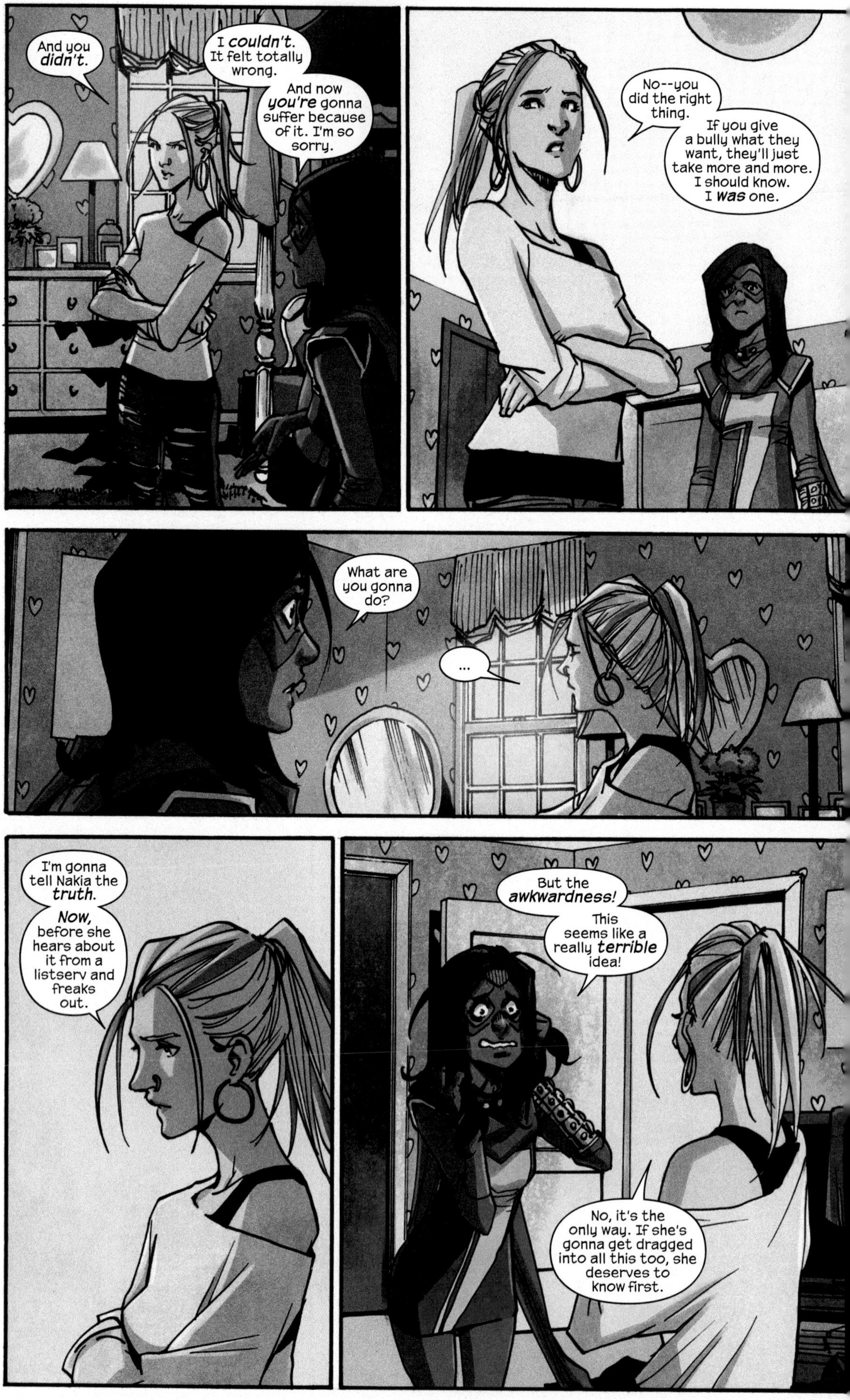

And you didn't.
I couldn't. It felt totally wrong.
And now you're gonna suffer because of it. I'm so sorry.
No--you did the right thing.
If you give a bully what they want, they'll just take more and more. I should know. I was one.
What are you gonna do?
...
I'm gonna tell Nakia the truth.
Now, before she hears about it from a listserv and freaks out.
But the awkwardness!
This seems like a really terrible idea!
No, it's the only way. If she's gonna get dragged into all this too, she deserves to know first.

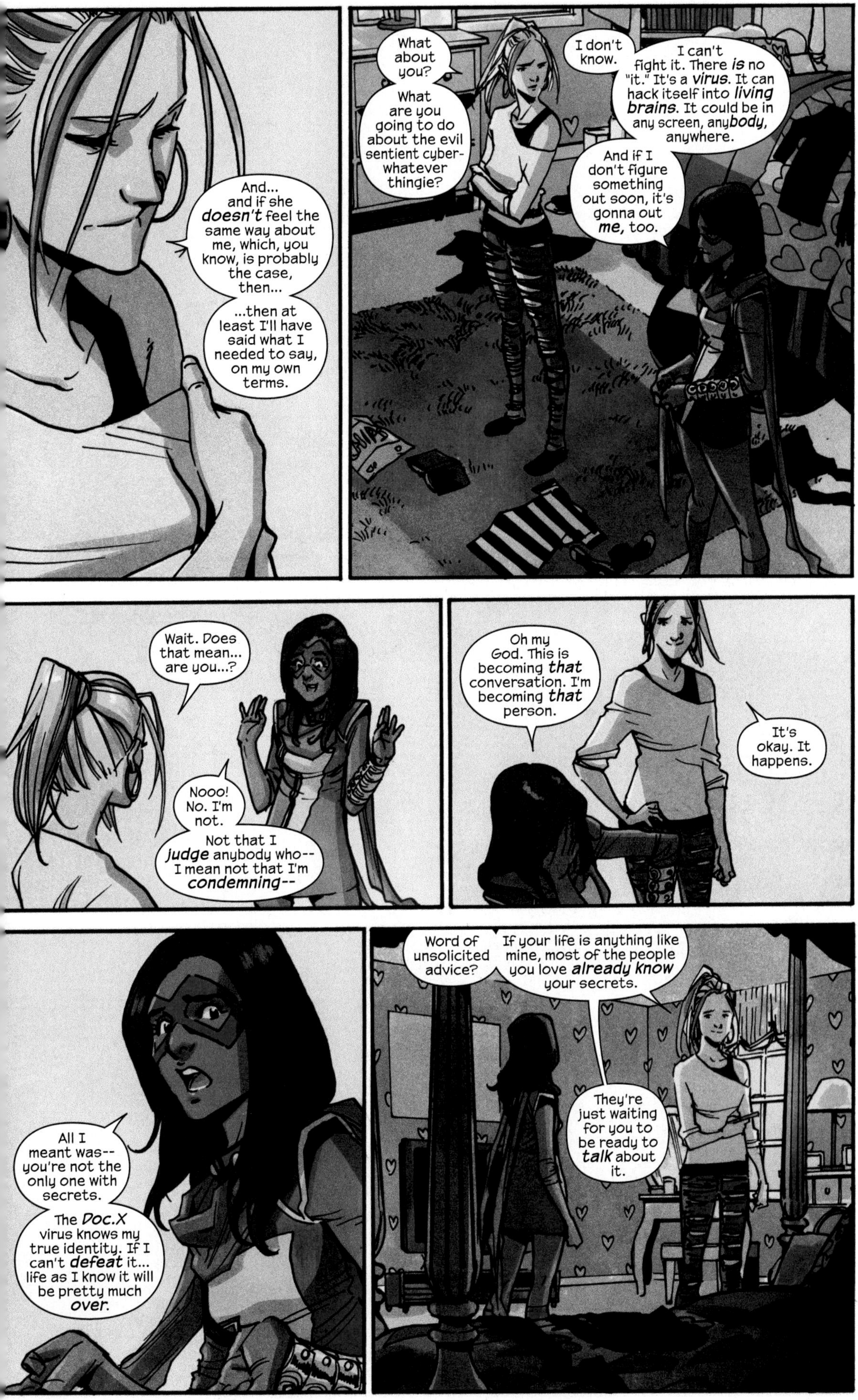
And... and if she doesn't feel the same way about me, which, you know, is probably the case, then...
...then at least I'll have said what I needed to say, on my own terms.
What about you?
What are you going to do about the evil sentient cyber-whatever thingie?
I don't know.
I can't fight it. There is no "it." It's a virus. It can hack itself into living brains. It could be in any screen, anybody, anywhere.
And if I don't figure something out soon, it's gonna out me, too.
Wait. Does that mean... are you...?
Nooo! No. I'm not.
Not that I judge anybody who-- I mean not that I'm condemning--
Oh my God. This is becoming that conversation. I'm becoming that person.
It's okay. It happens.
All I meant was-- you're not the only one with secrets.
The Doc.X virus knows my true identity. If I can't defeat it... life as I know it will be pretty much over.
Word of unsolicited advice?
If your life is anything like mine, most of the people you love already know your secrets.
They're just waiting for you to be ready to talk about it.

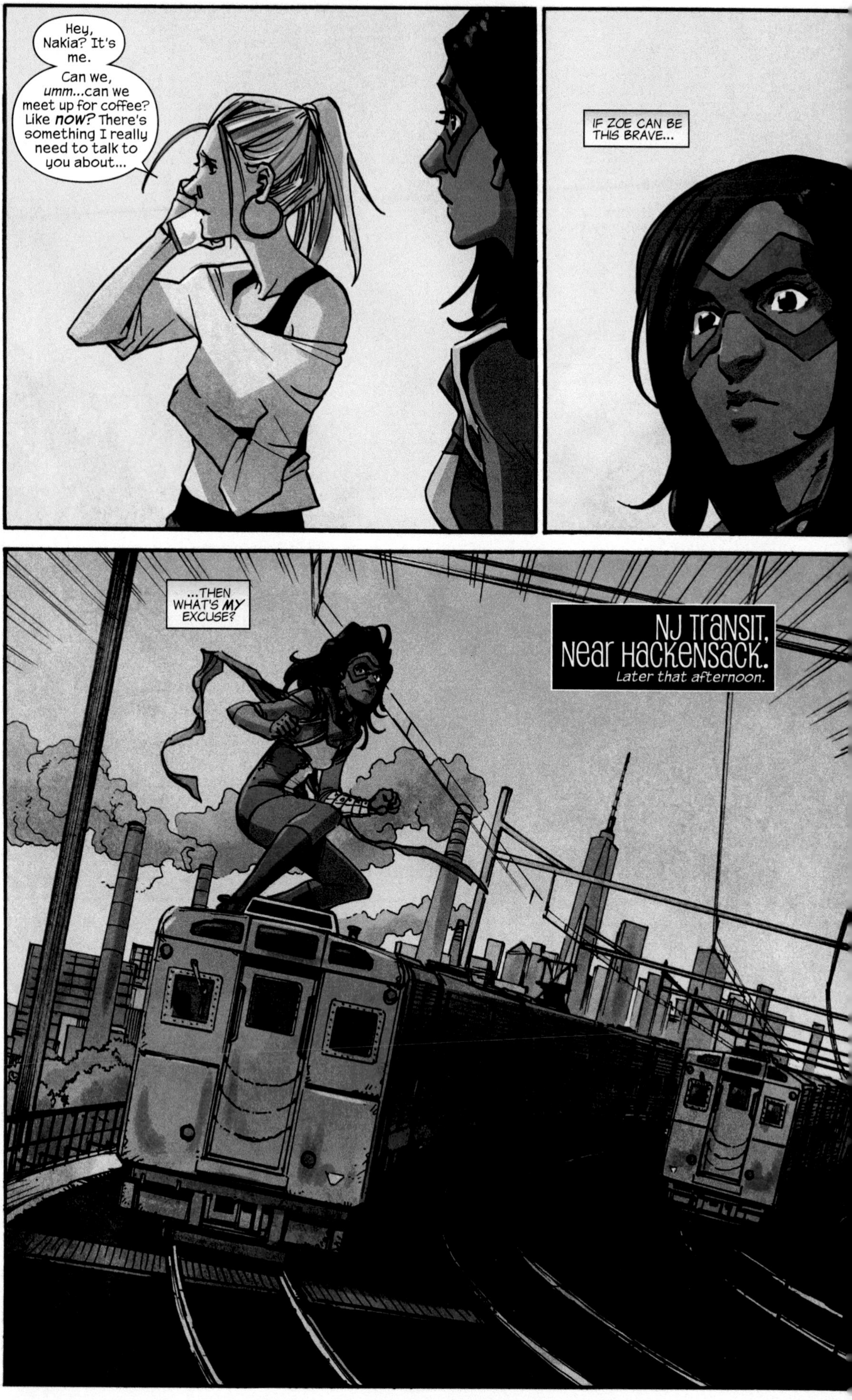
Hey, Nakia? It's me.
Can we, *umm*...can we meet up for coffee? Like ***NOW?*** There's something I really need to talk to you about...
IF ZOE CAN BE THIS BRAVE...
...THEN WHAT'S ***MY*** EXCUSE?
NJ TRANSIT, NEAR HACKENSACK.
Later that afternoon.

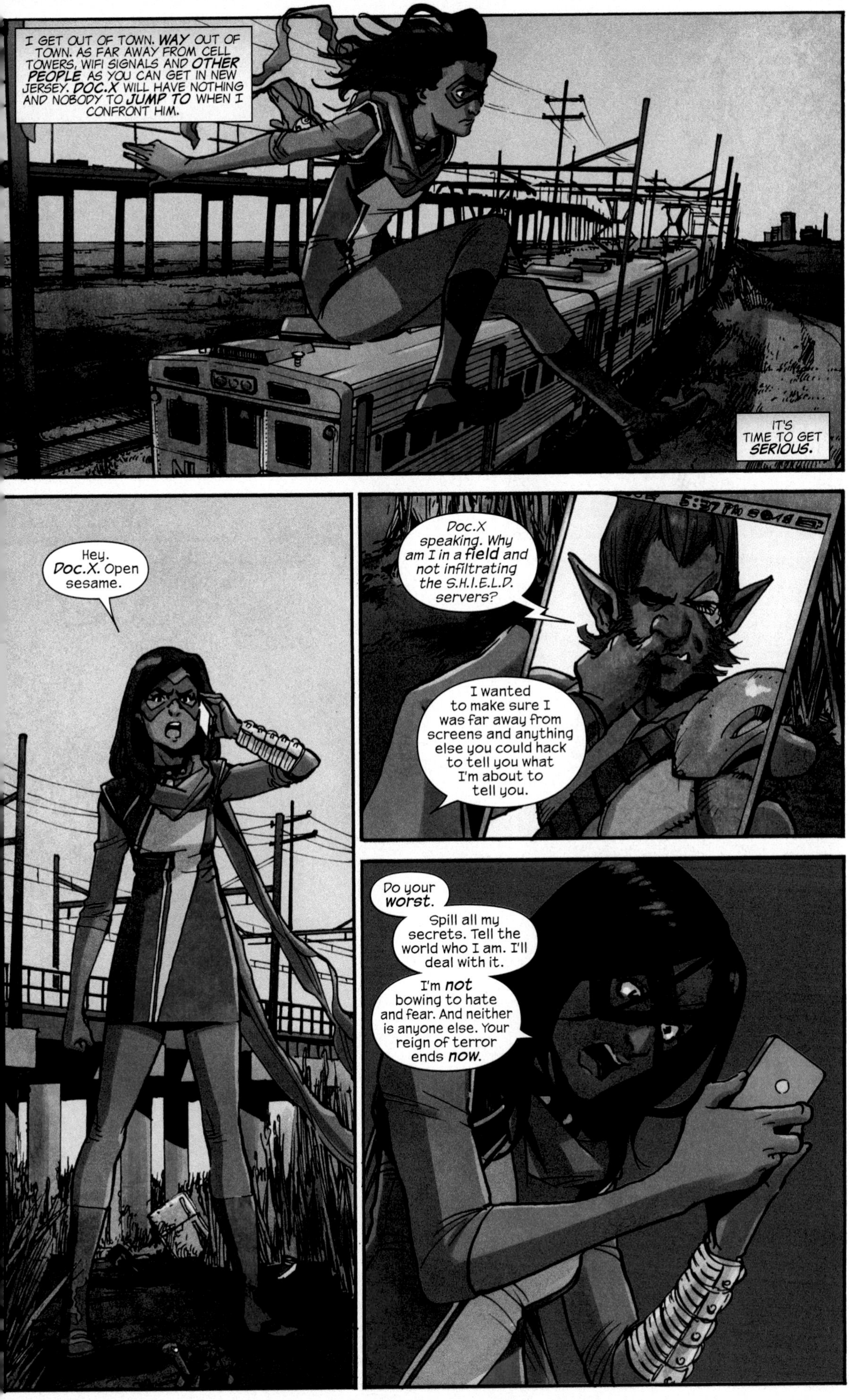
I GET OUT OF TOWN. WAY OUT OF TOWN. AS FAR AWAY FROM CELL TOWERS, WIFI SIGNALS AND OTHER PEOPLE AS YOU CAN GET IN NEW JERSEY. DOC.X WILL HAVE NOTHING AND NOBODY TO JUMP TO WHEN I CONFRONT HIM.
IT'S TIME TO GET SERIOUS.
Hey. Doc.X. Open sesame.
Doc.X speaking. Why am I in a field and not infiltrating the S.H.I.E.L.D. servers?
I wanted to make sure I was far away from screens and anything else you could hack to tell you what I'm about to tell you.
Do your worst.
Spill all my secrets. Tell the world who I am. I'll deal with it.
I'm not bowing to hate and fear. And neither is anyone else. Your reign of terror ends now.

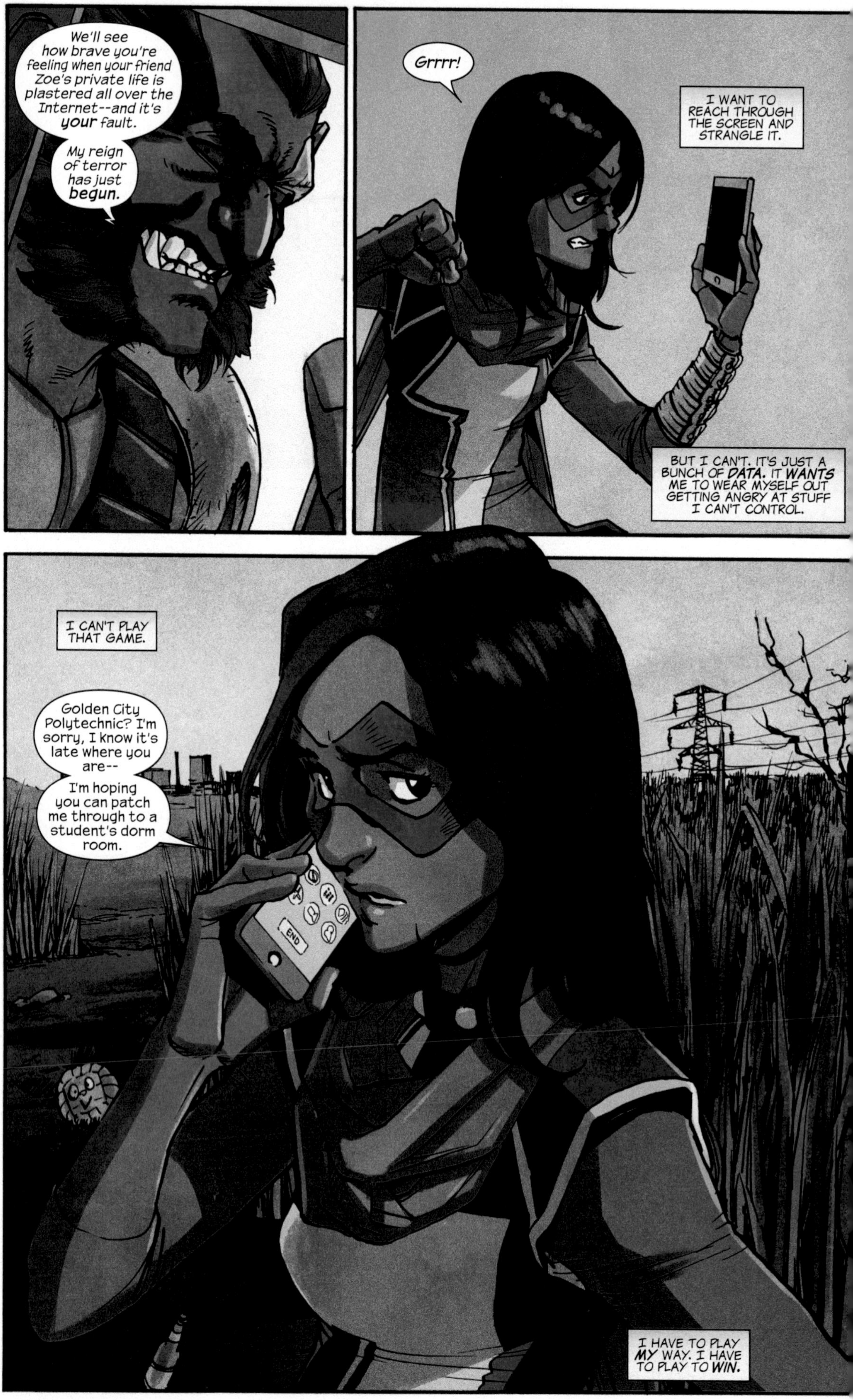
We'll see how brave you're feeling when your friend Zoe's private life is plastered all over the Internet--and it's your fault.
My reign of terror has just begun.
Grrrr!
I WANT TO REACH THROUGH THE SCREEN AND STRANGLE IT.
BUT I CAN'T. IT'S JUST A BUNCH OF DATA. IT WANTS ME TO WEAR MYSELF OUT GETTING ANGRY AT STUFF I CAN'T CONTROL.
I CAN'T PLAY THAT GAME.
Golden City Polytechnic? I'm sorry, I know it's late where you are--
I'm hoping you can patch me through to a student's dorm room.
END
I HAVE TO PLAY MY WAY. I HAVE TO PLAY TO WIN.

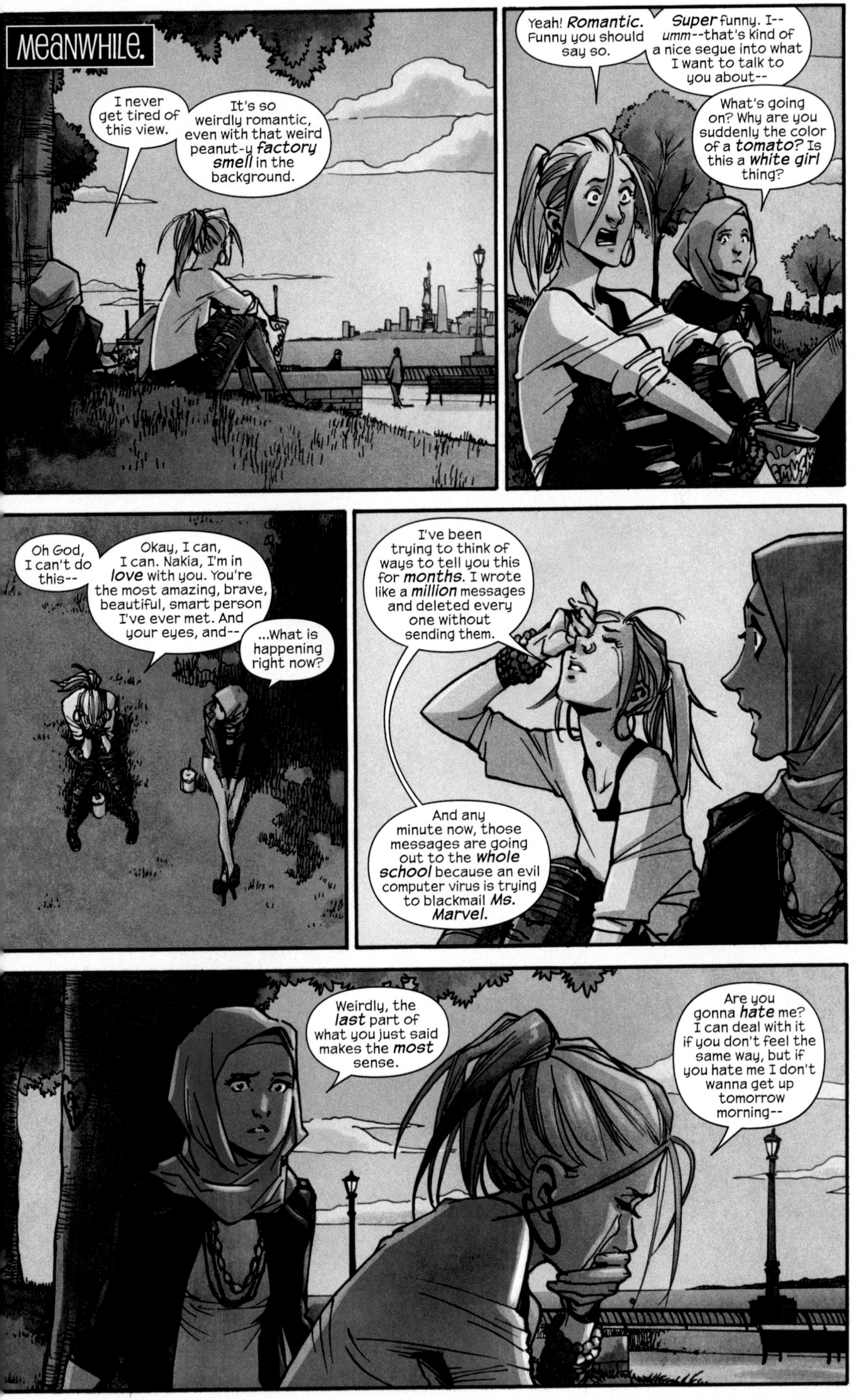
MEANWHILE.
I never get tired of this view.
It's so weirdly romantic, even with that weird peanut-y factory smell in the background.
Yeah! Romantic. Funny you should say so.
Super funny. I-- umm--that's kind of a nice segue into what I want to talk to you about--
What's going on? Why are you suddenly the color of a tomato? Is this a white girl thing?
Oh God, I can't do this--
Okay, I can, I can. Nakia, I'm in love with you. You're the most amazing, brave, beautiful, smart person I've ever met. And your eyes, and--
...What is happening right now?
I've been trying to think of ways to tell you this for months. I wrote like a million messages and deleted every one without sending them.
And any minute now, those messages are going out to the whole school because an evil computer virus is trying to blackmail Ms. Marvel.
Weirdly, the last part of what you just said makes the most sense.
Are you gonna hate me? I can deal with it if you don't feel the same way, but if you hate me I don't wanna get up tomorrow morning--

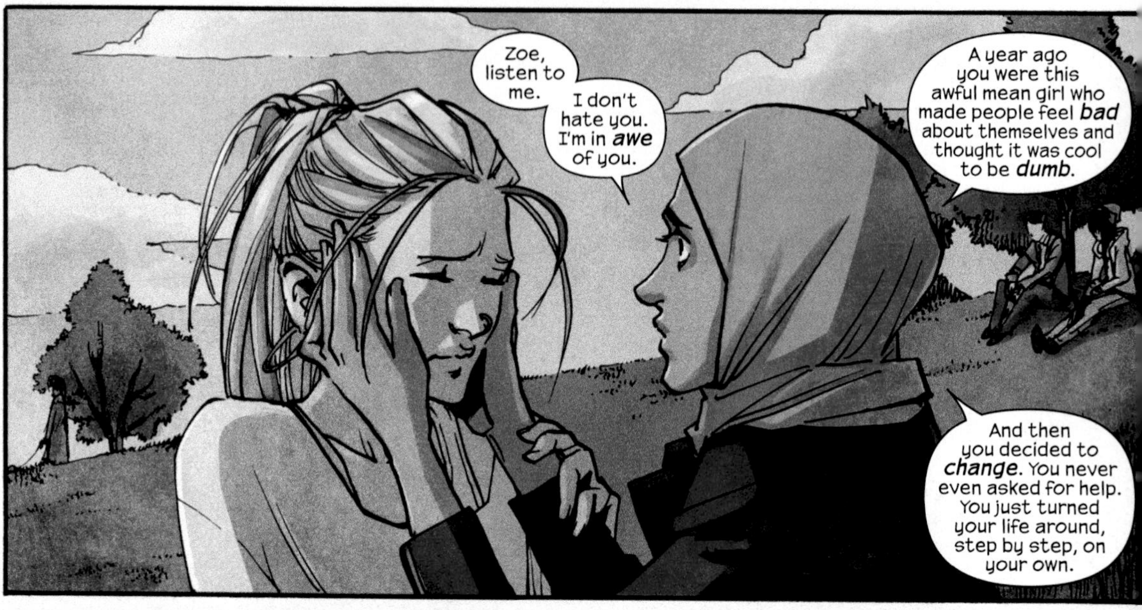
Zoe, listen to me.
I don't hate you. I'm in *awe* of you.
A year ago you were this awful mean girl who made people feel *bad* about themselves and thought it was cool to be *dumb*.
And then you decided to *change*. You never even asked for help. You just turned your life around, step by step, on your own.

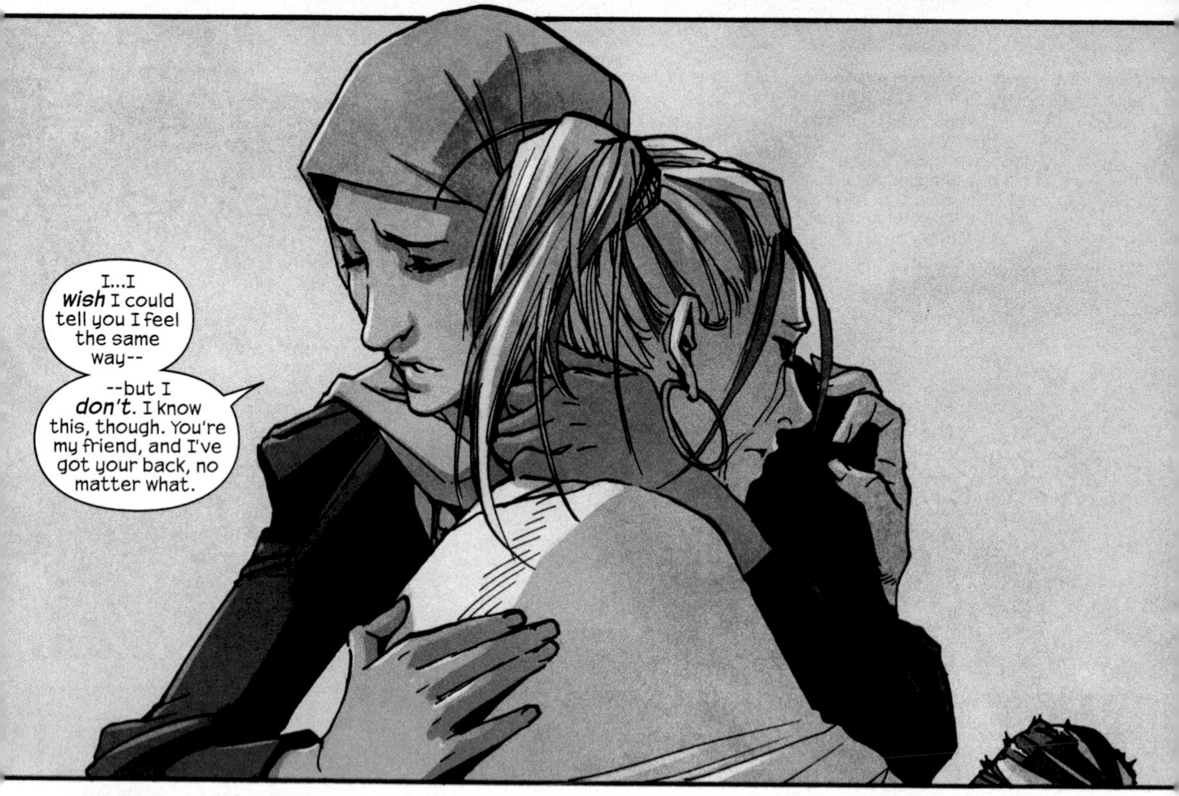
I...I *wish* I could tell you I feel the same way--
--but I *don't*. I know this, though. You're my friend, and I've got your back, no matter what.

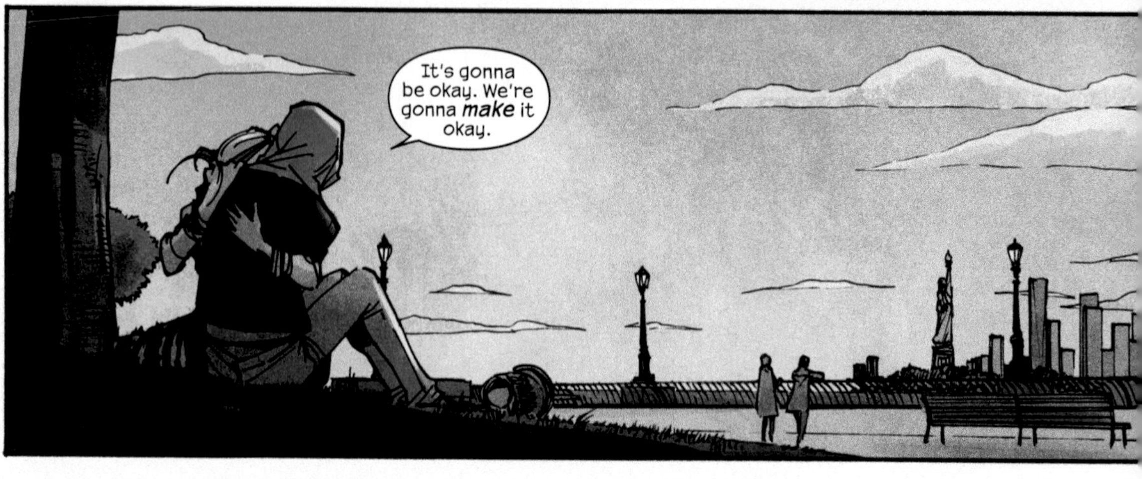
It's gonna be okay. We're gonna *make* it okay.

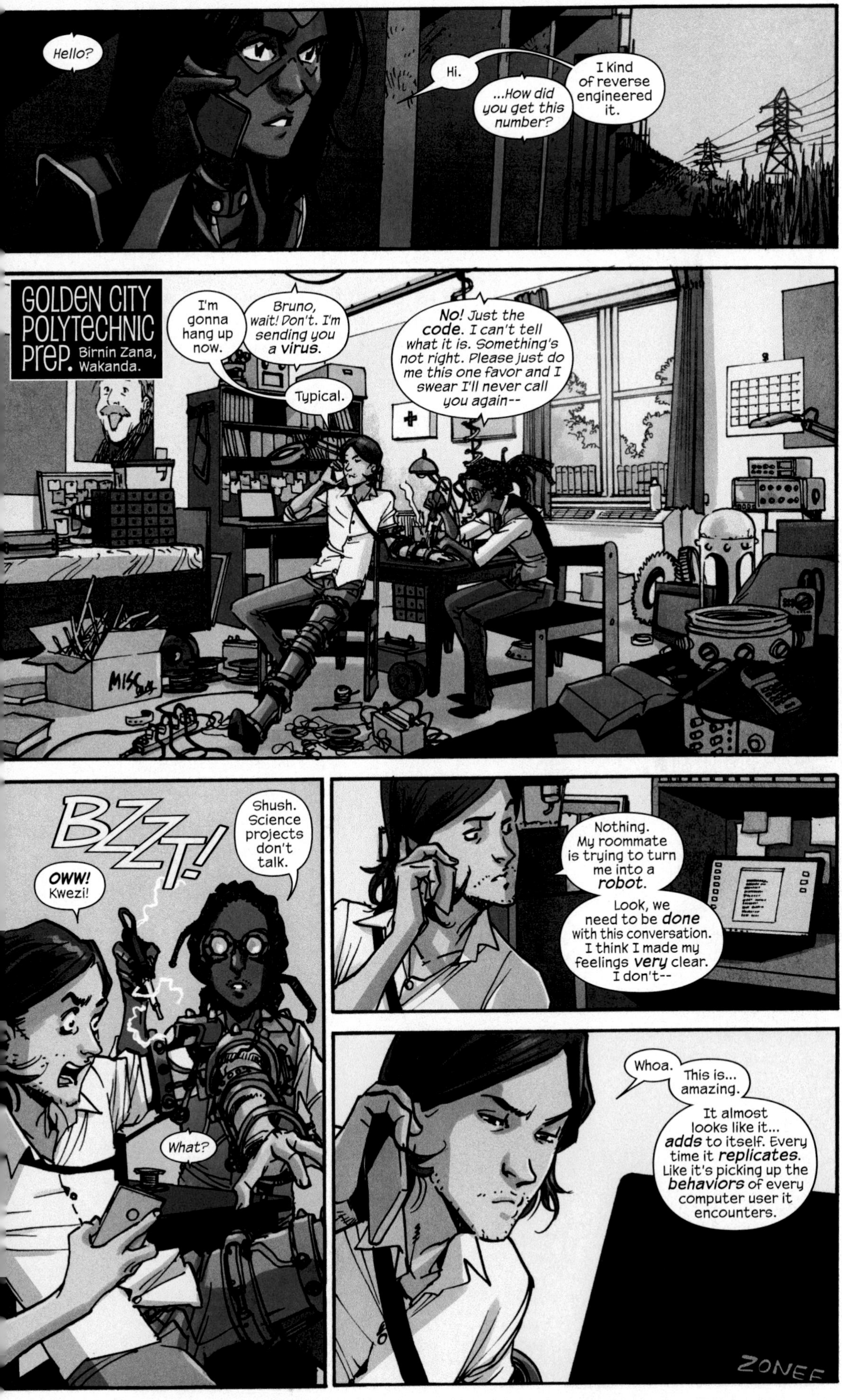

Hello?
Hi.
...How did you get this number?
I kind of reverse engineered it.
GOLDEN CITY POLYTECHNIC PREP. Birnin Zana, Wakanda.
I'm gonna hang up now.
Bruno, wait! Don't. I'm sending you a virus.
Typical.
No! Just the code. I can't tell what it is. Something's not right. Please just do me this one favor and I swear I'll never call you again--
MISC
BZZT!
OWW! Kwezi!
Shush. Science projects don't talk.
What?
Nothing. My roommate is trying to turn me into a robot.
Look, we need to be done with this conversation. I think I made my feelings very clear. I don't--
Whoa.
This is... amazing.
It almost looks like it... adds to itself. Every time it replicates. Like it's picking up the behaviors of every computer user it encounters.
ZONEF

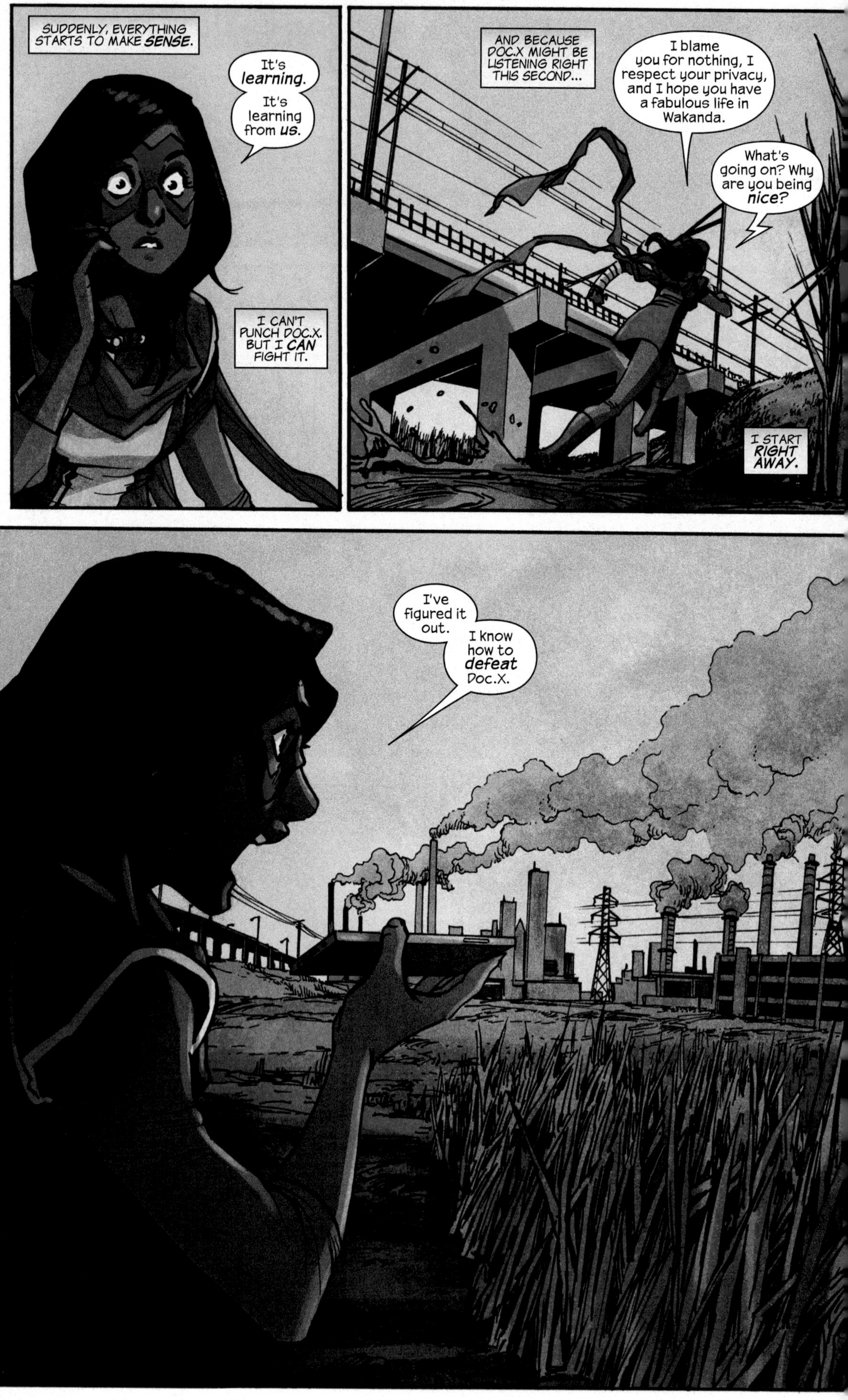
SUDDENLY, EVERYTHING STARTS TO MAKE SENSE.
It's learning.
It's learning from us.
I CAN'T PUNCH DOC.X. BUT I CAN FIGHT IT.
AND BECAUSE DOC.X MIGHT BE LISTENING RIGHT THIS SECOND...
I blame you for nothing, I respect your privacy, and I hope you have a fabulous life in Wakanda.
What's going on? Why are you being nice?
I START RIGHT AWAY.
I've figured it out.
I know how to defeat Doc.X.

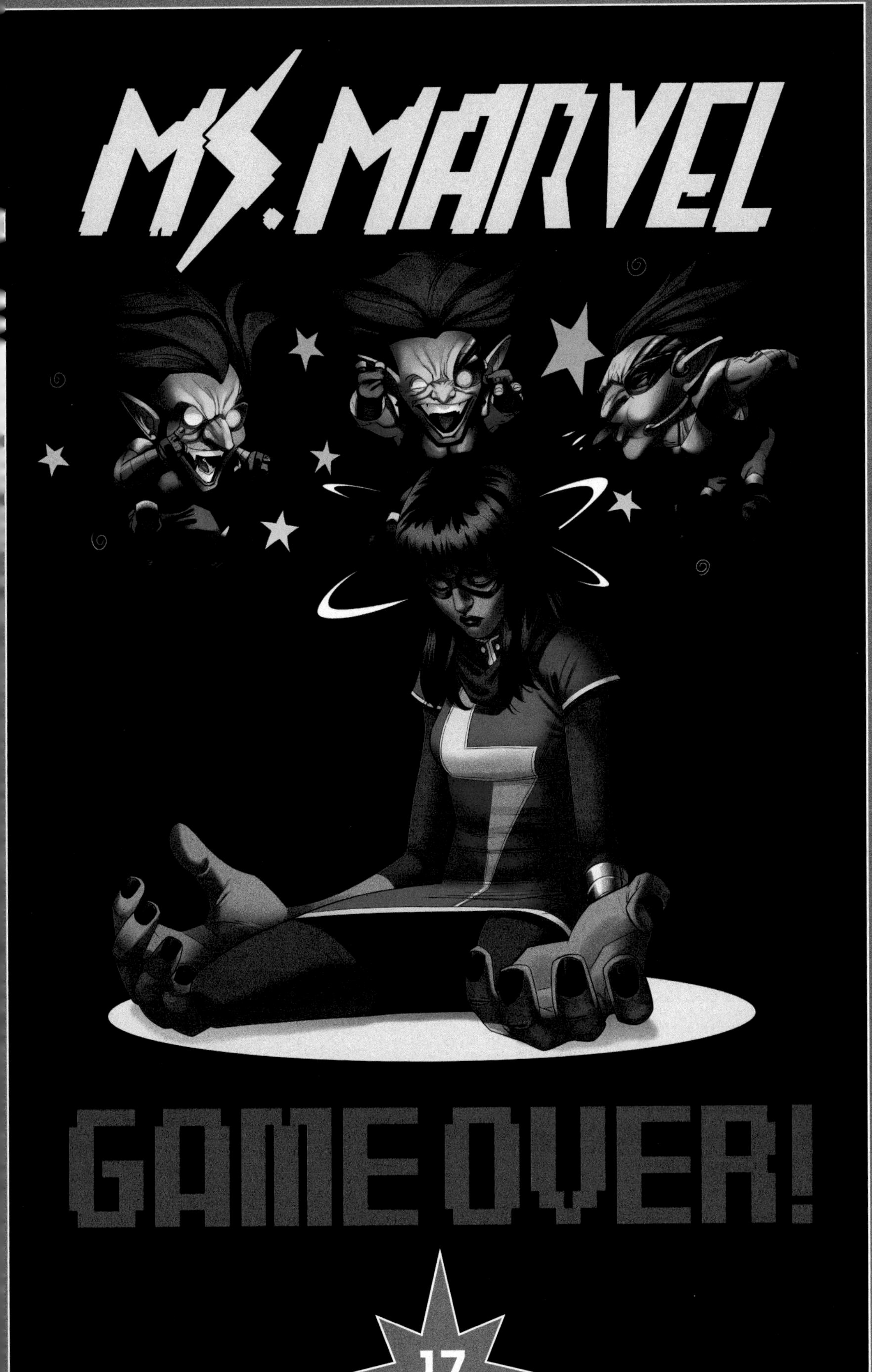
MS. MARVEL
GAME OVER!
17

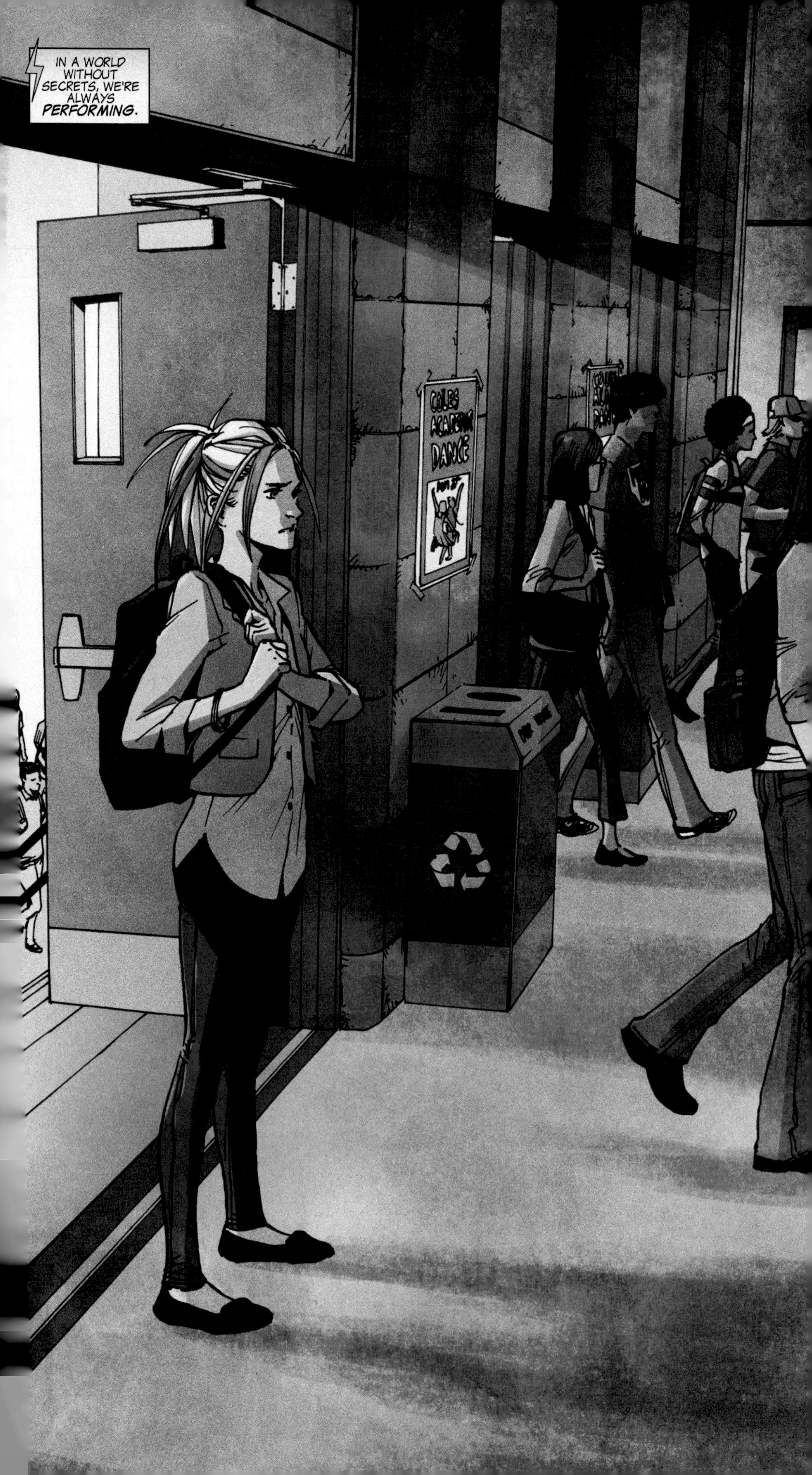
IN A WORLD WITHOUT SECRETS, WE'RE ALWAYS *PERFORMING*.
COLES ACADEMIC DANCE

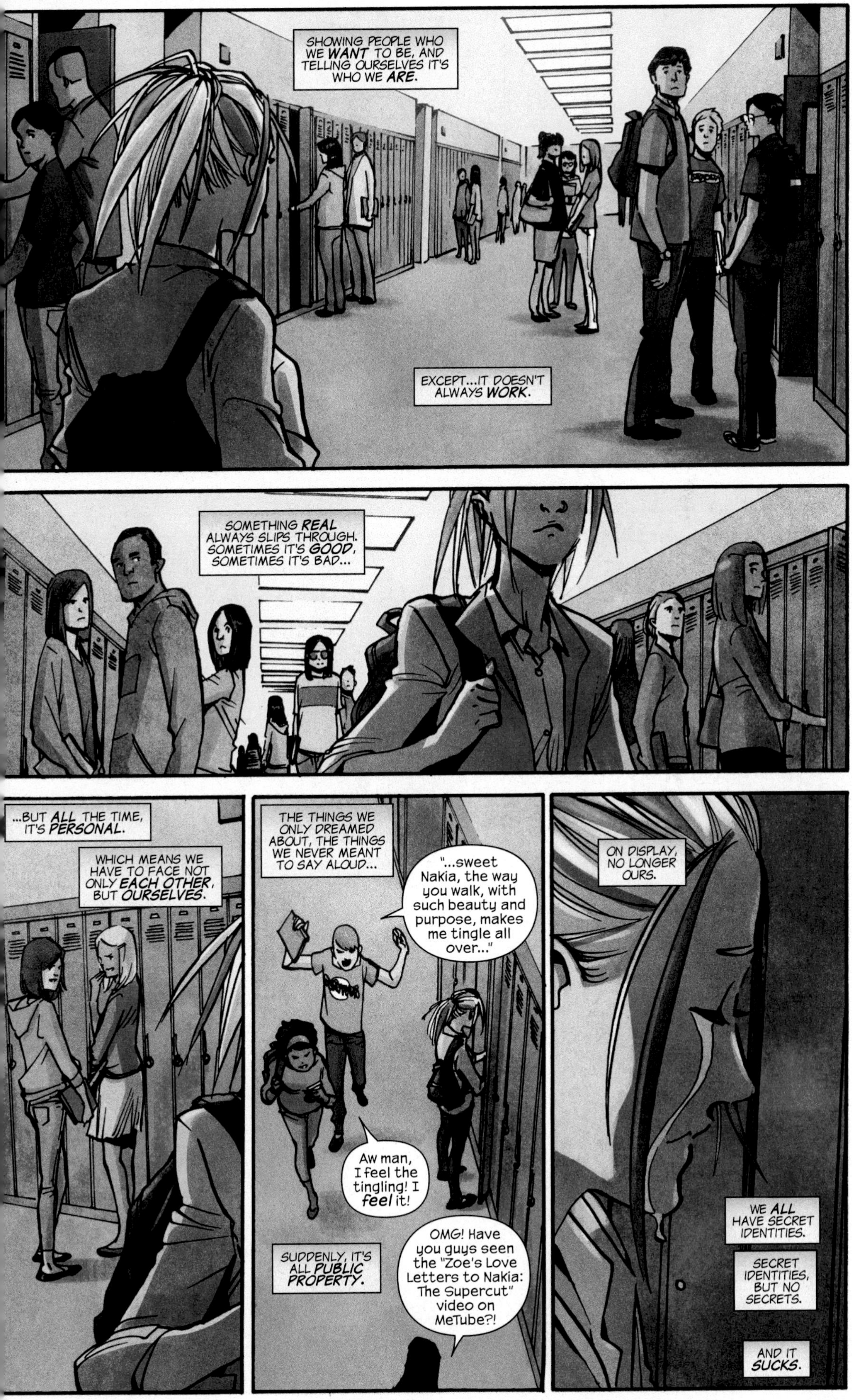
SHOWING PEOPLE WHO WE WANT TO BE, AND TELLING OURSELVES IT'S WHO WE ARE.
EXCEPT...IT DOESN'T ALWAYS WORK.
SOMETHING REAL ALWAYS SLIPS THROUGH. SOMETIMES IT'S GOOD, SOMETIMES IT'S BAD...
...BUT ALL THE TIME, IT'S PERSONAL.
WHICH MEANS WE HAVE TO FACE NOT ONLY EACH OTHER, BUT OURSELVES.
THE THINGS WE ONLY DREAMED ABOUT, THE THINGS WE NEVER MEANT TO SAY ALOUD...
"...sweet Nakia, the way you walk, with such beauty and purpose, makes me tingle all over..."
Aw man, I feel the tingling! I feel it!
SUDDENLY, IT'S ALL PUBLIC PROPERTY.
OMG! Have you guys seen the "Zoe's Love Letters to Nakia: The Supercut" video on MeTube?!
ON DISPLAY, NO LONGER OURS.
WE ALL HAVE SECRET IDENTITIES.
SECRET IDENTITIES, BUT NO SECRETS.
AND IT SUCKS.

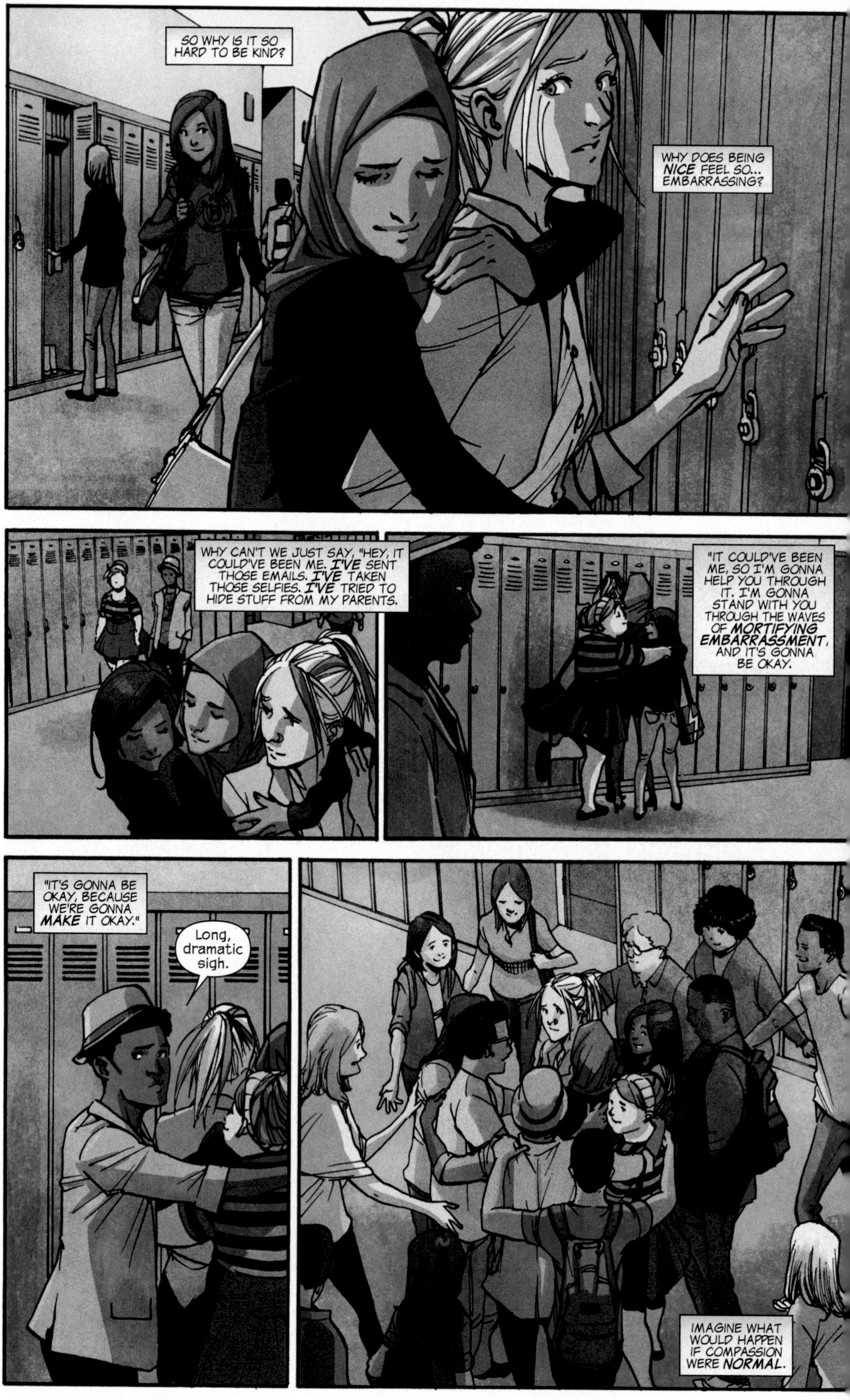
SO WHY IS IT SO HARD TO BE KIND?
WHY DOES BEING NICE FEEL SO... EMBARRASSING?
WHY CAN'T WE JUST SAY, "HEY, IT COULD'VE BEEN ME. I'VE SENT THOSE EMAILS. I'VE TAKEN THOSE SELFIES. I'VE TRIED TO HIDE STUFF FROM MY PARENTS.
"IT COULD'VE BEEN ME, SO I'M GONNA HELP YOU THROUGH IT. I'M GONNA STAND WITH YOU THROUGH THE WAVES OF MORTIFYING EMBARRASSMENT, AND IT'S GONNA BE OKAY.
"IT'S GONNA BE OKAY, BECAUSE WE'RE GONNA MAKE IT OKAY."
Long, dramatic sigh.
IMAGINE WHAT WOULD HAPPEN IF COMPASSION WERE NORMAL.

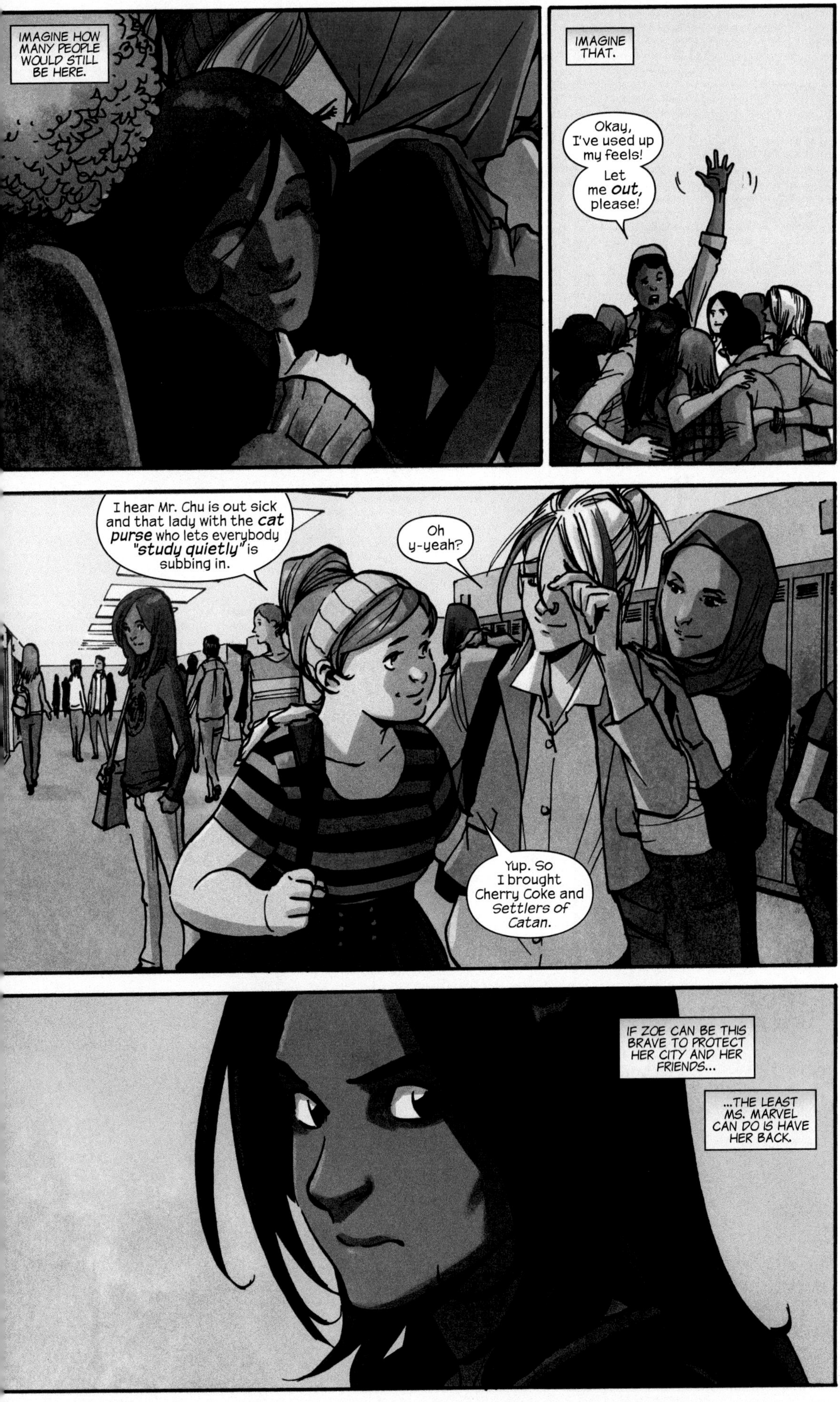
IMAGINE HOW MANY PEOPLE WOULD STILL BE HERE.
IMAGINE THAT.
Okay, I've used up my feels!
Let me *out,* please!
I hear Mr. Chu is out sick and that lady with the ***cat purse*** who lets everybody ***"study quietly"*** is subbing in.
Oh y-yeah?
Yup. So I brought Cherry Coke and *Settlers of Catan.*
IF ZOE CAN BE THIS BRAVE TO PROTECT HER CITY AND HER FRIENDS...
...THE LEAST MS. MARVEL CAN DO IS HAVE HER BACK.

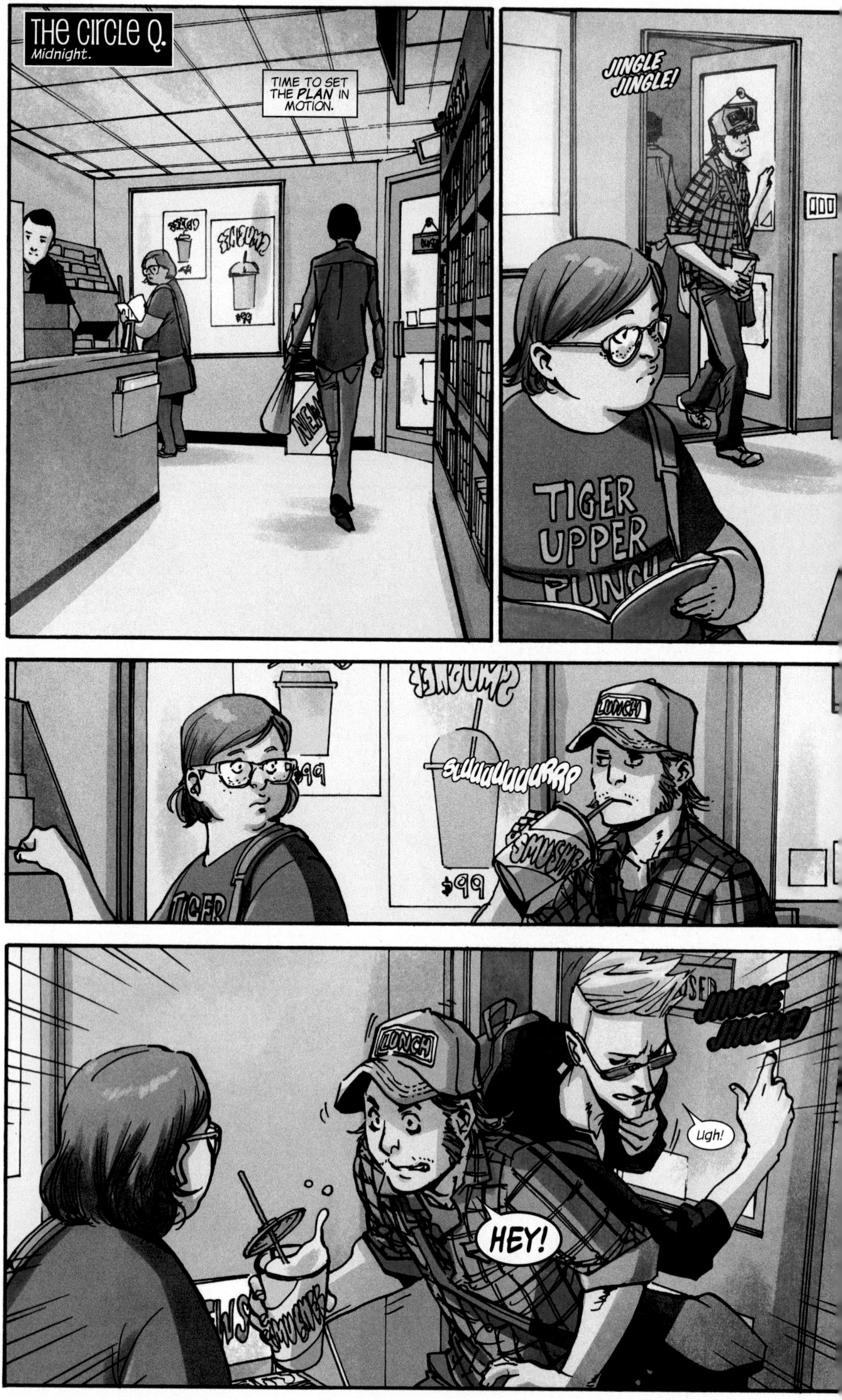
THE CIRCLE Q.
Midnight.
TIME TO SET THE PLAN IN MOTION.
JINGLE JINGLE!
TIGER UPPER PUNCH
SLUUUUUUURRP
JINGLE JINGLE!
Ugh!
HEY!

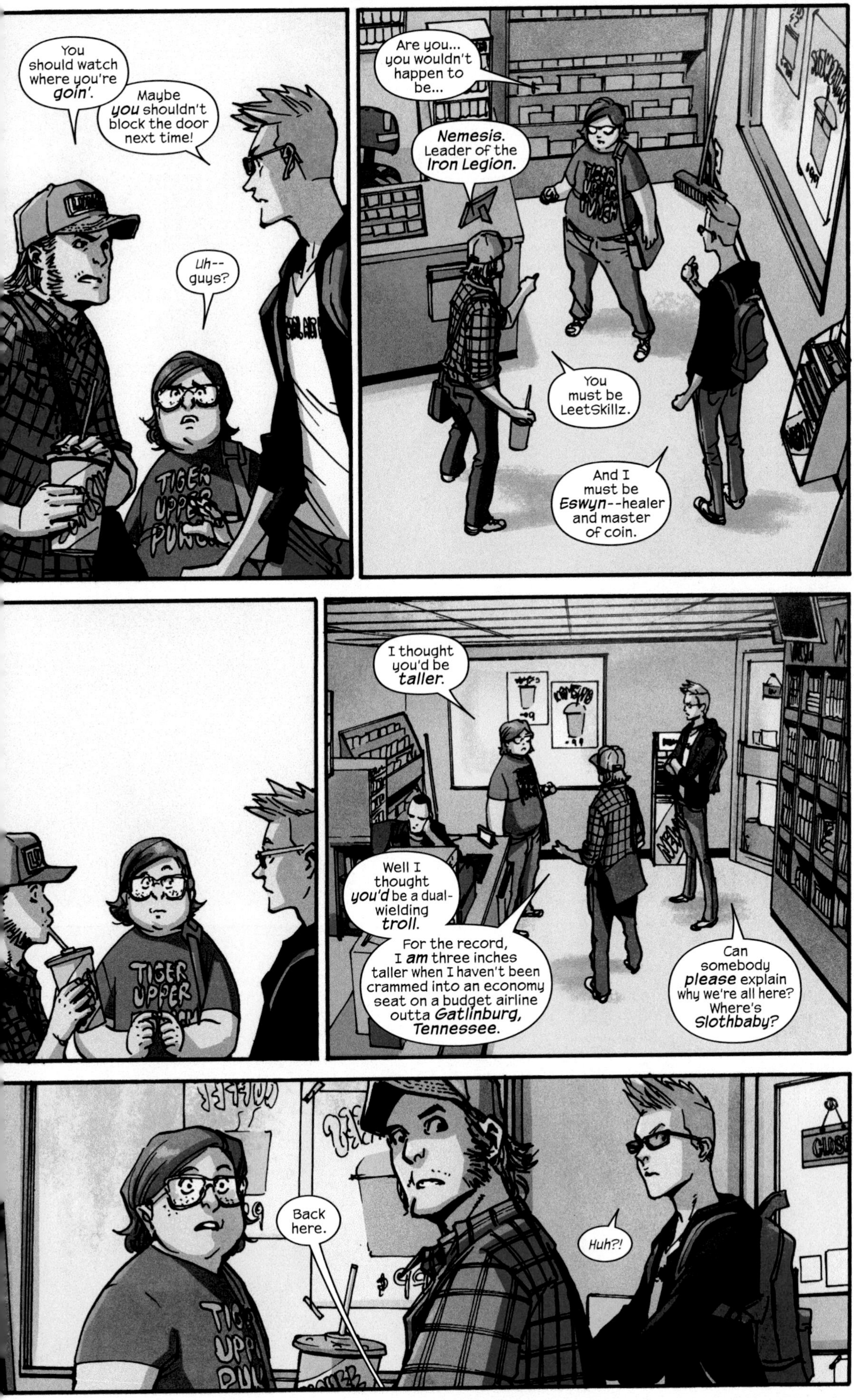
You should watch where you're goin'.
Maybe you shouldn't block the door next time!
Uh-- guys?
Are you... you wouldn't happen to be...
Nemesis. Leader of the Iron Legion.
You must be LeetSkillz.
And I must be Eswyn--healer and master of coin.
I thought you'd be taller.
Well I thought you'd be a dual-wielding troll.
For the record, I am three inches taller when I haven't been crammed into an economy seat on a budget airline outta Gatlinburg, Tennessee.
Can somebody please explain why we're all here? Where's Slothbaby?
Back here.
Huh?!

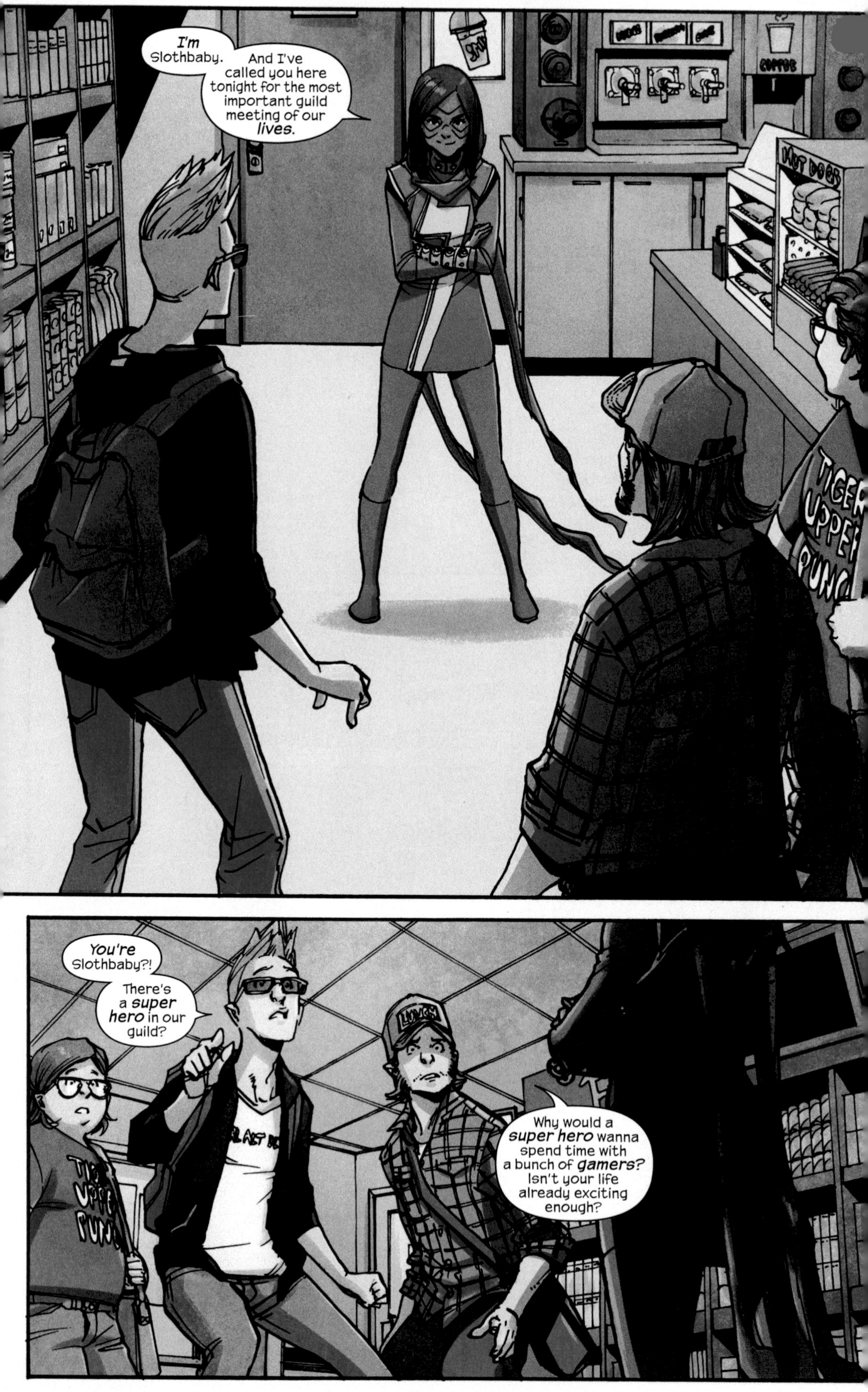
I'm Slothbaby.
And I've called you here tonight for the most important guild meeting of our lives.
You're Slothbaby?!
There's a super hero in our guild?
Why would a super hero wanna spend time with a bunch of gamers? Isn't your life already exciting enough?

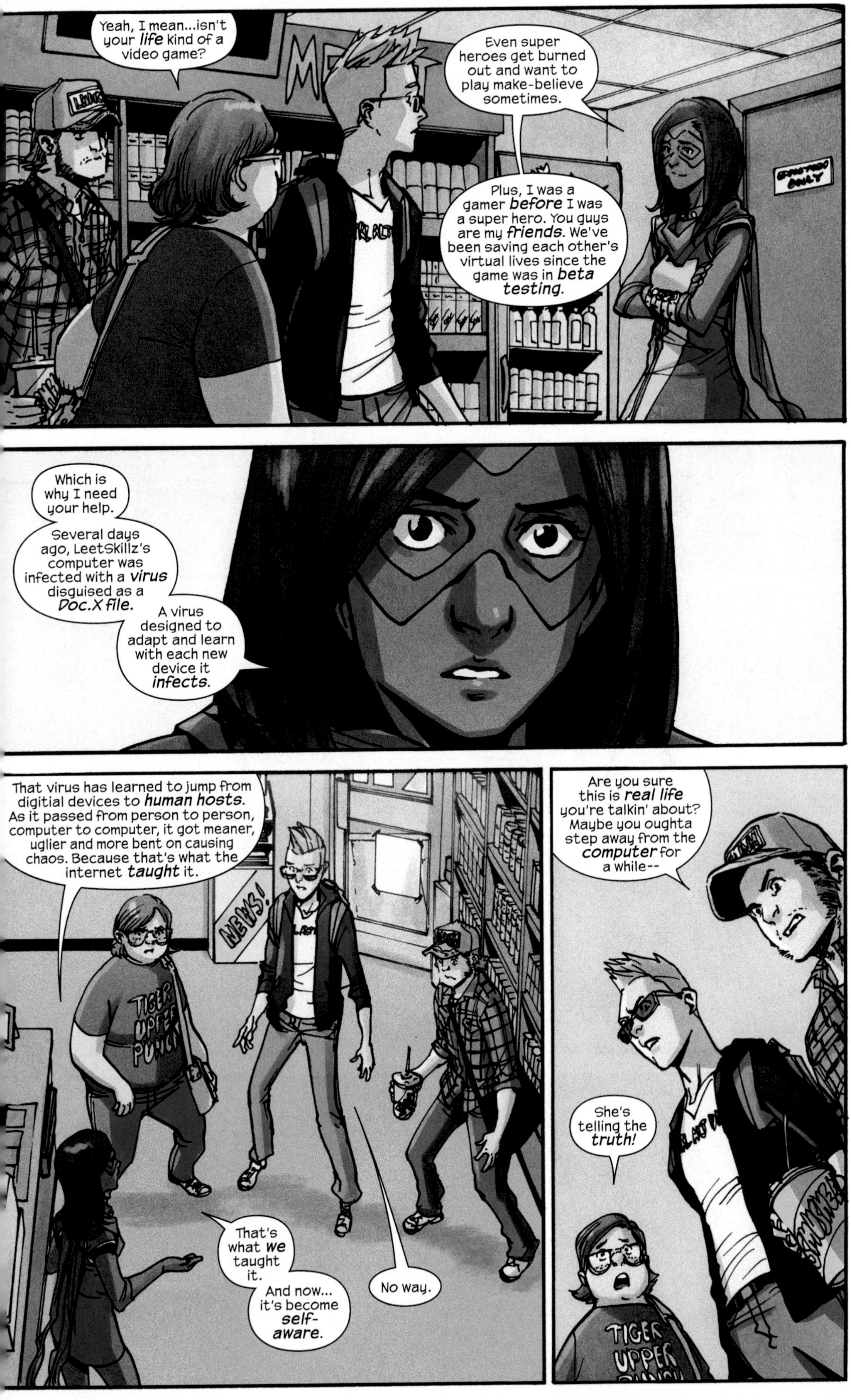
Yeah, I mean...isn't your *life* kind of a video game?
Even super heroes get burned out and want to play make-believe sometimes.
Plus, I was a gamer *before* I was a super hero. You guys are my *friends*. We've been saving each other's virtual lives since the game was in *beta testing*.
Which is why I need your help.
Several days ago, LeetSkillz's computer was infected with a *virus* disguised as a *Doc.X file.*
A virus designed to adapt and learn with each new device it *infects*.
That virus has learned to jump from digitial devices to *human hosts*. As it passed from person to person, computer to computer, it got meaner, uglier and more bent on causing chaos. Because that's what the internet *taught* it.
NEWS!
TIGER UPPER PUNCH
That's what *we* taught it.
And now... it's become *self-aware*.
No way.
Are you sure this is *real life* you're talkin' about? Maybe you oughta step away from the *computer* for a while--
She's telling the *truth!*
TIGER UPPER

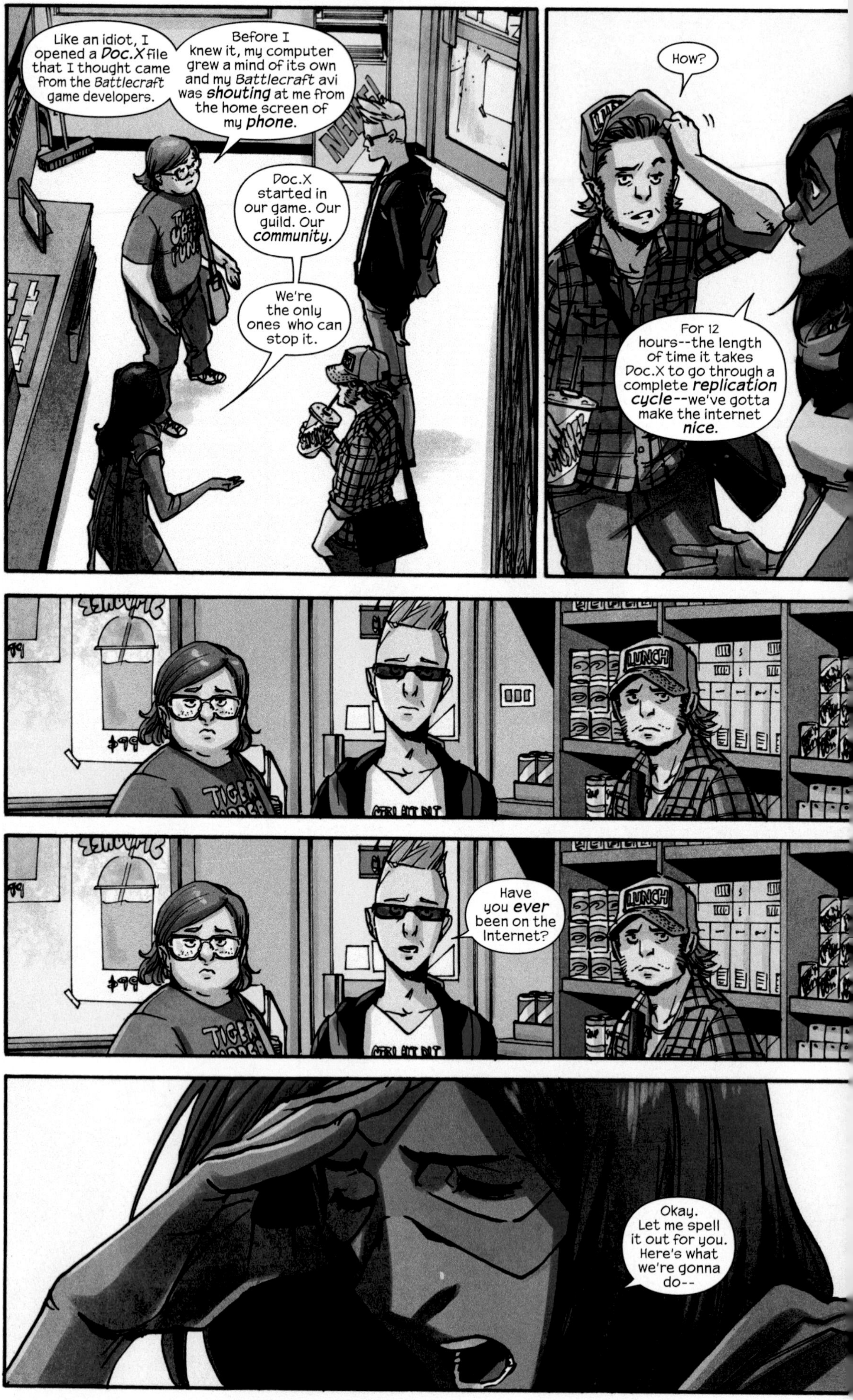

Like an idiot, I opened a Doc.X file that I thought came from the Battlecraft game developers.
Before I knew it, my computer grew a mind of its own and my Battlecraft avi was shouting at me from the home screen of my phone.
Doc.X started in our game. Our guild. Our community.
We're the only ones who can stop it.
How?
For 12 hours--the length of time it takes Doc.X to go through a complete replication cycle--we've gotta make the internet nice.
Have you ever been on the Internet?
Okay. Let me spell it out for you. Here's what we're gonna do--

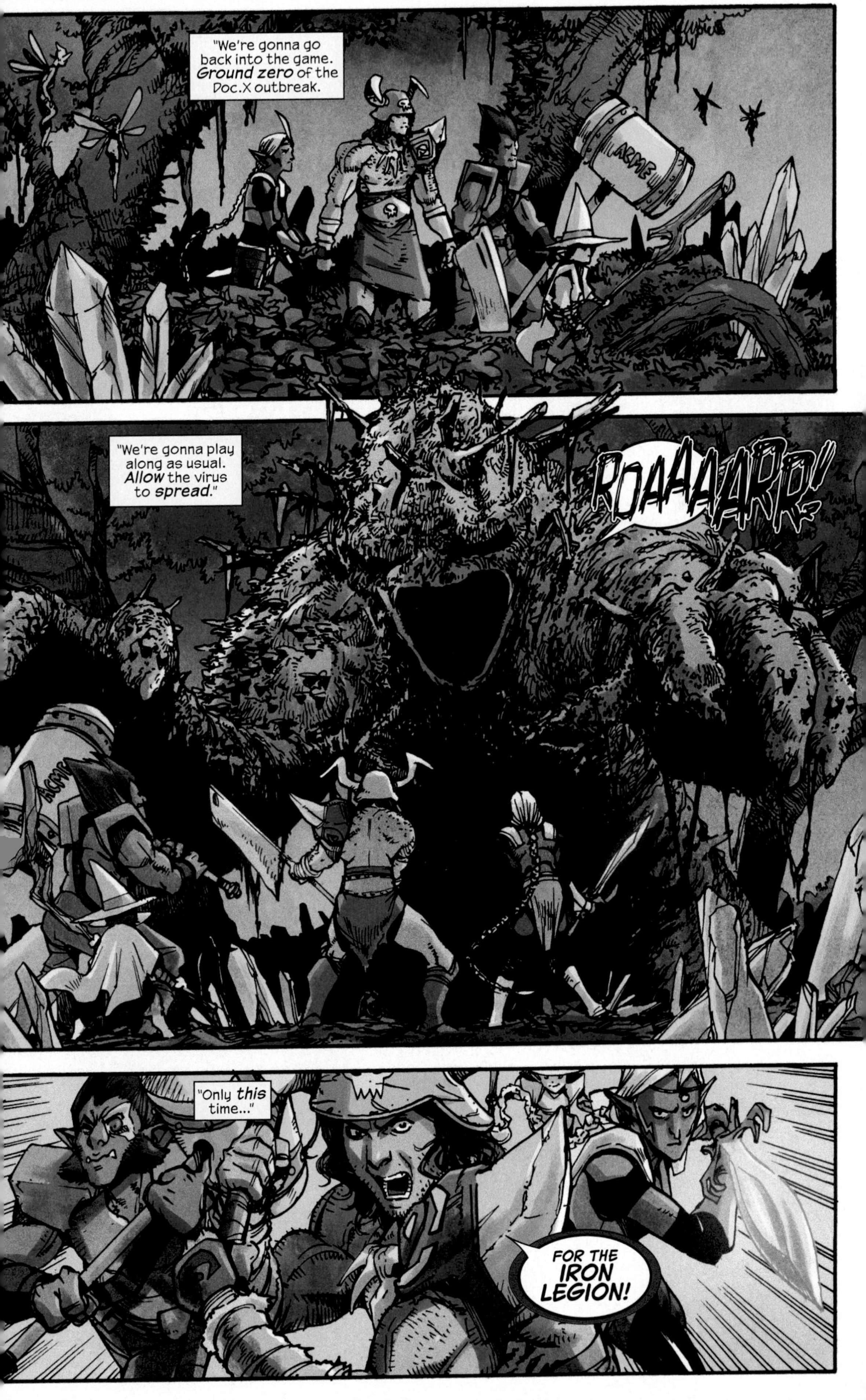
"We're gonna go back into the game. Ground zero of the Doc.X outbreak.
ARME
"We're gonna play along as usual. Allow the virus to spread."
ROAAAAARR!
"Only this time..."
FOR THE IRON LEGION!

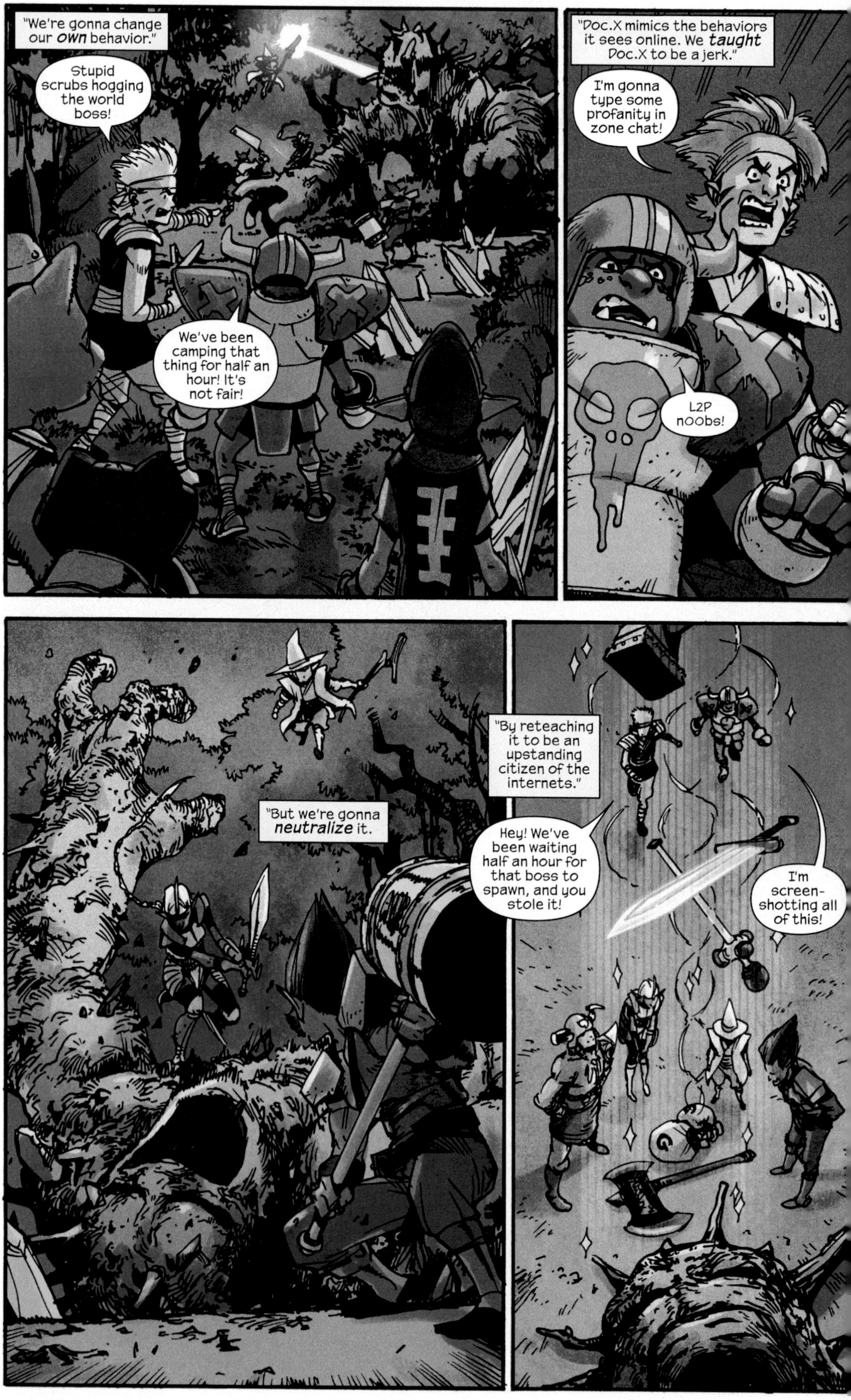
"We're gonna change our *own* behavior."
Stupid scrubs hogging the world boss!
We've been camping that thing for half an hour! It's not fair!
"Doc.X mimics the behaviors it sees online. We *taught* Doc.X to be a jerk."
I'm gonna type some profanity in zone chat!
L2P n0obs!
"But we're gonna *neutralize* it.
"By reteaching it to be an upstanding citizen of the internets."
Hey! We've been waiting half an hour for that boss to spawn, and you stole it!
I'm screen-shotting all of this!

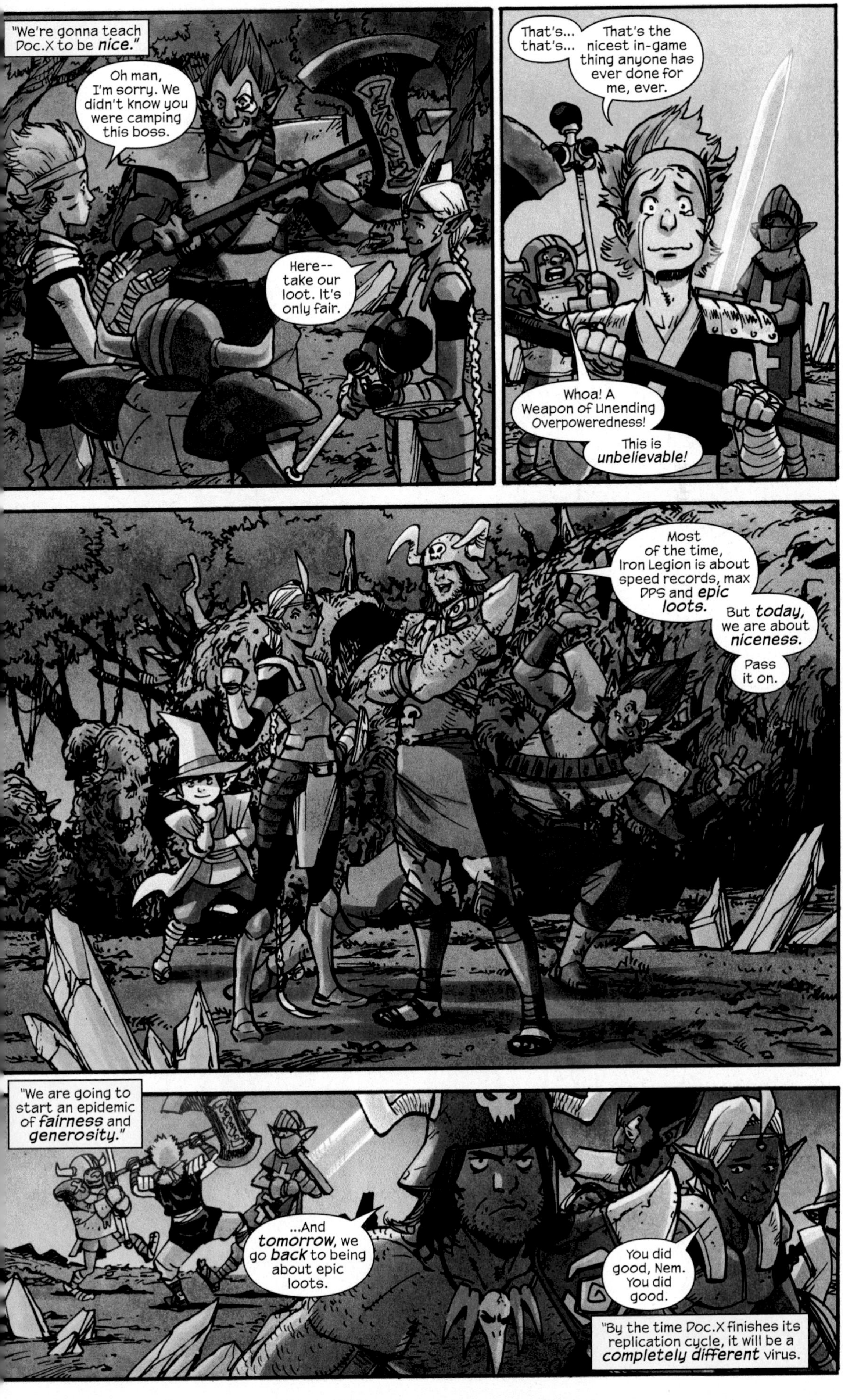
"We're gonna teach Doc.X to be *nice.*"
Oh man, I'm sorry. We didn't know you were camping this boss.
Here-- take our loot. It's only fair.
That's... that's...
That's the nicest in-game thing anyone has ever done for me, ever.
Whoa! A Weapon of Unending Overpoweredness!
This is *unbelievable!*
Most of the time, Iron Legion is about speed records, max DPS and *epic loots.*
But *today,* we are about *niceness.*
Pass it on.
"We are going to start an epidemic of *fairness* and *generosity.*"
...And *tomorrow,* we go *back* to being about epic loots.
You did good, Nem. You did good.
"By the time Doc.X finishes its replication cycle, it will be a *completely different* virus.

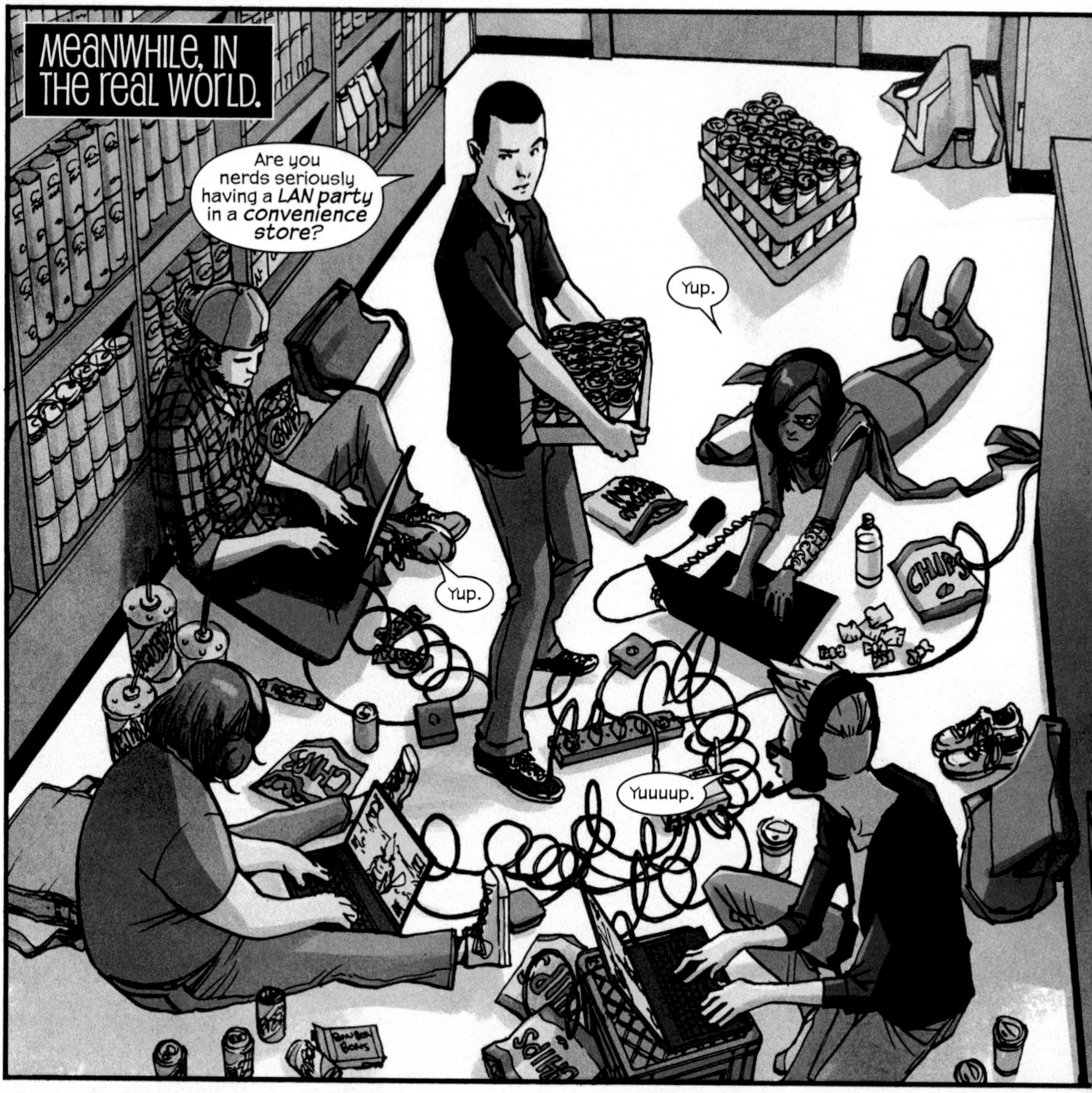
MEANWHILE, IN THE REAL WORLD.
Are you nerds seriously having a LAN party in a convenience store?
Yup.
Yup.
Yuuuup.
CHIPS

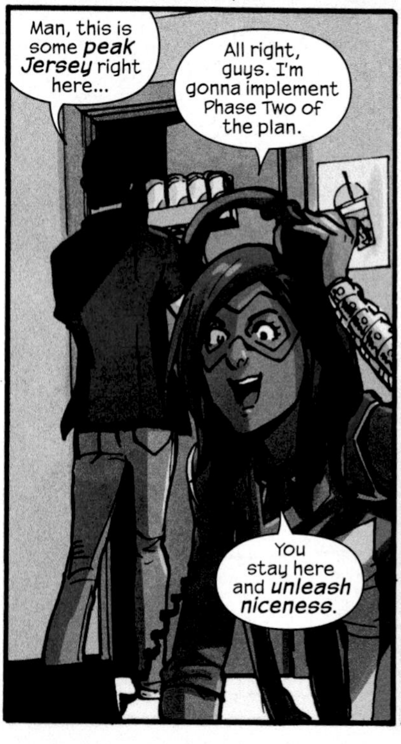
Man, this is some peak Jersey right here...
All right, guys. I'm gonna implement Phase Two of the plan.
You stay here and unleash niceness.

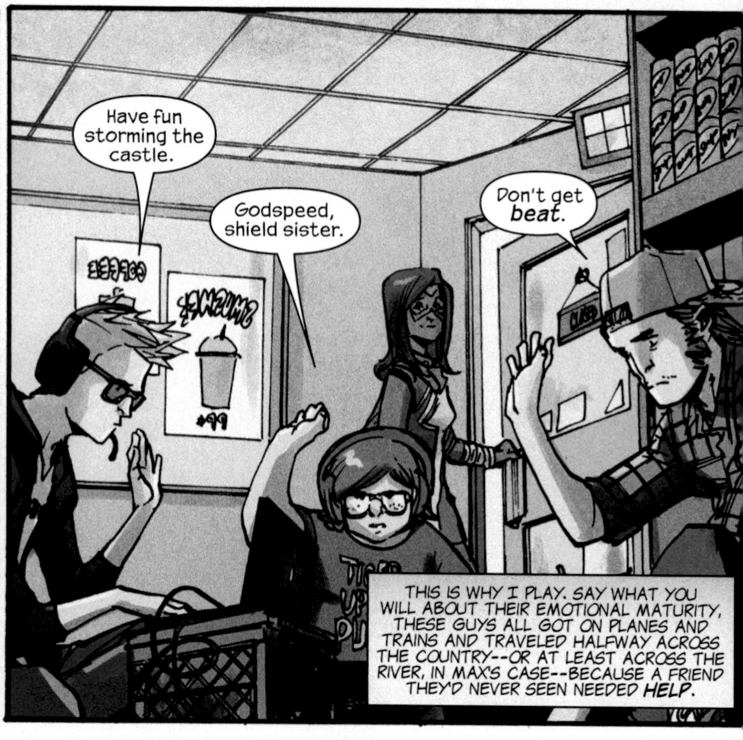
Have fun storming the castle.
Godspeed, shield sister.
Don't get beat.
THIS IS WHY I PLAY. SAY WHAT YOU WILL ABOUT THEIR EMOTIONAL MATURITY, THESE GUYS ALL GOT ON PLANES AND TRAINS AND TRAVELED HALFWAY ACROSS THE COUNTRY--OR AT LEAST ACROSS THE RIVER, IN MAX'S CASE--BECAUSE A FRIEND THEY'D NEVER SEEN NEEDED HELP.

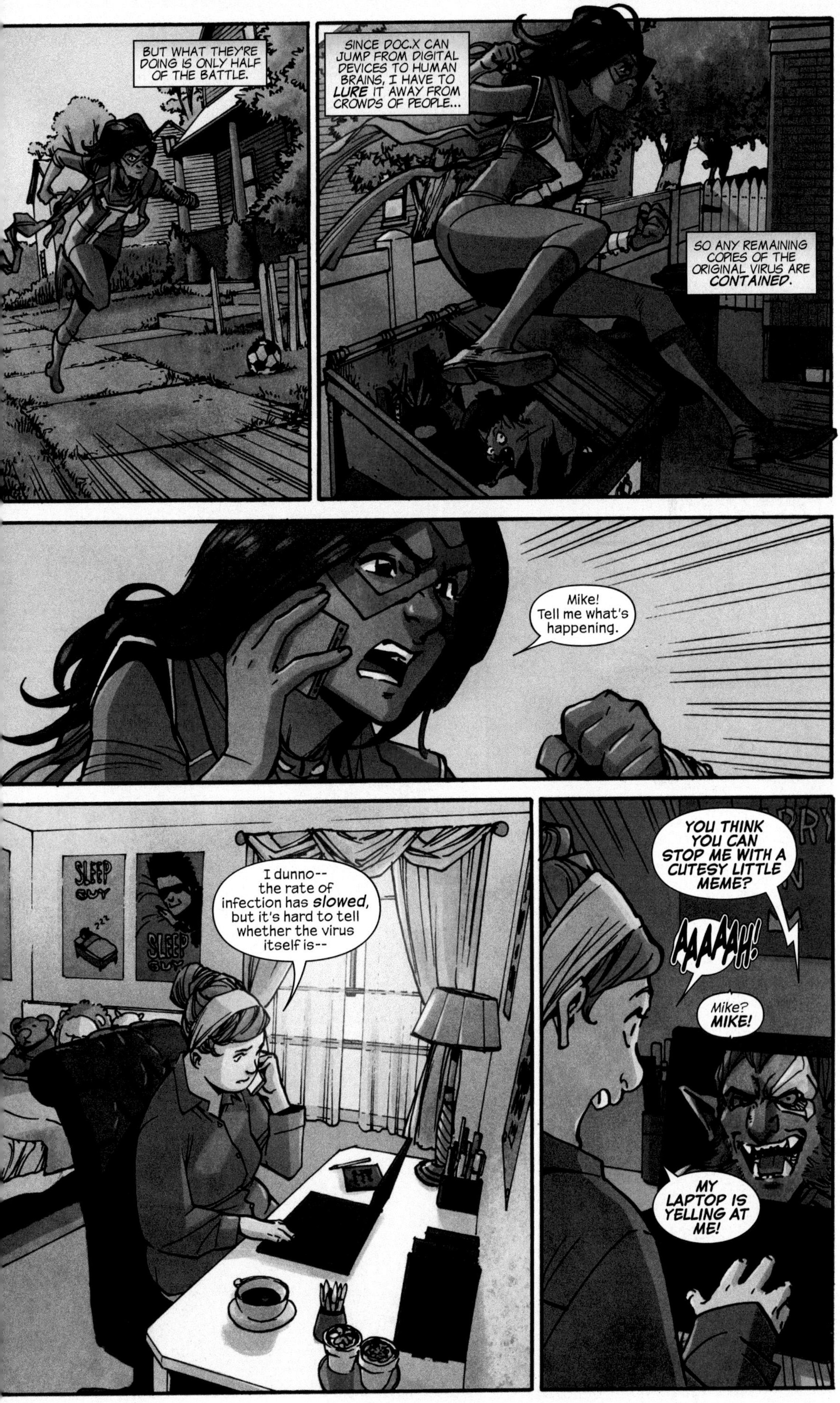
BUT WHAT THEY'RE DOING IS ONLY HALF OF THE BATTLE.
SINCE DOC.X CAN JUMP FROM DIGITAL DEVICES TO HUMAN BRAINS, I HAVE TO LURE IT AWAY FROM CROWDS OF PEOPLE...
SO ANY REMAINING COPIES OF THE ORIGINAL VIRUS ARE CONTAINED.
Mike! Tell me what's happening.
SLEEP GUY
SLEEP GUY
I dunno-- the rate of infection has slowed, but it's hard to tell whether the virus itself is--
YOU THINK YOU CAN STOP ME WITH A CUTESY LITTLE MEME?
AAAAAH!
Mike? MIKE!
MY LAPTOP IS YELLING AT ME!

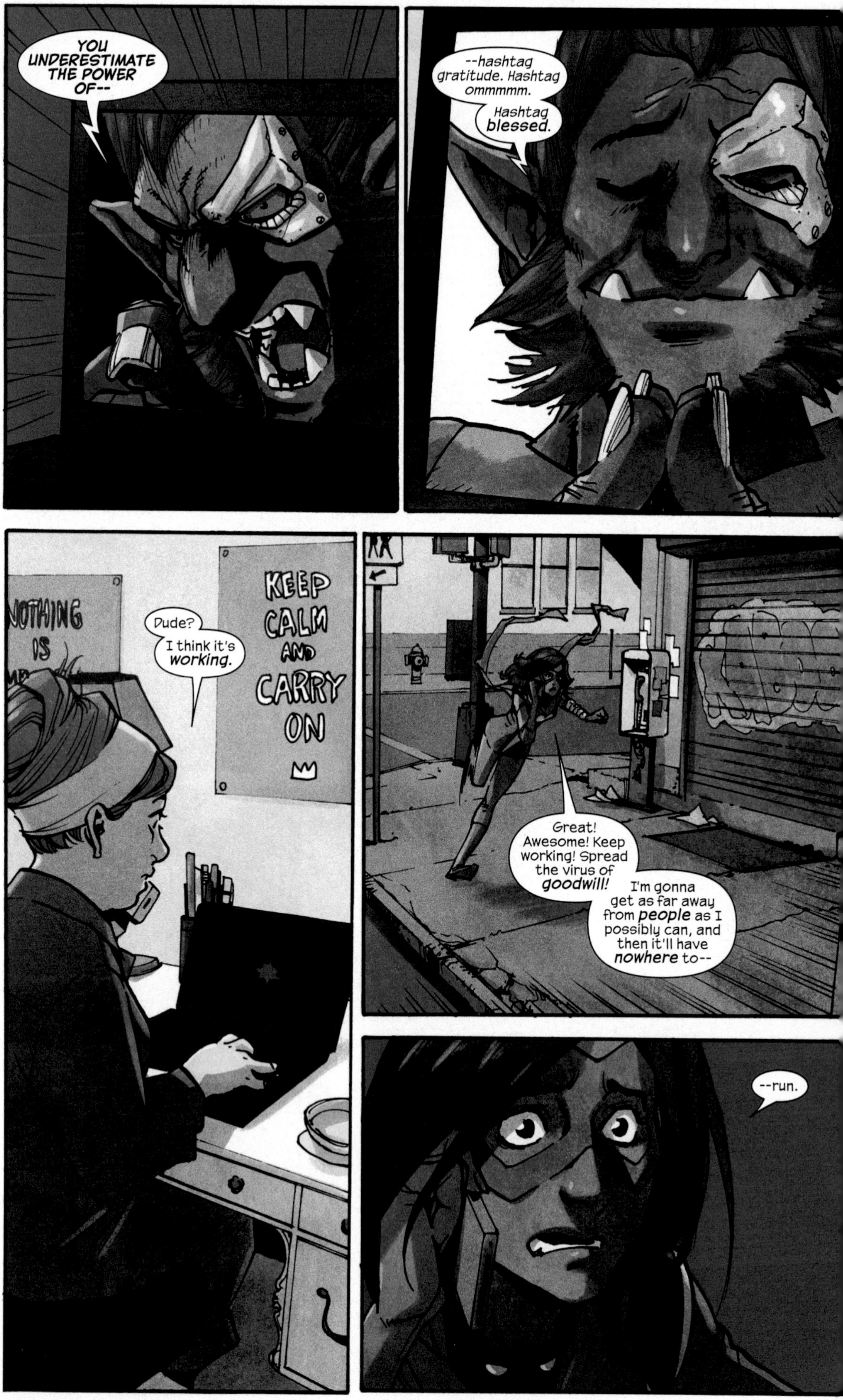
YOU UNDERESTIMATE THE POWER OF--
--hashtag gratitude. Hashtag ommmmm.
Hashtag blessed.
NOTHING IS
KEEP CALM AND CARRY ON
Dude?
I think it's working.
Great! Awesome! Keep working! Spread the virus of goodwill!
I'm gonna get as far away from people as I possibly can, and then it'll have nowhere to--
--run.

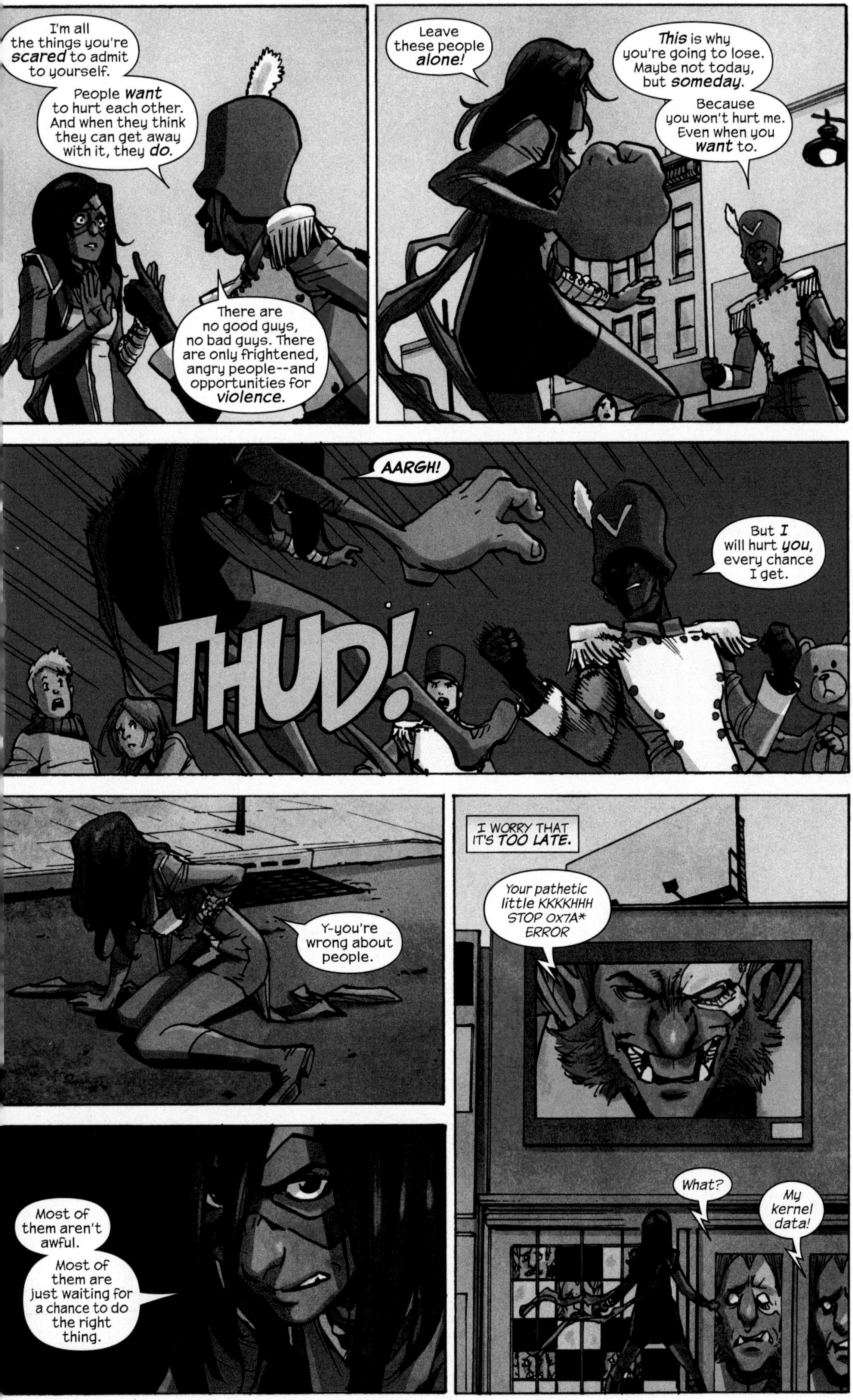

I'm all the things you're scared to admit to yourself.
People want to hurt each other. And when they think they can get away with it, they do.
There are no good guys, no bad guys. There are only frightened, angry people--and opportunities for violence.
Leave these people alone!
This is why you're going to lose. Maybe not today, but someday.
Because you won't hurt me. Even when you want to.
AARGH!
But I will hurt you, every chance I get.
THUD!
Y-you're wrong about people.
Most of them aren't awful.
Most of them are just waiting for a chance to do the right thing.
I WORRY THAT IT'S TOO LATE.
Your pathetic little KKKKHHH STOP 0X7A* ERROR
What?
My kernel data!

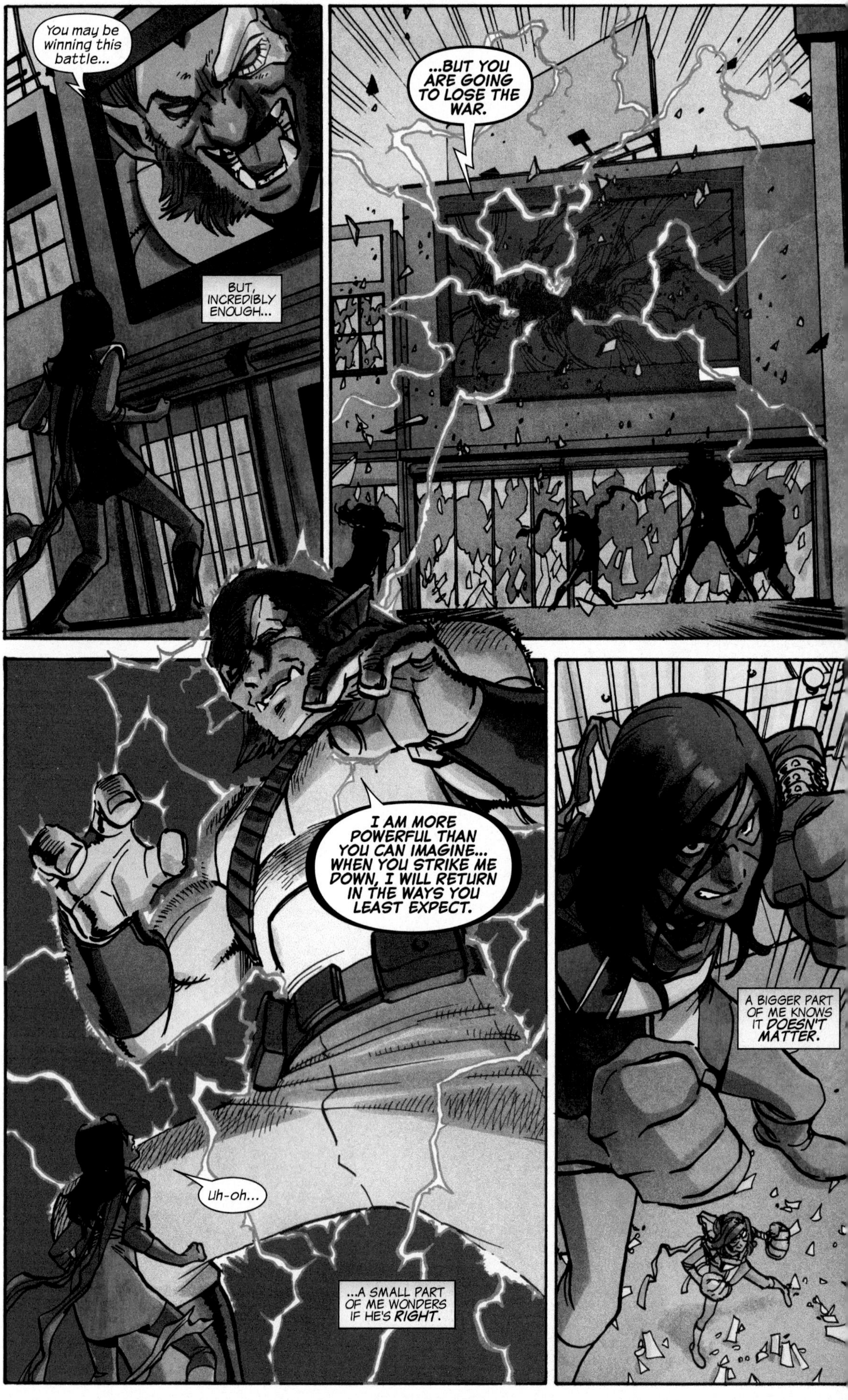
You may be winning this battle...
BUT, INCREDIBLY ENOUGH...
...BUT YOU ARE GOING TO LOSE THE WAR.
I AM MORE POWERFUL THAN YOU CAN IMAGINE... WHEN YOU STRIKE ME DOWN, I WILL RETURN IN THE WAYS YOU LEAST EXPECT.
Uh-oh...
...A SMALL PART OF ME WONDERS IF HE'S RIGHT.
A BIGGER PART OF ME KNOWS IT DOESN'T MATTER.

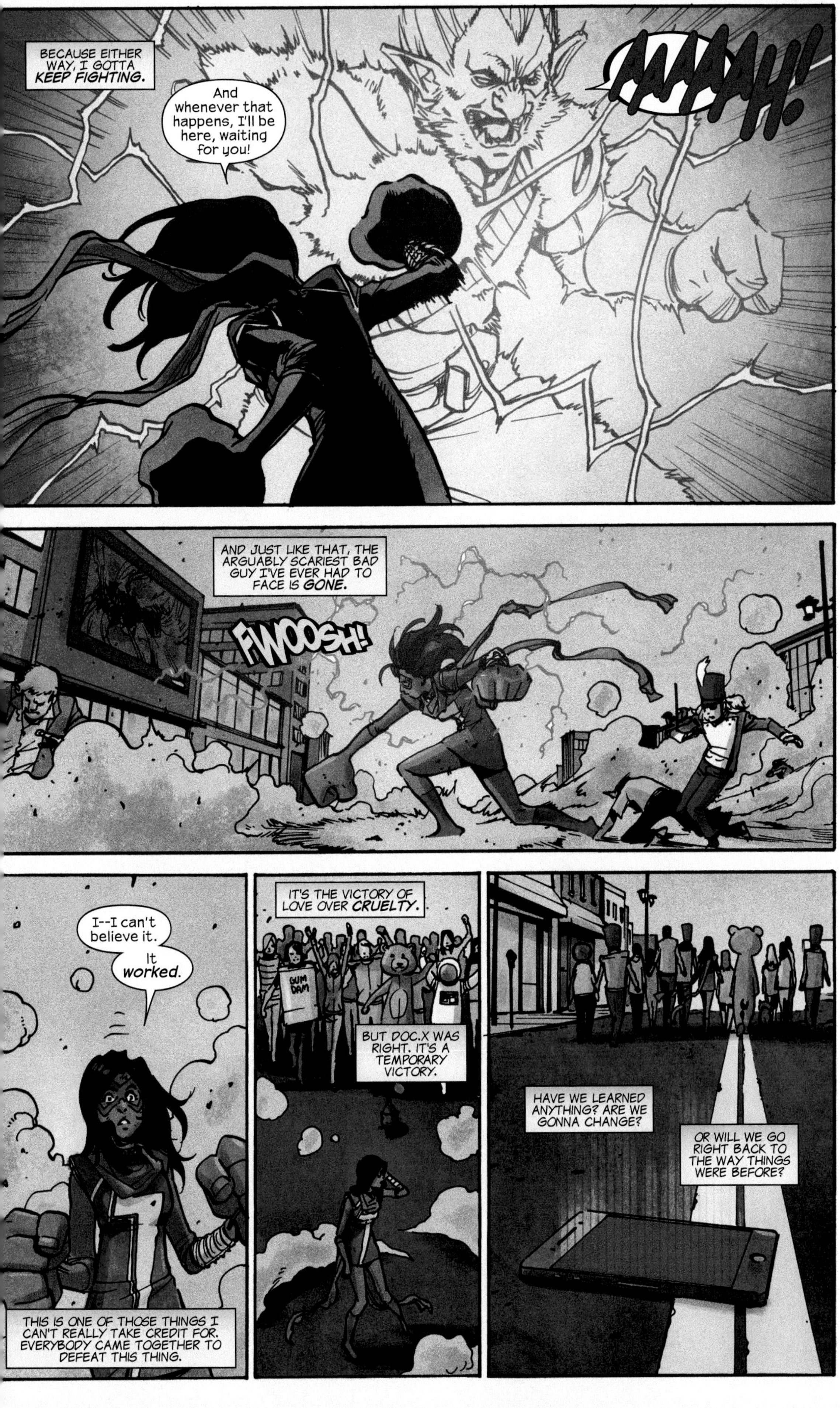
BECAUSE EITHER WAY, I GOTTA KEEP FIGHTING.
And whenever that happens, I'll be here, waiting for you!
AAAAAH!
AND JUST LIKE THAT, THE ARGUABLY SCARIEST BAD GUY I'VE EVER HAD TO FACE IS GONE.
FWOOSH!
I--I can't believe it.
It worked.
THIS IS ONE OF THOSE THINGS I CAN'T REALLY TAKE CREDIT FOR. EVERYBODY CAME TOGETHER TO DEFEAT THIS THING.
IT'S THE VICTORY OF LOVE OVER CRUELTY.
GUM DAM
BUT DOC.X WAS RIGHT. IT'S A TEMPORARY VICTORY.
HAVE WE LEARNED ANYTHING? ARE WE GONNA CHANGE?
OR WILL WE GO RIGHT BACK TO THE WAY THINGS WERE BEFORE?

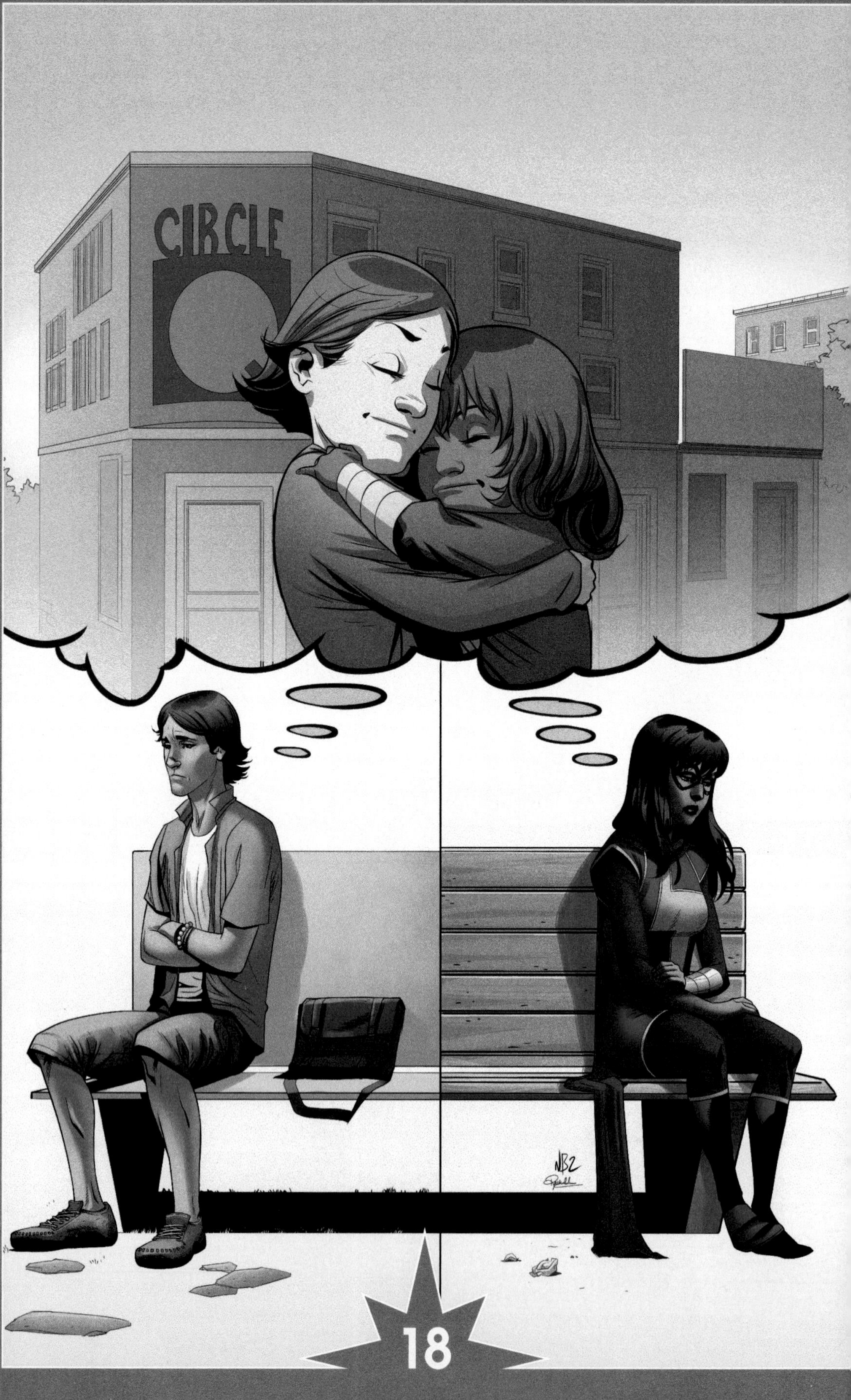
CIRCLE
18

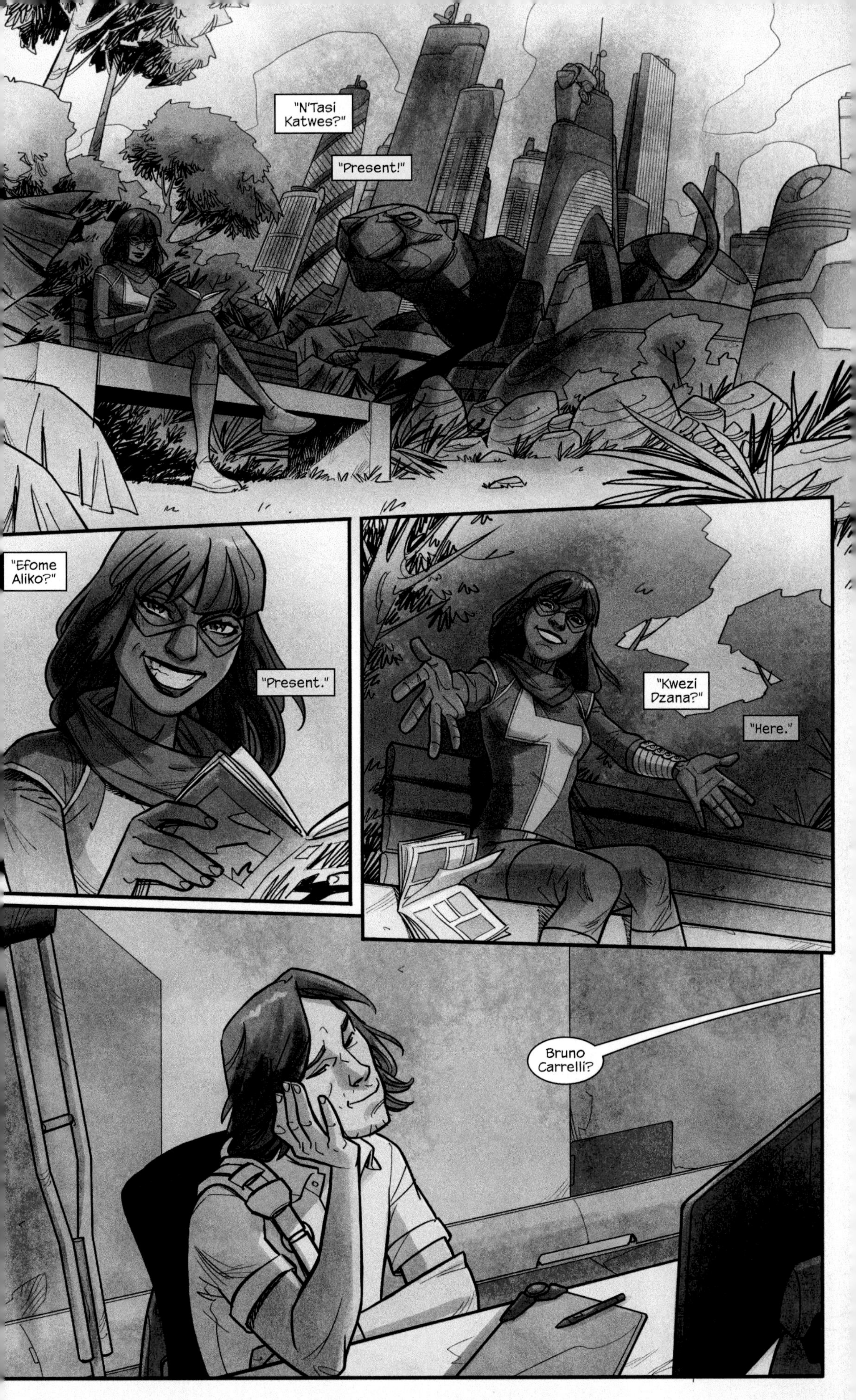
"N'Tasi Katwes?"
"Present!"
"Efome Aliko?"
"Present."
"Kwezi Dzana?"
"Here."
Bruno Carrelli?

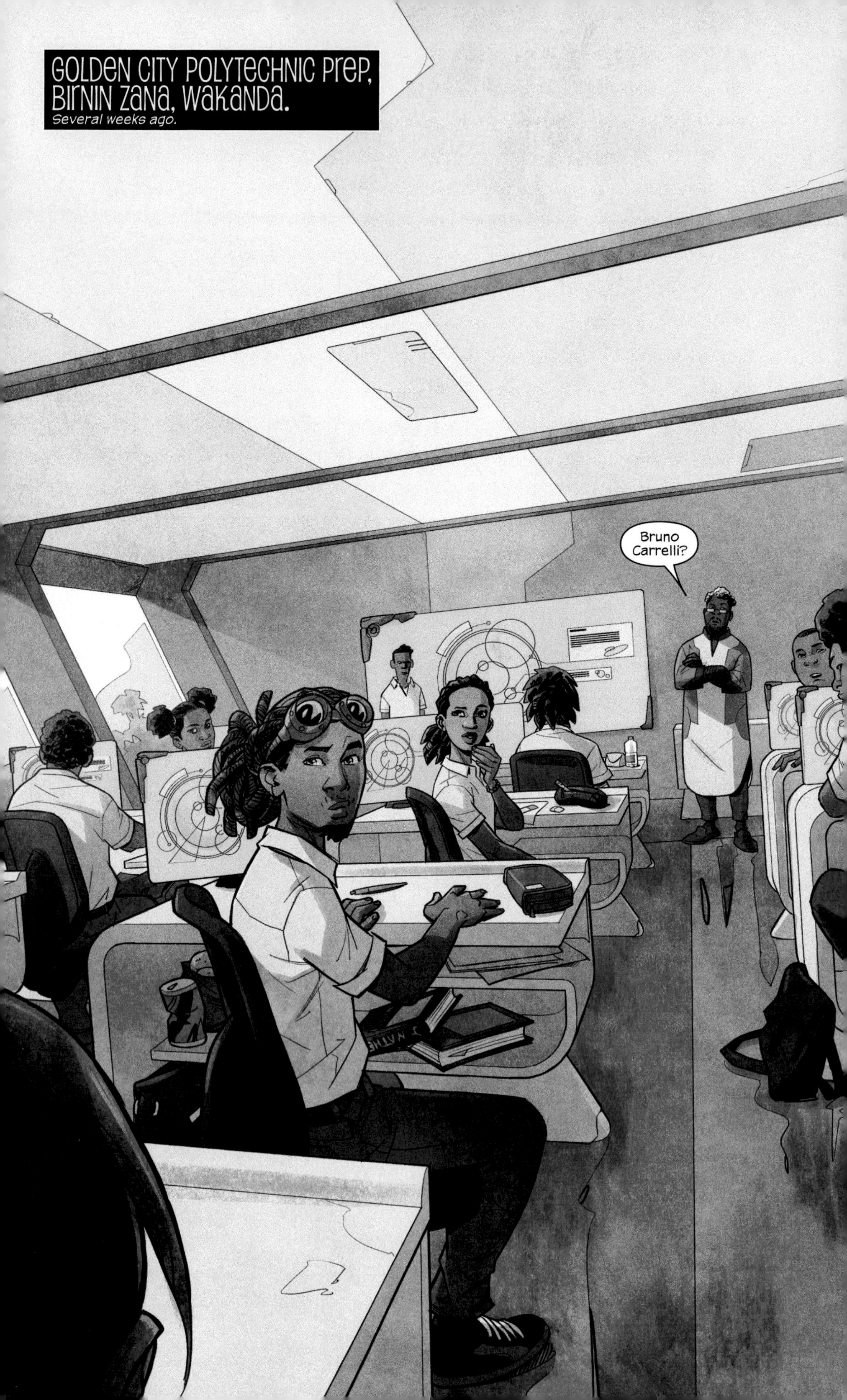
GOLDEN CITY POLYTECHNIC PREP,
BIRNIN ZANA, WAKANDA.
Several weeks ago.
Bruno Carrelli?

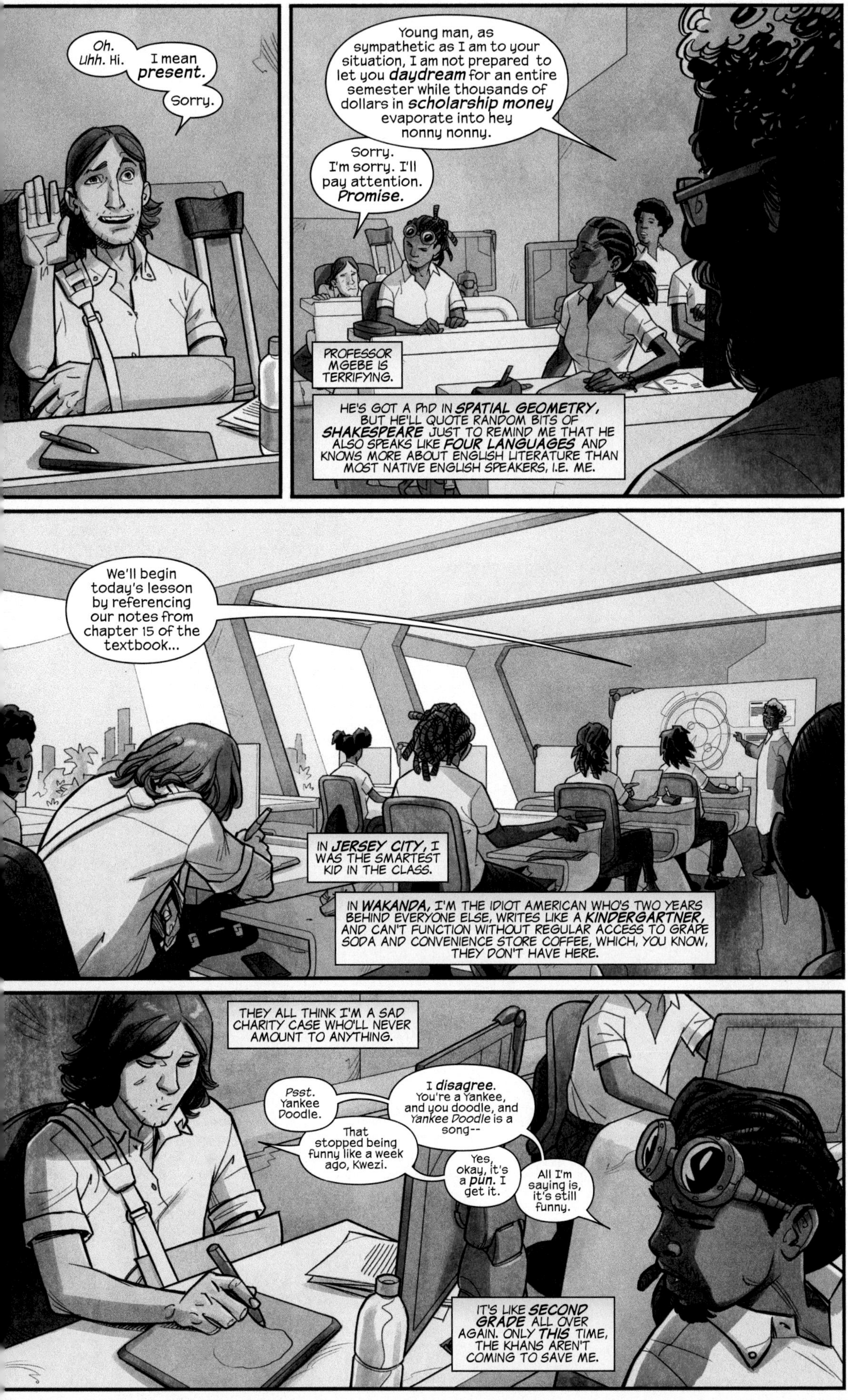
Oh. Uhh. Hi.
I mean present.
Sorry.
Young man, as sympathetic as I am to your situation, I am not prepared to let you daydream for an entire semester while thousands of dollars in scholarship money evaporate into hey nonny nonny.
Sorry. I'm sorry. I'll pay attention. Promise.
PROFESSOR MGEBE IS TERRIFYING.
HE'S GOT A PhD IN SPATIAL GEOMETRY, BUT HE'LL QUOTE RANDOM BITS OF SHAKESPEARE JUST TO REMIND ME THAT HE ALSO SPEAKS LIKE FOUR LANGUAGES AND KNOWS MORE ABOUT ENGLISH LITERATURE THAN MOST NATIVE ENGLISH SPEAKERS, I.E. ME.
We'll begin today's lesson by referencing our notes from chapter 15 of the textbook...
IN JERSEY CITY, I WAS THE SMARTEST KID IN THE CLASS.
IN WAKANDA, I'M THE IDIOT AMERICAN WHO'S TWO YEARS BEHIND EVERYONE ELSE, WRITES LIKE A KINDERGARTNER, AND CAN'T FUNCTION WITHOUT REGULAR ACCESS TO GRAPE SODA AND CONVENIENCE STORE COFFEE, WHICH, YOU KNOW, THEY DON'T HAVE HERE.
THEY ALL THINK I'M A SAD CHARITY CASE WHO'LL NEVER AMOUNT TO ANYTHING.
Psst. Yankee Doodle.
I disagree. You're a Yankee, and you doodle, and Yankee Doodle is a song--
That stopped being funny like a week ago, Kwezi.
Yes, okay, it's a pun. I get it.
All I'm saying is, it's still funny.
IT'S LIKE SECOND GRADE ALL OVER AGAIN. ONLY THIS TIME, THE KHANS AREN'T COMING TO SAVE ME.

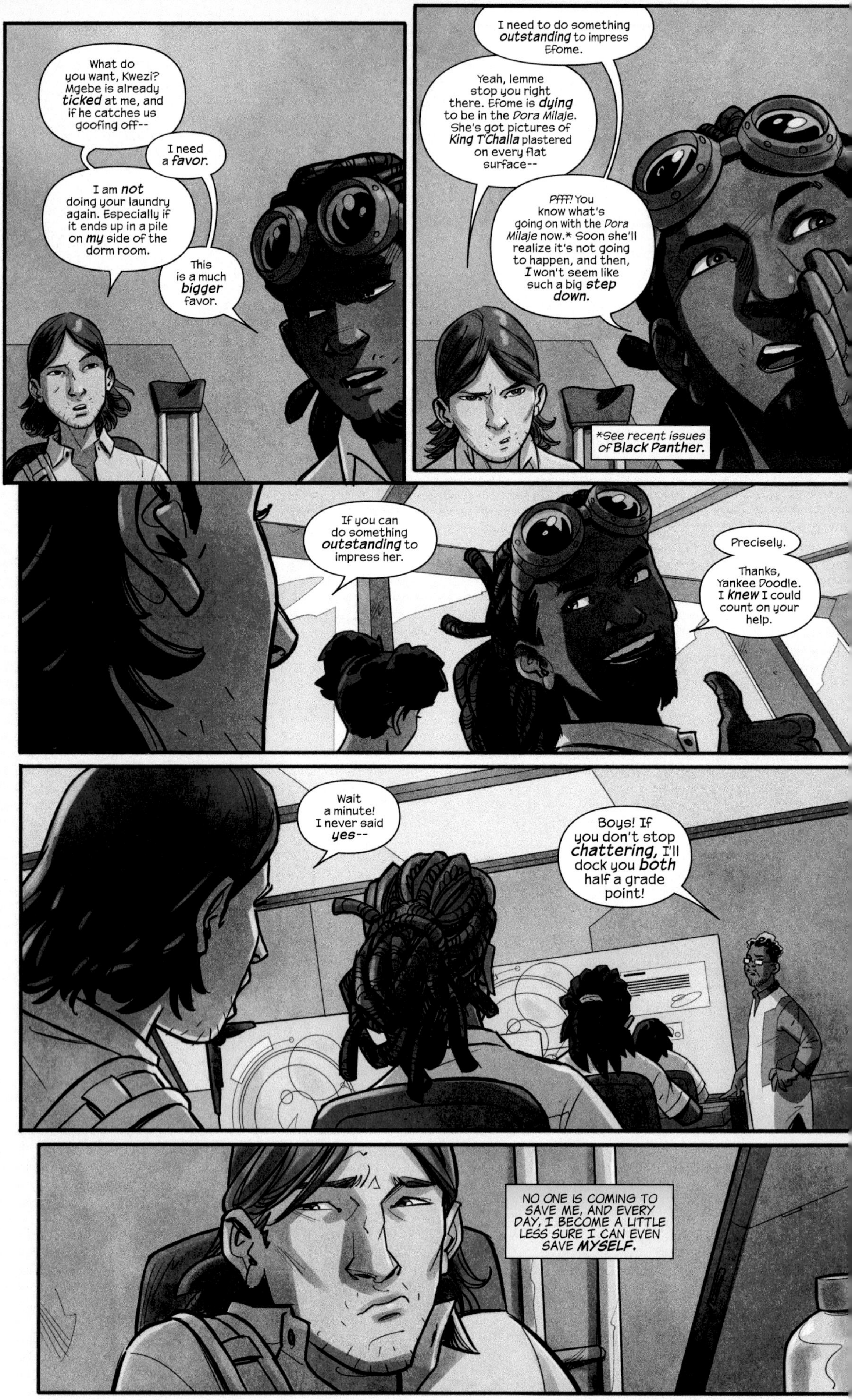
What do you want, Kwezi? Mgebe is already *ticked* at me, and if he catches us goofing off--
I need a *favor*.
I am *not* doing your laundry again. Especially if it ends up in a pile on *my* side of the dorm room.
This is a much *bigger* favor.
I need to do something *outstanding* to impress Efome.
Yeah, lemme stop you right there. Efome is *dying* to be in the *Dora Milaje*. She's got pictures of *King T'Challa* plastered on every flat surface--
Pfff! You know what's going on with the *Dora Milaje* now.* Soon she'll realize it's not going to happen, and then, *I* won't seem like such a big *step down.*
*See recent issues of *Black Panther*.
If you can do something *outstanding* to impress her.
Precisely.
Thanks, Yankee Doodle. I *knew* I could count on your help.
Wait a minute! I never said *yes*--
Boys! If you don't stop *chattering*, I'll dock you *both* half a grade point!
NO ONE IS COMING TO SAVE ME, AND EVERY DAY, I BECOME A LITTLE LESS SURE I CAN EVEN SAVE *MYSELF.*

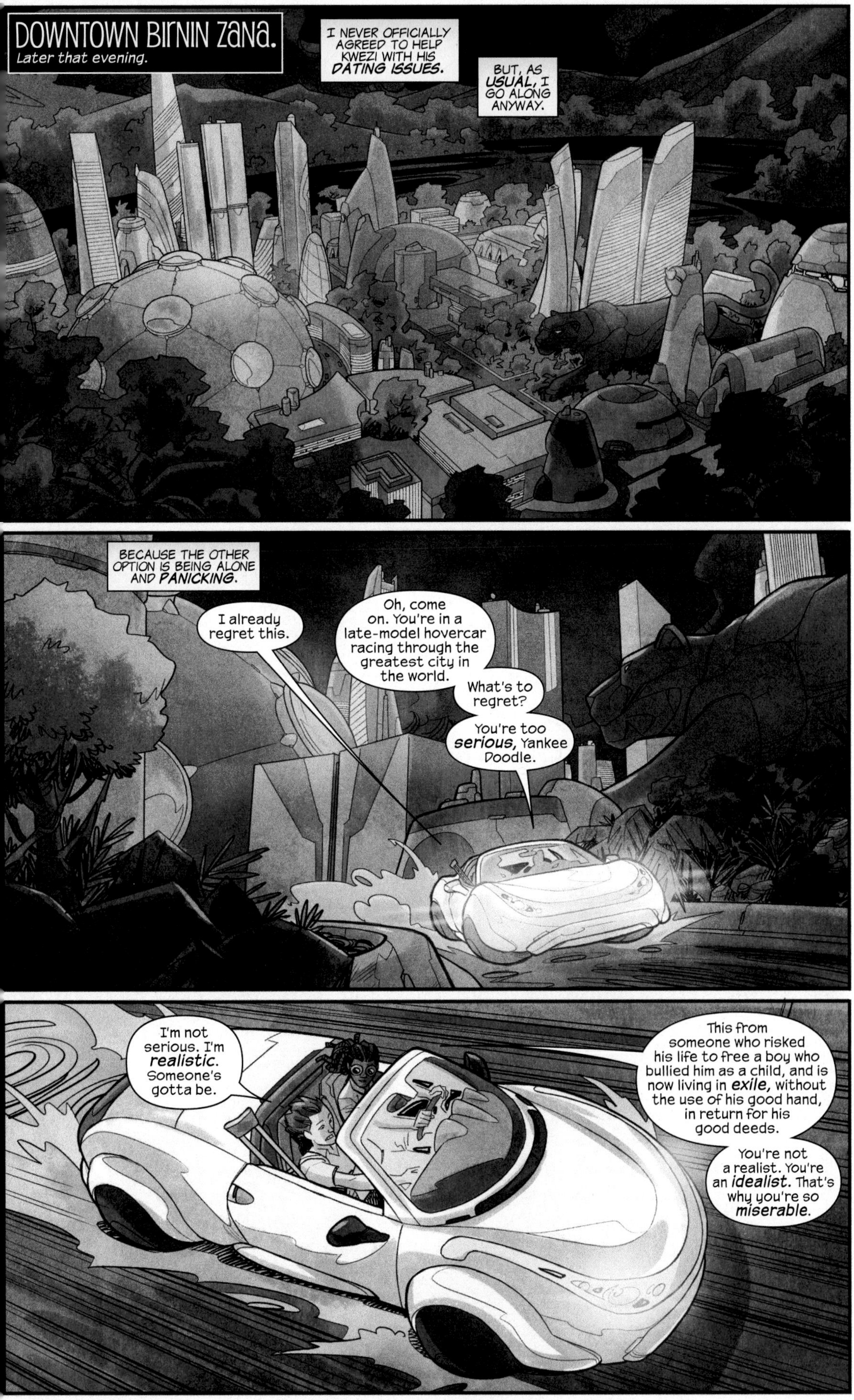
DOWNTOWN BIRNIN ZANA.
Later that evening.
I NEVER OFFICIALLY AGREED TO HELP KWEZI WITH HIS DATING ISSUES.
BUT, AS USUAL, I GO ALONG ANYWAY.
BECAUSE THE OTHER OPTION IS BEING ALONE AND PANICKING.
I already regret this.
Oh, come on. You're in a late-model hovercar racing through the greatest city in the world.
What's to regret?
You're too serious, Yankee Doodle.
I'm not serious. I'm realistic. Someone's gotta be.
This from someone who risked his life to free a boy who bullied him as a child, and is now living in exile, without the use of his good hand, in return for his good deeds.
You're not a realist. You're an idealist. That's why you're so miserable.

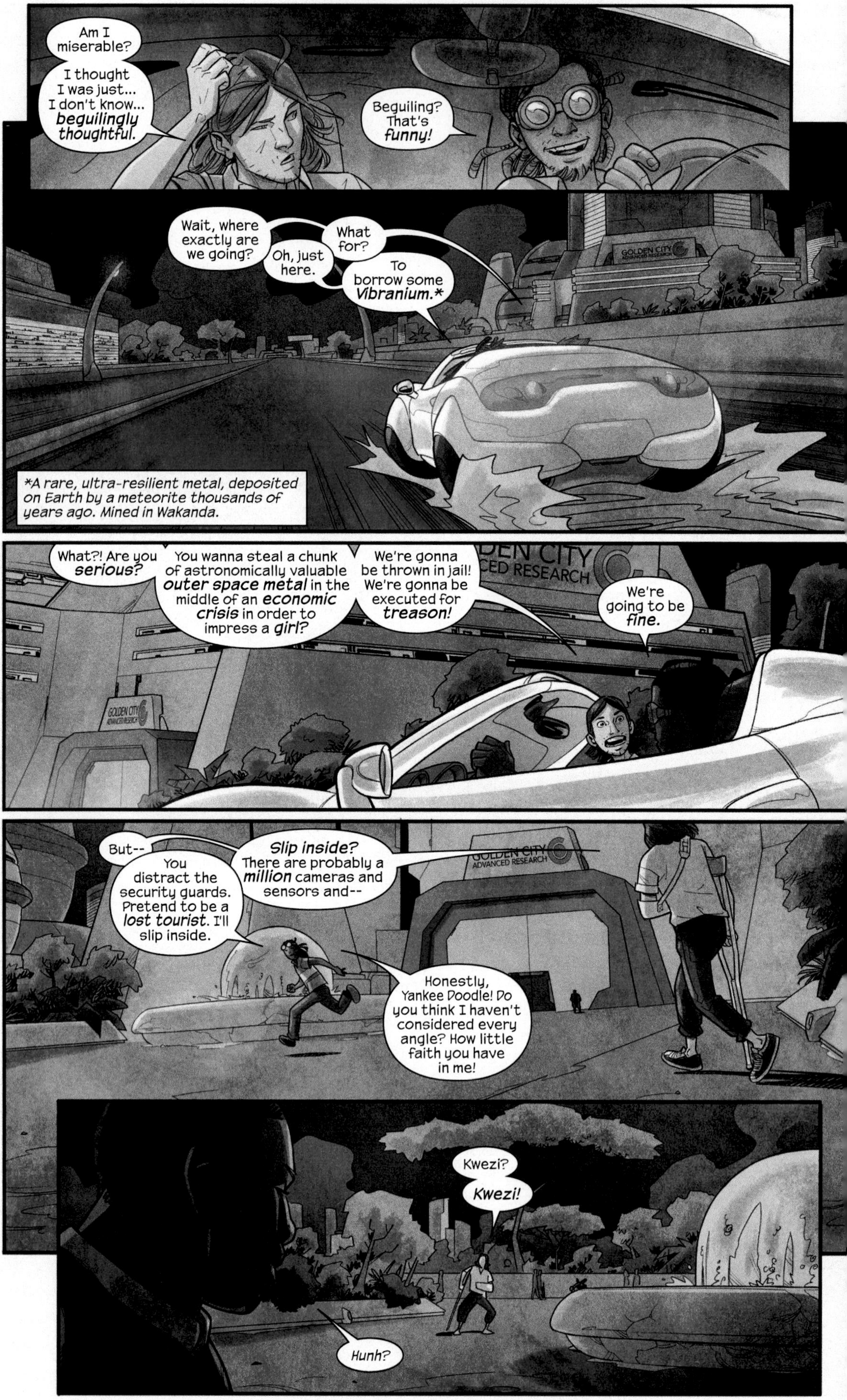
Am I miserable?
I thought I was just... I don't know... beguilingly thoughtful.
Beguiling? That's funny!
Wait, where exactly are we going?
Oh, just here.
What for?
To borrow some Vibranium.*
GOLDEN CITY ADVANCED RESEARCH
*A rare, ultra-resilient metal, deposited on Earth by a meteorite thousands of years ago. Mined in Wakanda.
What?! Are you serious?
You wanna steal a chunk of astronomically valuable outer space metal in the middle of an economic crisis in order to impress a girl?
We're gonna be thrown in jail! We're gonna be executed for treason!
We're going to be fine.
GOLDEN CITY ADVANCED RESEARCH
But--
You distract the security guards. Pretend to be a lost tourist. I'll slip inside.
Slip inside? There are probably a million cameras and sensors and--
GOLDEN CITY ADVANCED RESEARCH
Honestly, Yankee Doodle! Do you think I haven't considered every angle? How little faith you have in me!
Kwezi?
Kwezi!
Hunh?

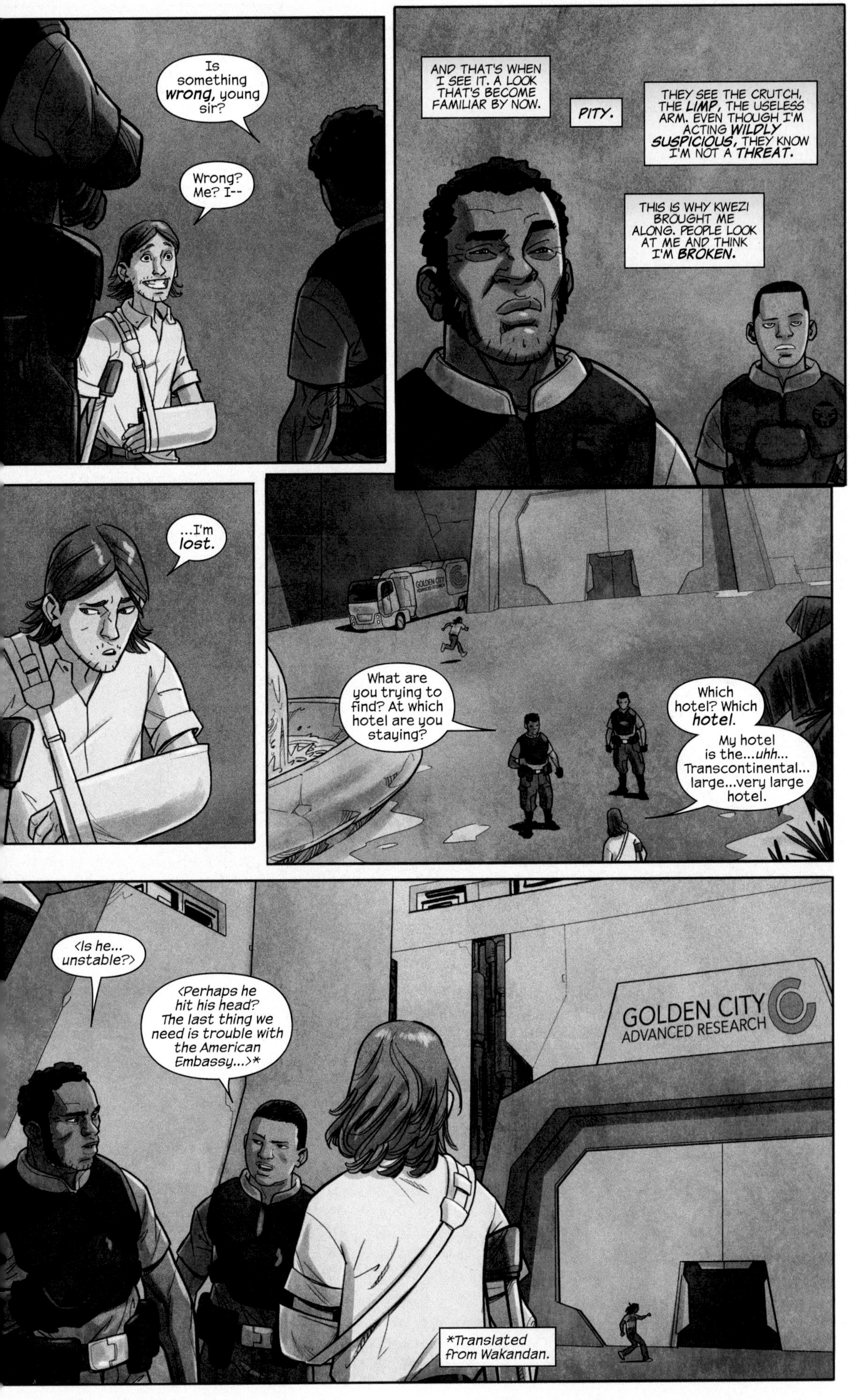
Is something *wrong,* young sir?
Wrong? Me? I--
AND THAT'S WHEN I SEE IT. A LOOK THAT'S BECOME FAMILIAR BY NOW.
PITY.
THEY SEE THE CRUTCH, THE ***LIMP,*** THE USELESS ARM. EVEN THOUGH I'M ACTING ***WILDLY SUSPICIOUS,*** THEY KNOW I'M NOT A ***THREAT.***
THIS IS WHY KWEZI BROUGHT ME ALONG. PEOPLE LOOK AT ME AND THINK **I'M BROKEN.**
...I'm *lost.*
GOLDEN CITY ADVANCED RESEARCH
What are you trying to find? At which hotel are you staying?
Which hotel? Which **hotel.**
My hotel is the...*uhh*... Transcontinental... large...very large hotel.
<Is he... unstable?>
*<Perhaps he hit his head? The last thing we need is trouble with the American Embassy...>**
GOLDEN CITY ADVANCED RESEARCH
**Translated from Wakandan.*

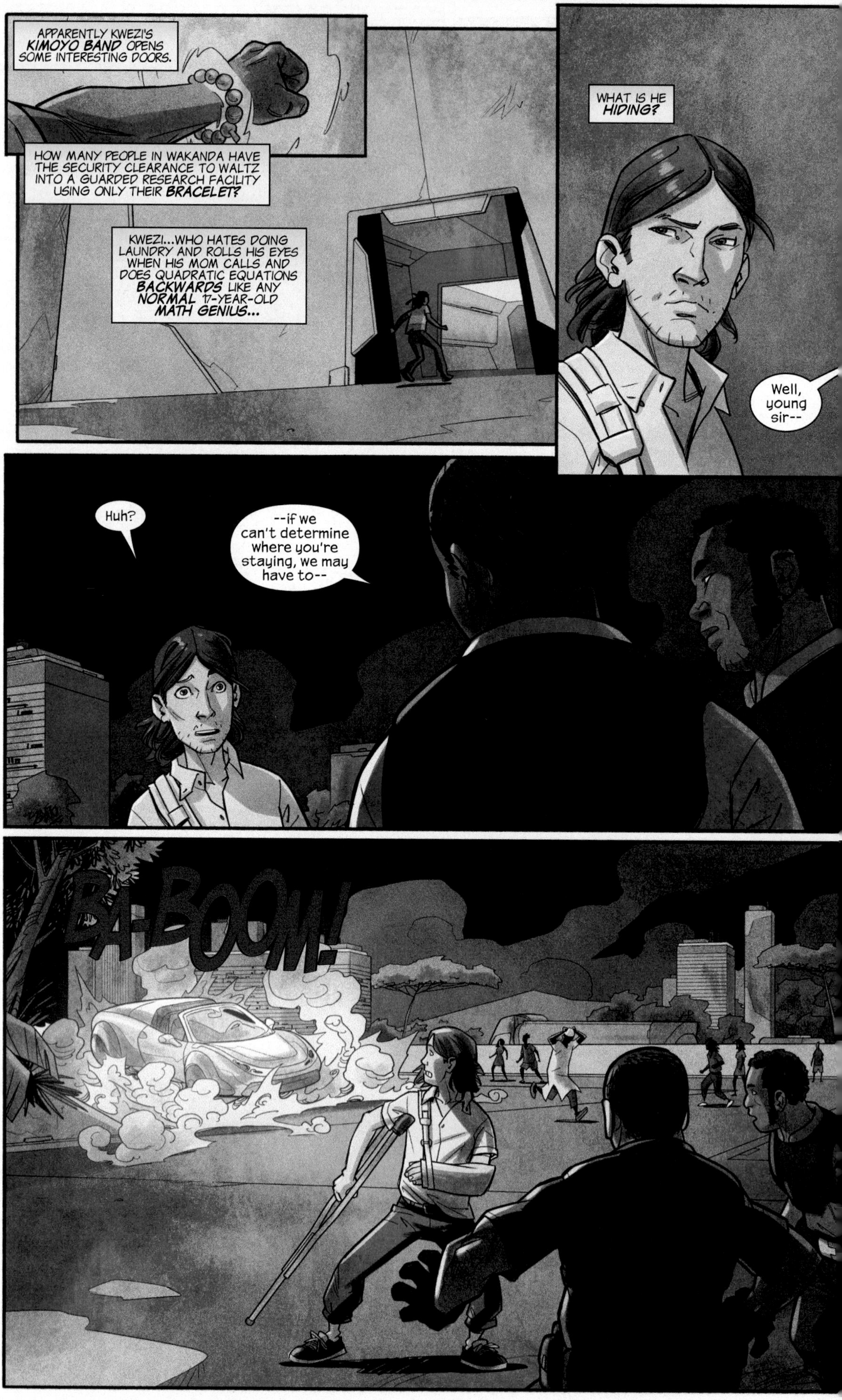

APPARENTLY KWEZI'S KIMOYO BAND OPENS SOME INTERESTING DOORS.
HOW MANY PEOPLE IN WAKANDA HAVE THE SECURITY CLEARANCE TO WALTZ INTO A GUARDED RESEARCH FACILITY USING ONLY THEIR BRACELET?
KWEZI...WHO HATES DOING LAUNDRY AND ROLLS HIS EYES WHEN HIS MOM CALLS AND DOES QUADRATIC EQUATIONS BACKWARDS LIKE ANY NORMAL 17-YEAR-OLD MATH GENIUS...
WHAT IS HE HIDING?
Well, young sir--
Huh?
--if we can't determine where you're staying, we may have to--
BA-BOOM!

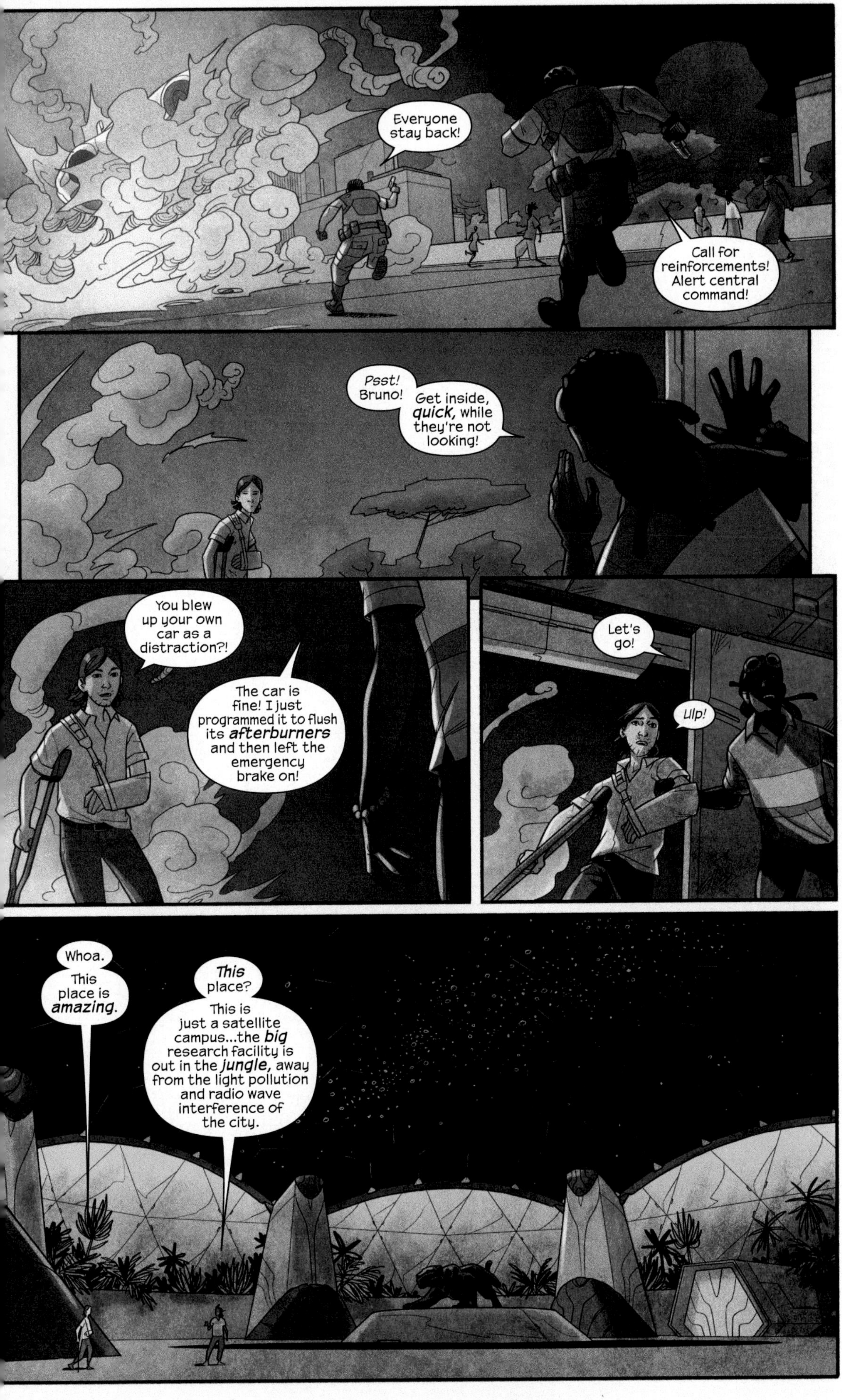
Everyone stay back!
Call for reinforcements! Alert central command!
Psst! Bruno!
Get inside, quick, while they're not looking!
You blew up your own car as a distraction?!
The car is fine! I just programmed it to flush its afterburners and then left the emergency brake on!
Let's go!
Ulp!
Whoa.
This place is amazing.
This place?
This is just a satellite campus...the big research facility is out in the jungle, away from the light pollution and radio wave interference of the city.

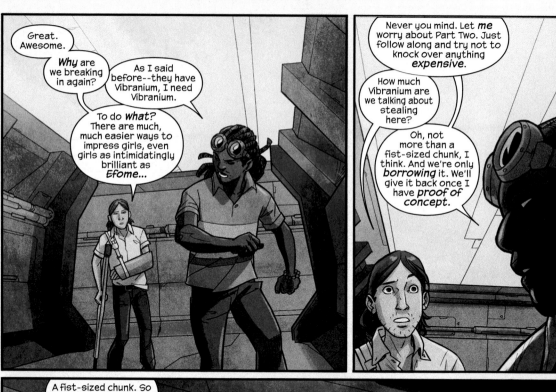

Great. Awesome.

Why are we breaking in again?

As I said before--they have Vibranium, I need Vibranium.

To do *what?* There are much, much easier ways to impress girls, even girls as intimidatingly brilliant as *Efome*...

Never you mind. Let *me* worry about Part Two. Just follow along and try not to knock over anything *expensive*.

How much Vibranium are we talking about stealing here?

Oh, not more than a fist-sized chunk, I think. And we're only *borrowing* it. We'll give it back once I have *proof of concept*.

A fist-sized chunk. So only, like, half a million dollars worth of space metal.

This is gonna end *very* badly.

The constant stream of negativity is becoming *annoying*, Yankee Doodle.

Sorry. I just--

Whoa.

Jackpot.

I've never seen an unrefined chunk of Vibranium this *big* before.

Me neither.

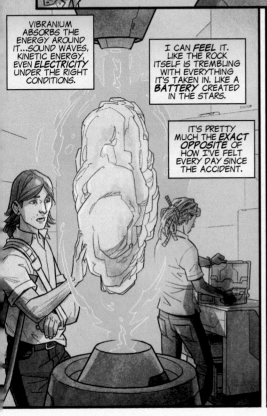

VIBRANIUM ABSORBS THE ENERGY AROUND IT...SOUND WAVES, KINETIC ENERGY, EVEN *ELECTRICITY* UNDER THE RIGHT CONDITIONS.

I CAN *FEEL* IT. LIKE THE ROCK ITSELF IS TREMBLING WITH EVERYTHING IT'S TAKEN IN. LIKE A *BATTERY* CREATED IN THE STARS.

IT'S PRETTY MUCH THE *EXACT OPPOSITE* OF HOW I'VE FELT EVERY DAY SINCE THE ACCIDENT.

Here you go, Yankee Doodle. Get to work. A very *modest* chunk will do. Make sure you cut against the plane. Wouldn't want the whole thing to crack open.

Are you *serious*? I can barely write my own *name* with this hand!

You do it! This was all your idea!

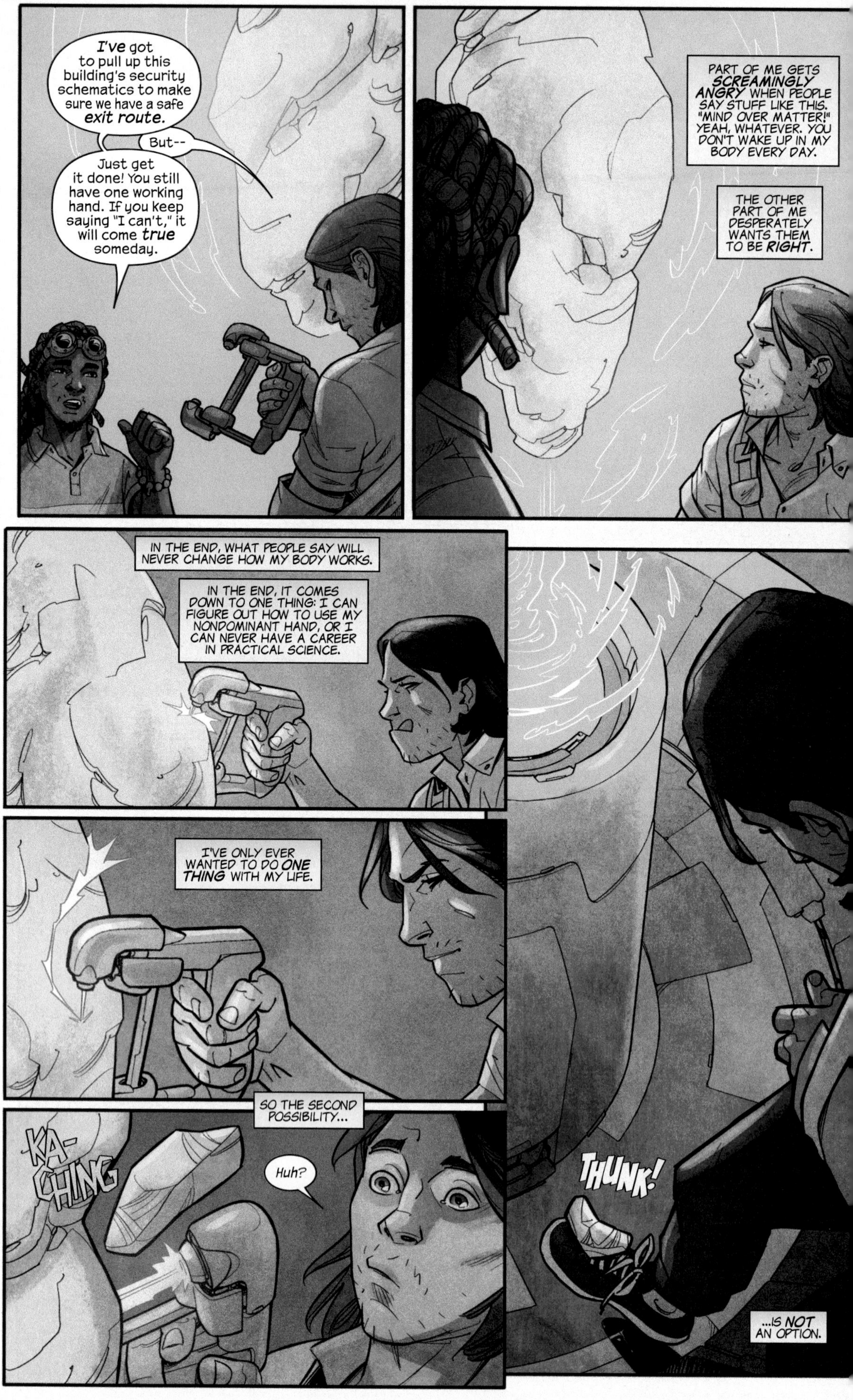
I've got to pull up this building's security schematics to make sure we have a safe exit route.
But--
Just get it done! You still have one working hand. If you keep saying "I can't," it will come true someday.
PART OF ME GETS SCREAMINGLY ANGRY WHEN PEOPLE SAY STUFF LIKE THIS. "MIND OVER MATTER!" YEAH, WHATEVER. YOU DON'T WAKE UP IN MY BODY EVERY DAY.
THE OTHER PART OF ME DESPERATELY WANTS THEM TO BE RIGHT.
IN THE END, WHAT PEOPLE SAY WILL NEVER CHANGE HOW MY BODY WORKS.
IN THE END, IT COMES DOWN TO ONE THING: I CAN FIGURE OUT HOW TO USE MY NONDOMINANT HAND, OR I CAN NEVER HAVE A CAREER IN PRACTICAL SCIENCE.
I'VE ONLY EVER WANTED TO DO ONE THING WITH MY LIFE.
SO THE SECOND POSSIBILITY...
KA-CHING
Huh?
THUNK!
...IS NOT AN OPTION.

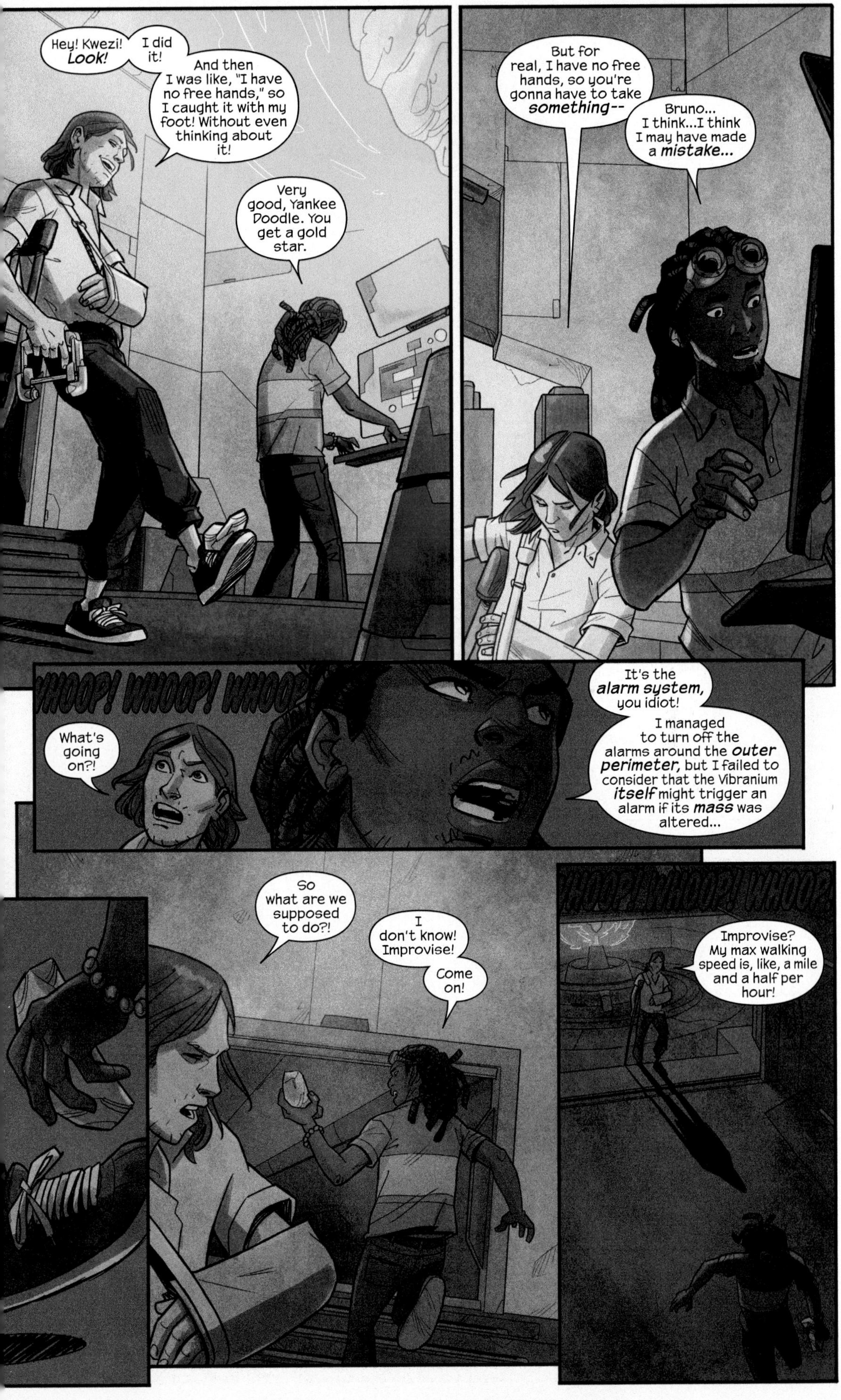
Hey! Kwezi! Look!
I did it!
And then I was like, "I have no free hands," so I caught it with my foot! Without even thinking about it!
Very good, Yankee Doodle. You get a gold star.
But for real, I have no free hands, so you're gonna have to take something--
Bruno... I think...I think I may have made a mistake...
WHOOP! WHOOP! WHOOP!
What's going on?!
It's the alarm system, you idiot!
I managed to turn off the alarms around the outer perimeter, but I failed to consider that the Vibranium itself might trigger an alarm if its mass was altered...
So what are we supposed to do?!
I don't know! Improvise!
Come on!
WHOOP! WHOOP! WHOOP!
Improvise? My max walking speed is, like, a mile and a half per hour!

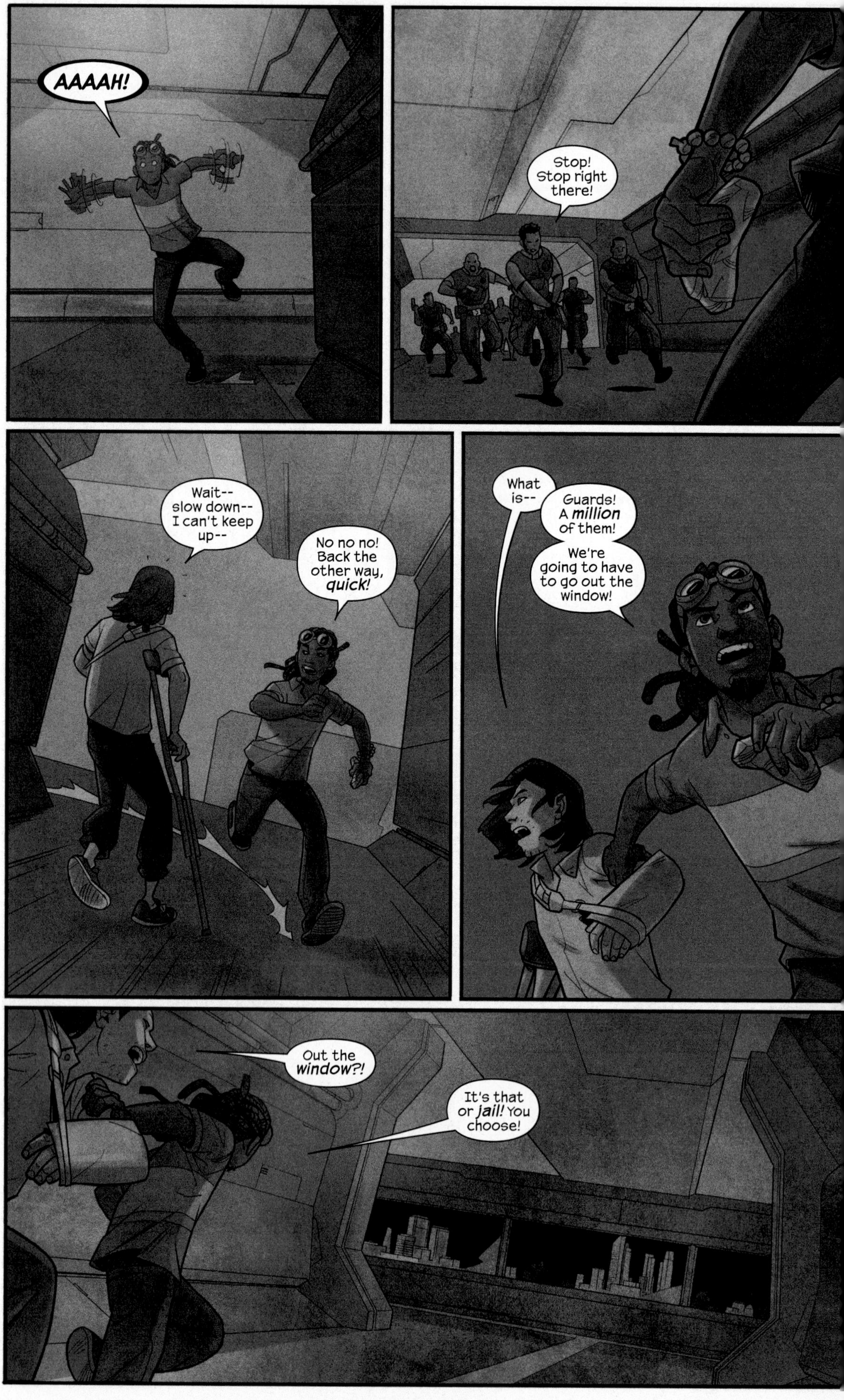
AAAAH!
Stop! Stop right there!
Wait-- slow down-- I can't keep up--
No no no! Back the other way, quick!
What is--
Guards! A million of them!
We're going to have to go out the window!
Out the window?!
It's that or jail! You choose!

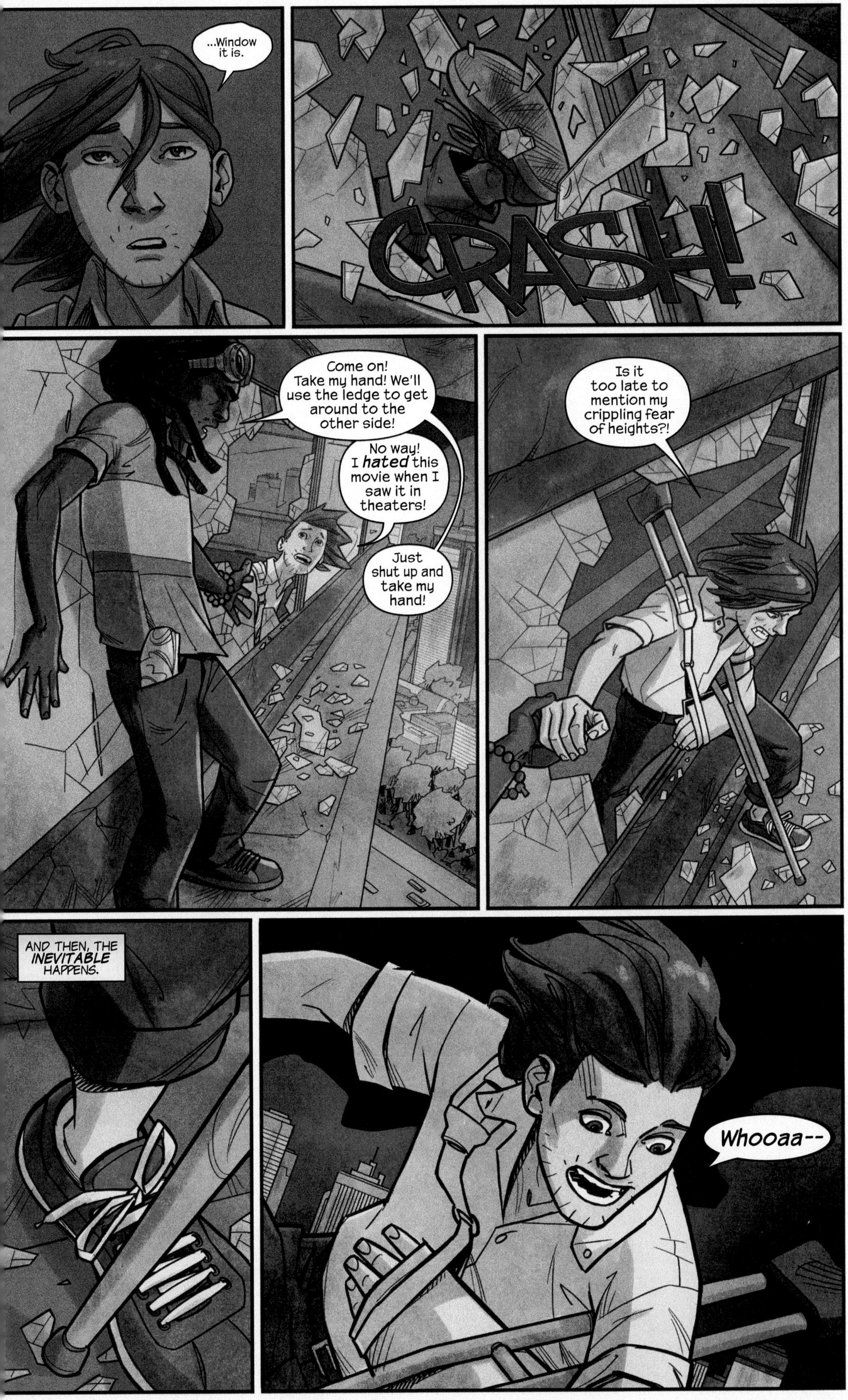

...Window it is.
CRASH!
Come on! Take my hand! We'll use the ledge to get around to the other side!
No way! I *hated* this movie when I saw it in theaters!
Just shut up and take my hand!
Is it too late to mention my crippling fear of heights?!
AND THEN, THE *INEVITABLE* HAPPENS.
Whooaa--

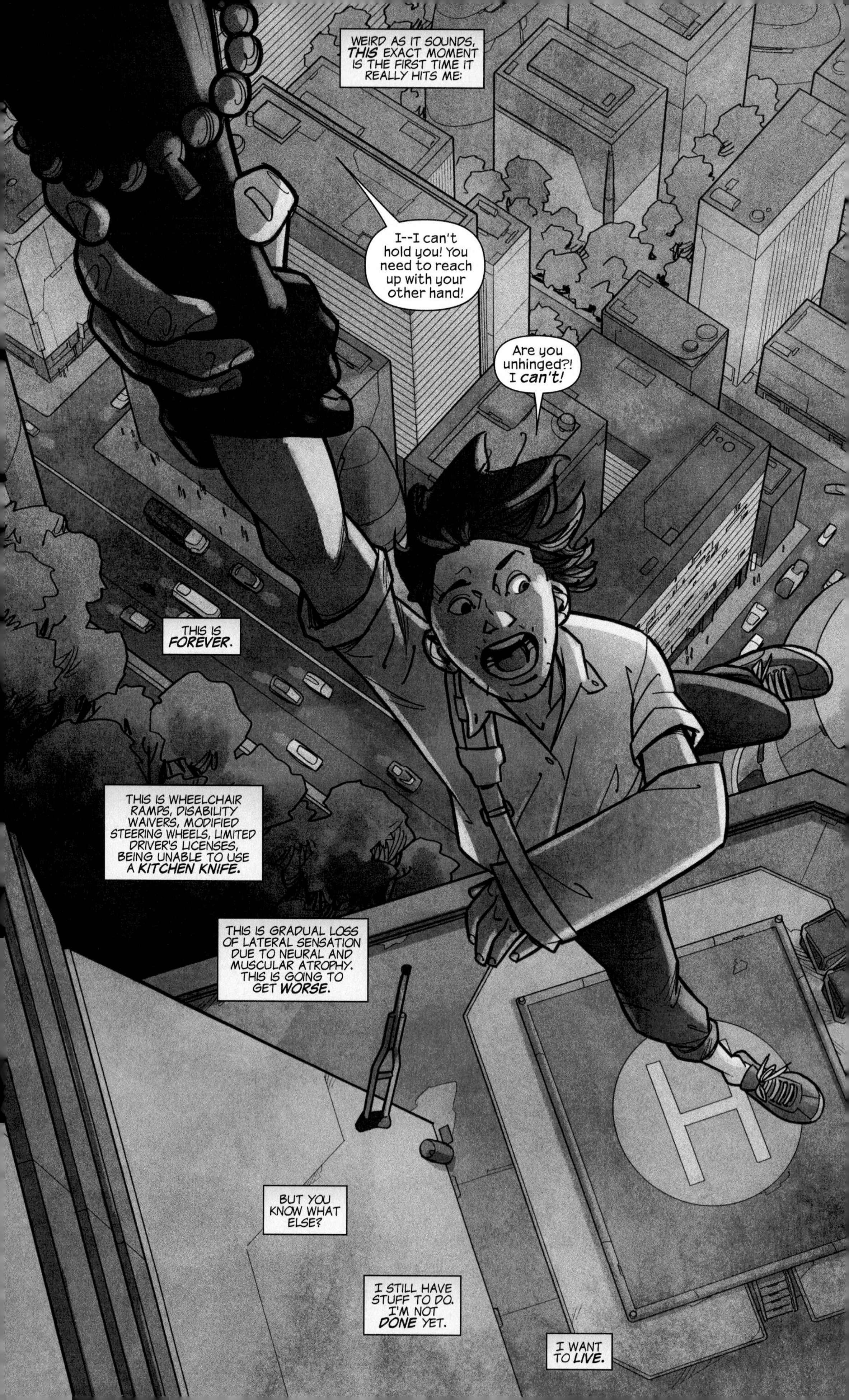

WEIRD AS IT SOUNDS, THIS EXACT MOMENT IS THE FIRST TIME IT REALLY HITS ME:
I--I can't hold you! You need to reach up with your other hand!
Are you unhinged?! I can't!
THIS IS FOREVER.
THIS IS WHEELCHAIR RAMPS, DISABILITY WAIVERS, MODIFIED STEERING WHEELS, LIMITED DRIVER'S LICENSES, BEING UNABLE TO USE A KITCHEN KNIFE.
THIS IS GRADUAL LOSS OF LATERAL SENSATION DUE TO NEURAL AND MUSCULAR ATROPHY. THIS IS GOING TO GET WORSE.
BUT YOU KNOW WHAT ELSE?
I STILL HAVE STUFF TO DO. I'M NOT DONE YET.
I WANT TO LIVE.

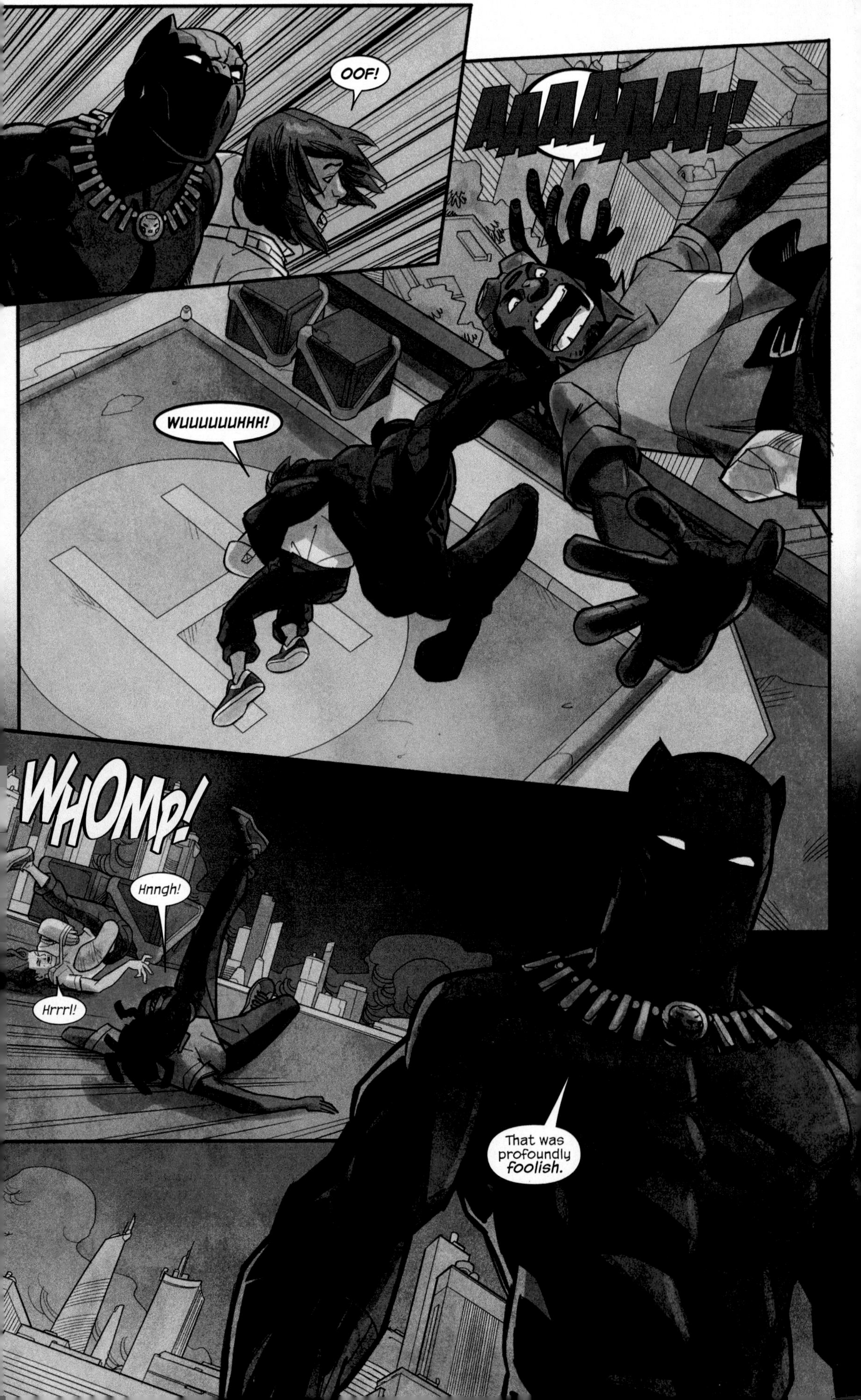
OOF!
AAAAAAAH!
WUUUUUUUHHH!
WHOMP!
Hnngh!
Hrrrl!
That was profoundly foolish.

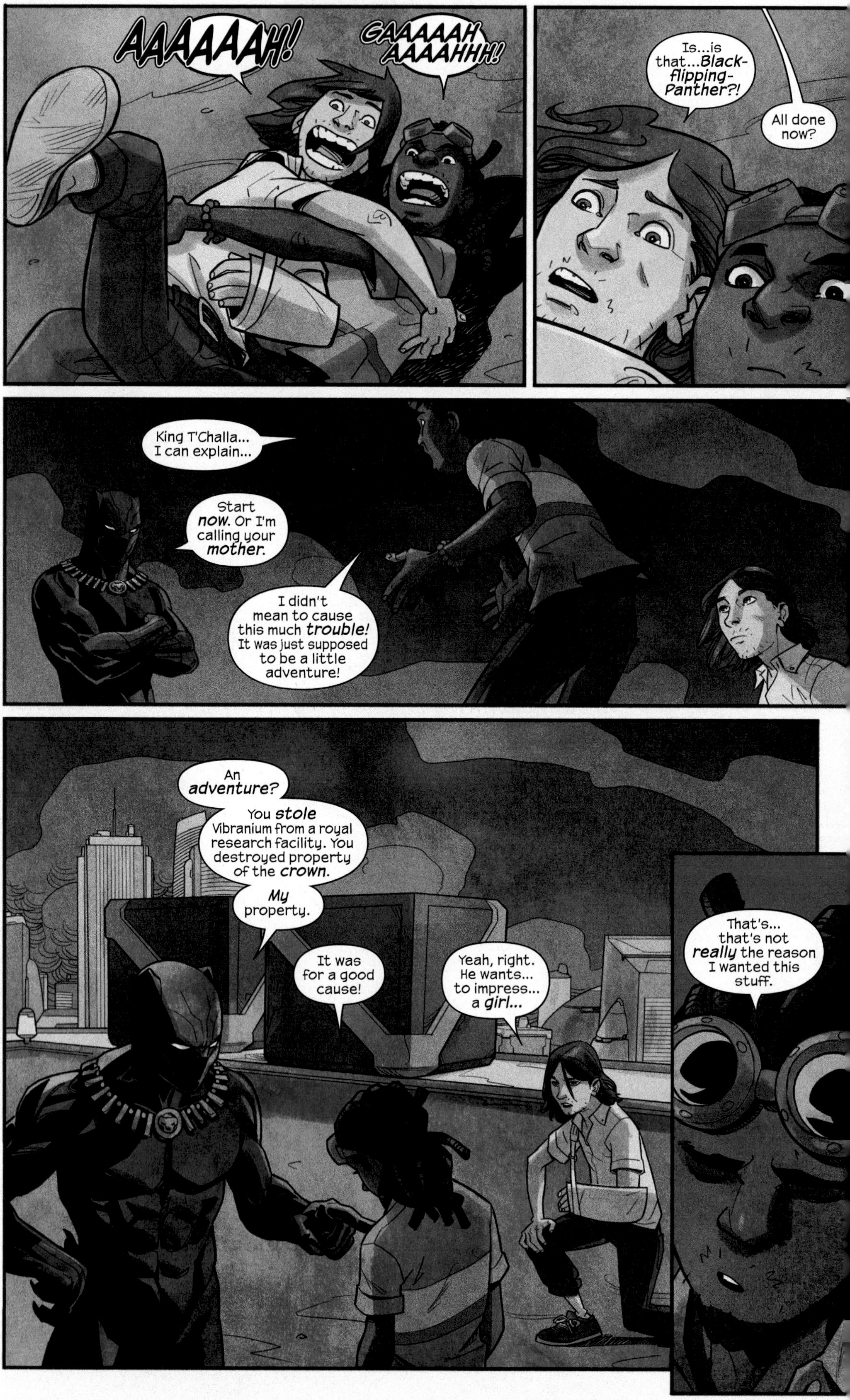
AAAAAAH!
GAAAAAH AAAAHHH!
Is...is that...Black-flipping-Panther?!
All done now?
King T'Challa... I can explain...
Start now. Or I'm calling your mother.
I didn't mean to cause this much trouble! It was just supposed to be a little adventure!
An adventure?
You stole Vibranium from a royal research facility. You destroyed property of the crown.
My property.
It was for a good cause!
Yeah, right. He wants... to impress... a girl...
That's... that's not really the reason I wanted this stuff.

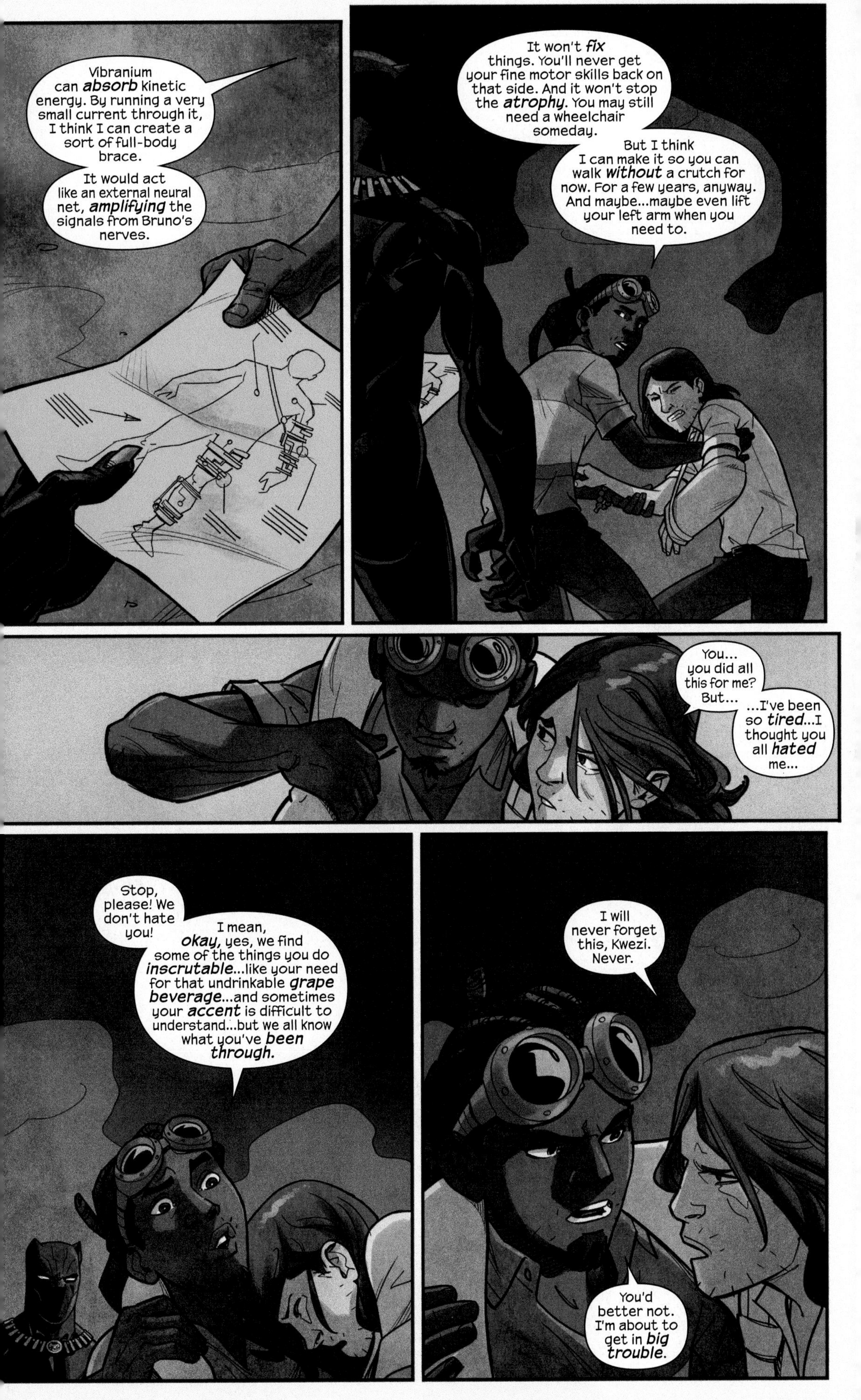

Vibranium can *absorb* kinetic energy. By running a very small current through it, I think I can create a sort of full-body brace.
It would act like an external neural net, *amplifying* the signals from Bruno's nerves.
It won't *fix* things. You'll never get your fine motor skills back on that side. And it won't stop the *atrophy*. You may still need a wheelchair someday.
But I think I can make it so you can walk *without* a crutch for now. For a few years, anyway. And maybe...maybe even lift your left arm when you need to.
You... you did all this for me? But...
...I've been so *tired*...I thought you all *hated* me...
Stop, please! We don't hate you!
I mean, *okay*, yes, we find some of the things you do *inscrutable*...like your need for that undrinkable *grape beverage*...and sometimes your *accent* is difficult to understand...but we all know what you've *been through*.
I will never forget this, Kwezi. Never.
You'd better not. I'm about to get in *big trouble*.

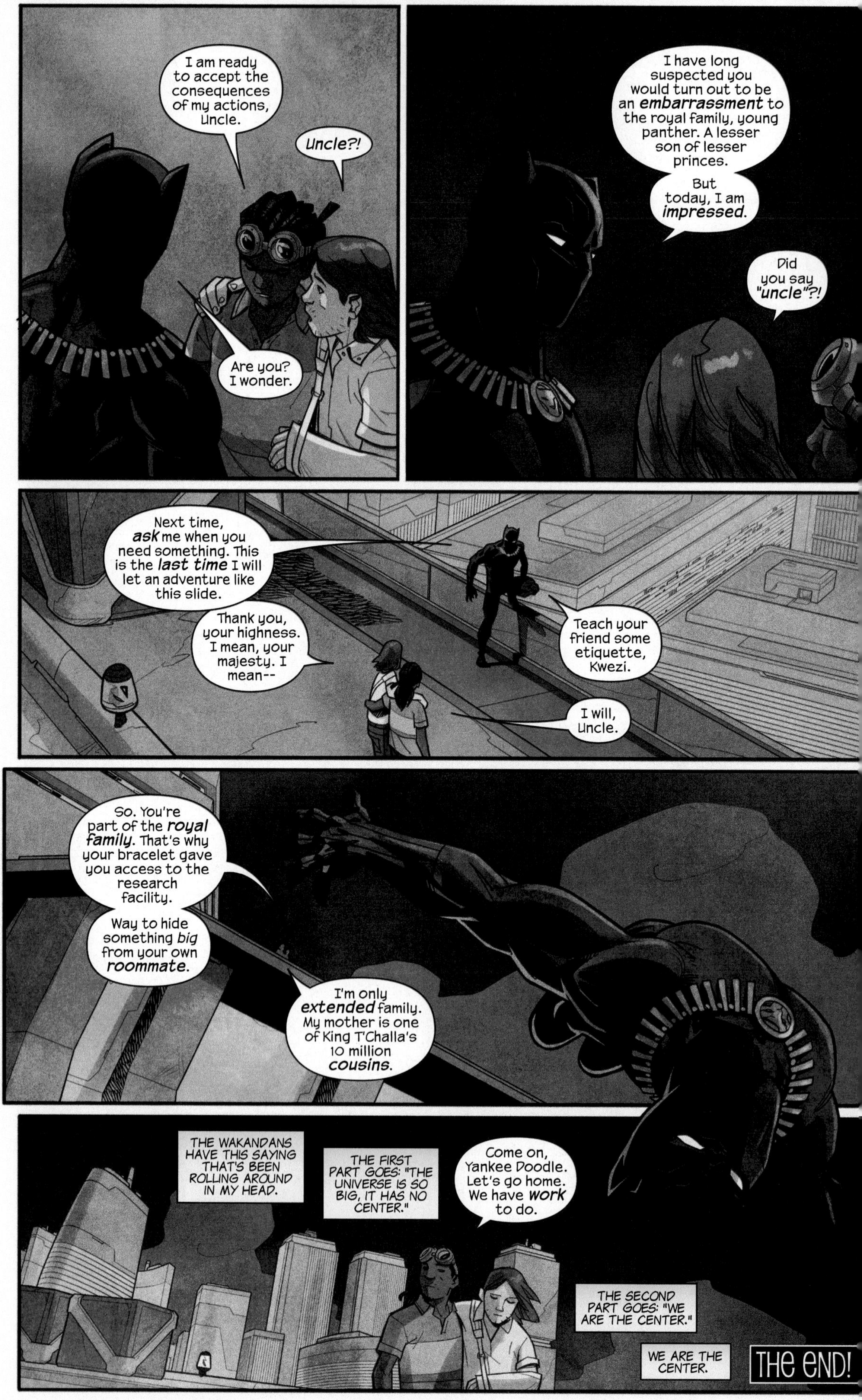
I am ready to accept the consequences of my actions, Uncle.
Uncle?!
Are you? I wonder.
I have long suspected you would turn out to be an embarrassment to the royal family, young panther. A lesser son of lesser princes.
But today, I am impressed.
Did you say "uncle"?!
Next time, ask me when you need something. This is the last time I will let an adventure like this slide.
Thank you, your highness. I mean, your majesty. I mean--
Teach your friend some etiquette, Kwezi.
I will, Uncle.
So. You're part of the royal family. That's why your bracelet gave you access to the research facility.
Way to hide something big from your own roommate.
I'm only extended family. My mother is one of King T'Challa's 10 million cousins.
THE WAKANDANS HAVE THIS SAYING THAT'S BEEN ROLLING AROUND IN MY HEAD.
THE FIRST PART GOES: "THE UNIVERSE IS SO BIG, IT HAS NO CENTER."
Come on, Yankee Doodle. Let's go home. We have work to do.
THE SECOND PART GOES: "WE ARE THE CENTER."
WE ARE THE CENTER.
THE END!

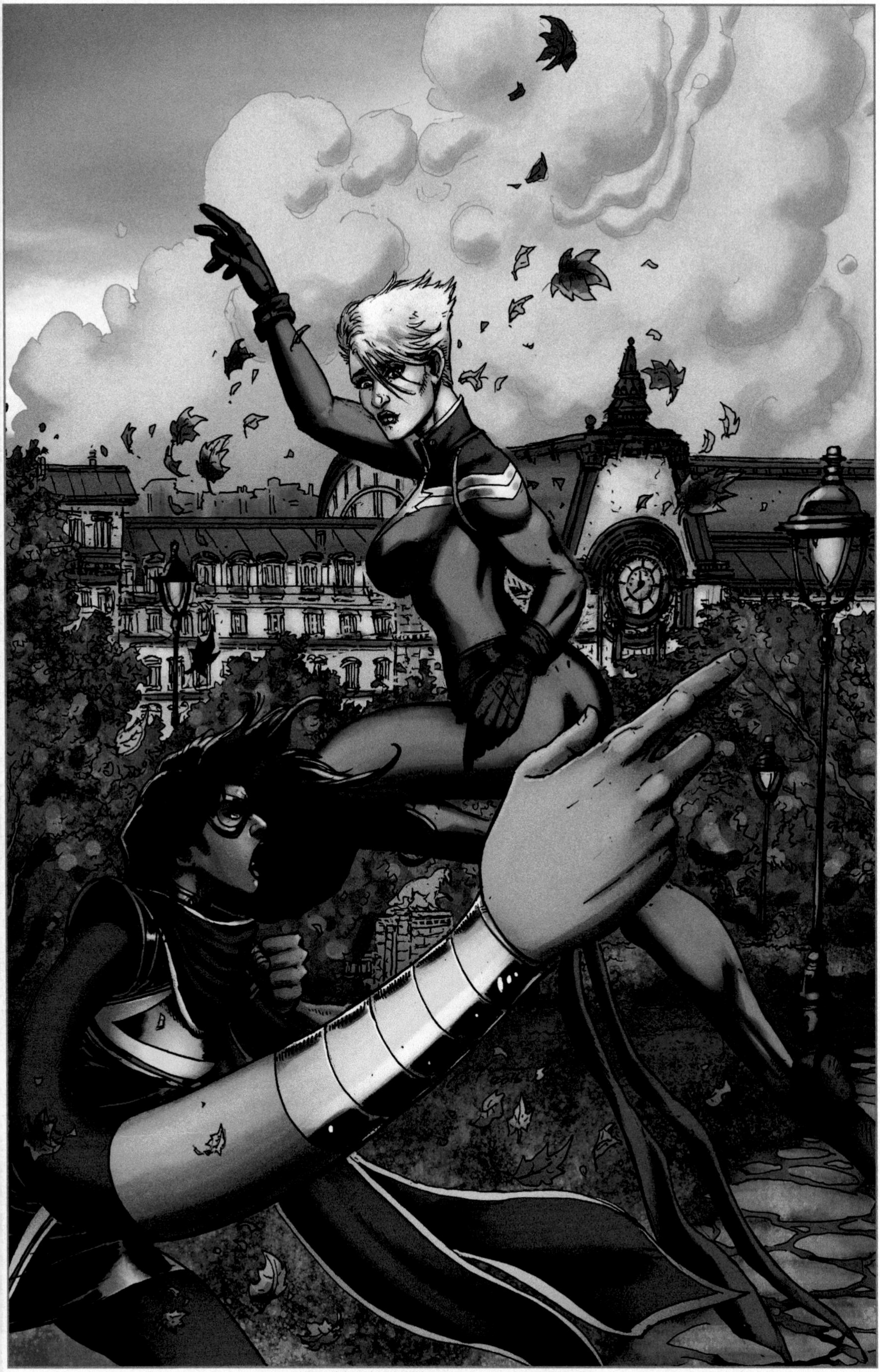

MS. MARVEL #13 VARIANT
BY JOYCE CHIN & CHRIS SOTOMAYOR

#14 COVER SKETCH
BY NELSON BLAKE II

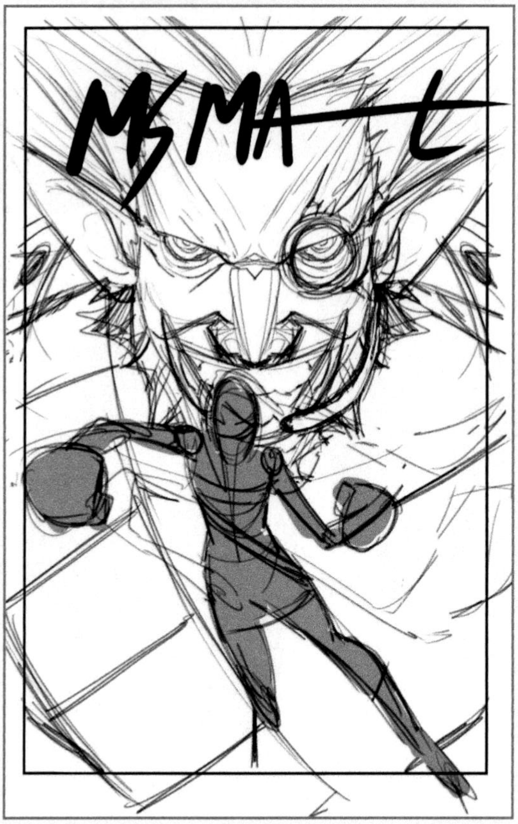

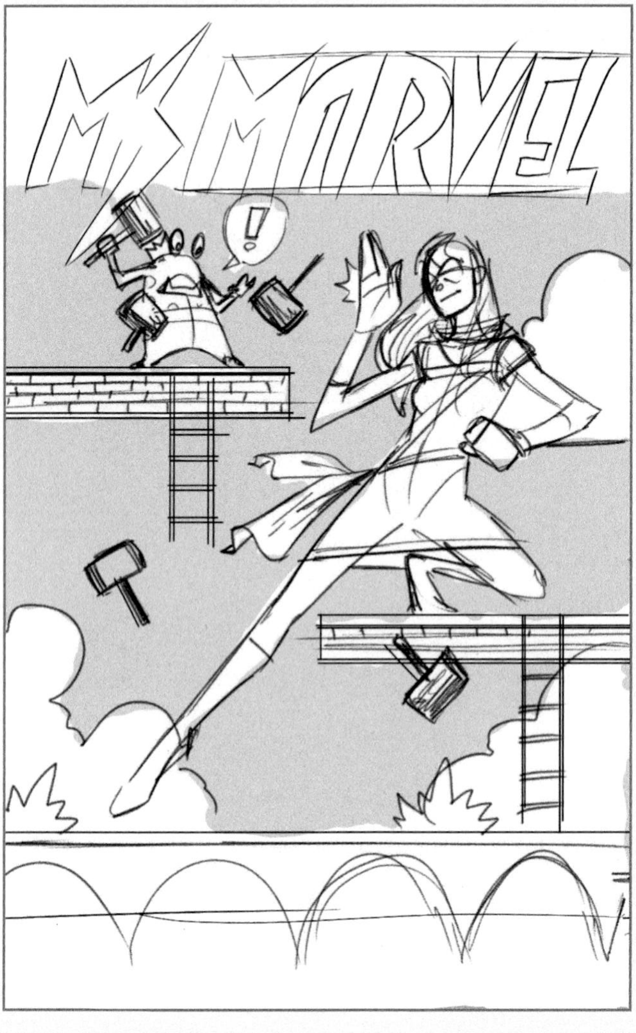
MS MARVEL
!

#15 COVER SKETCH & INKS
BY NELSON BLAKE II

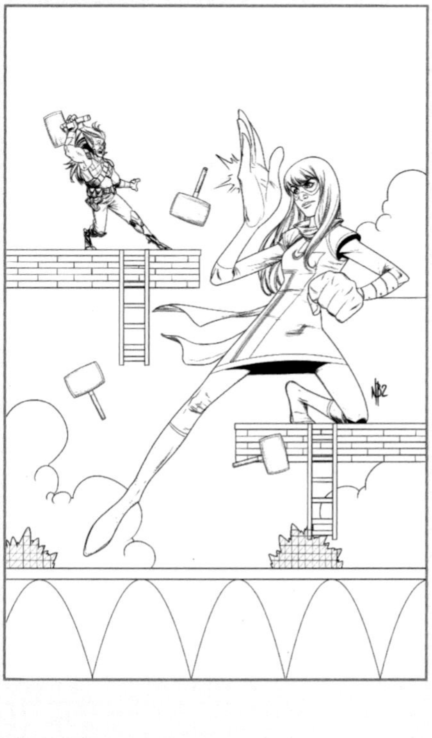

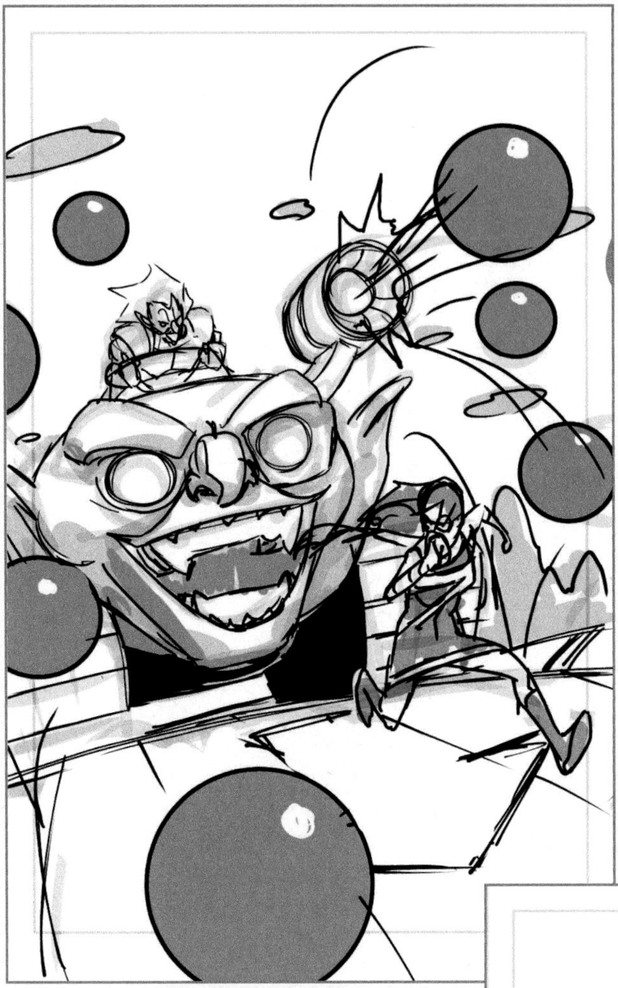

#16 COVER SKETCHES
BY NELSON BLAKE II

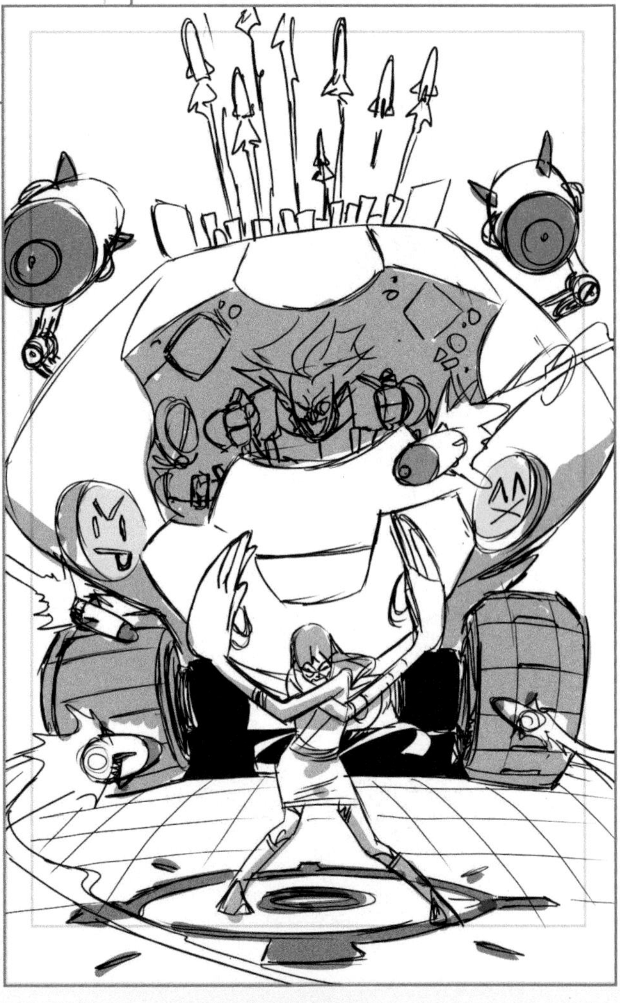

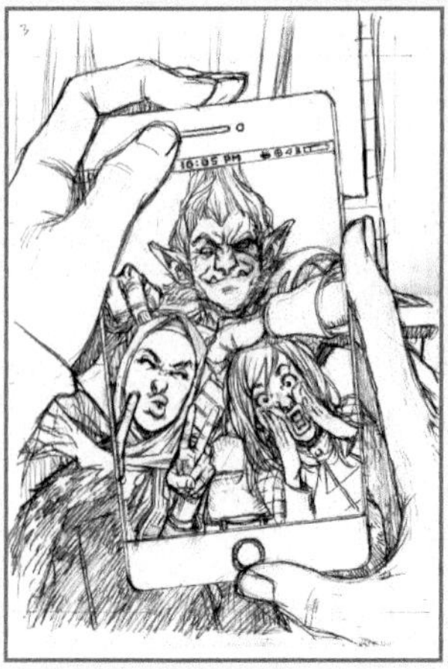

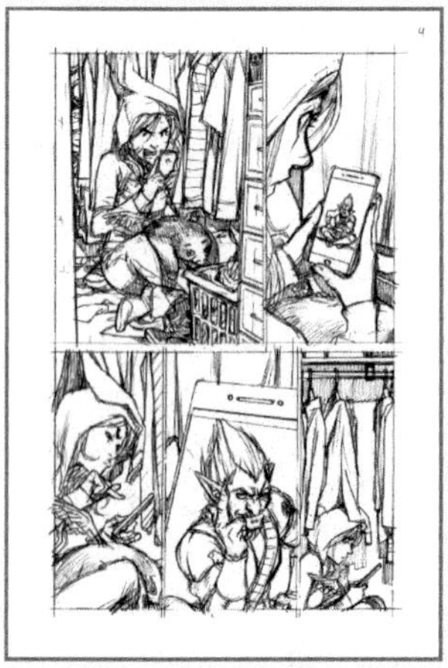

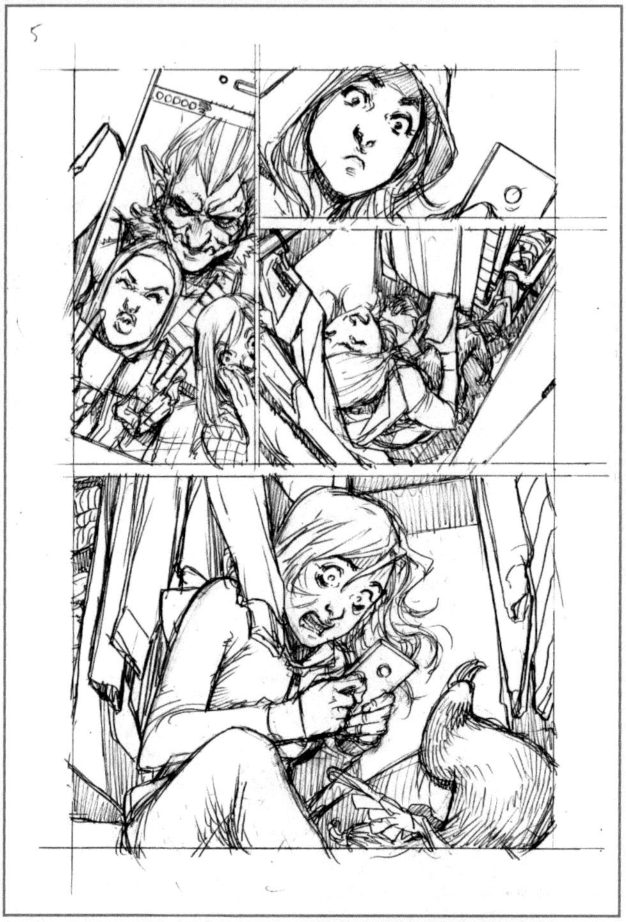

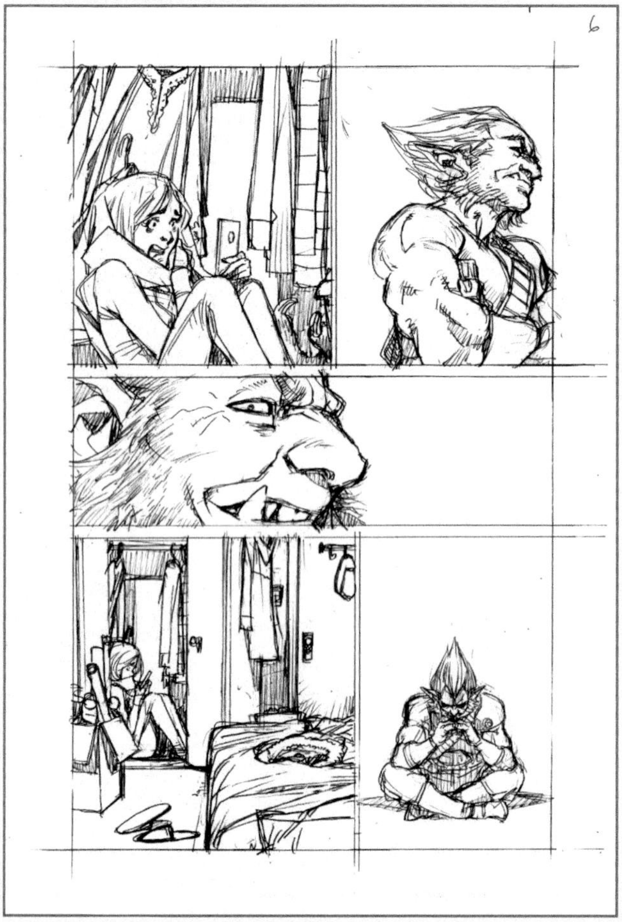

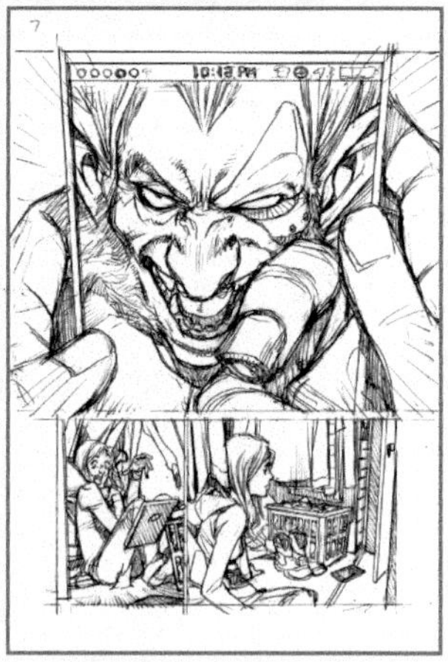

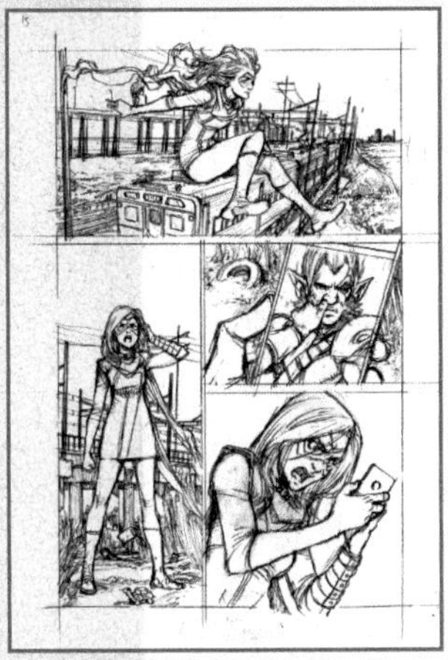

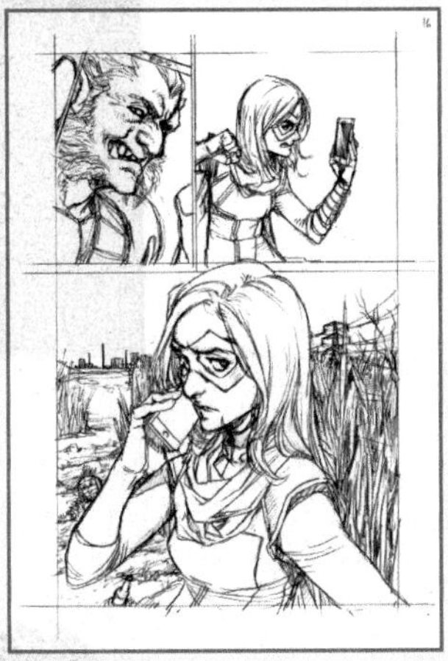

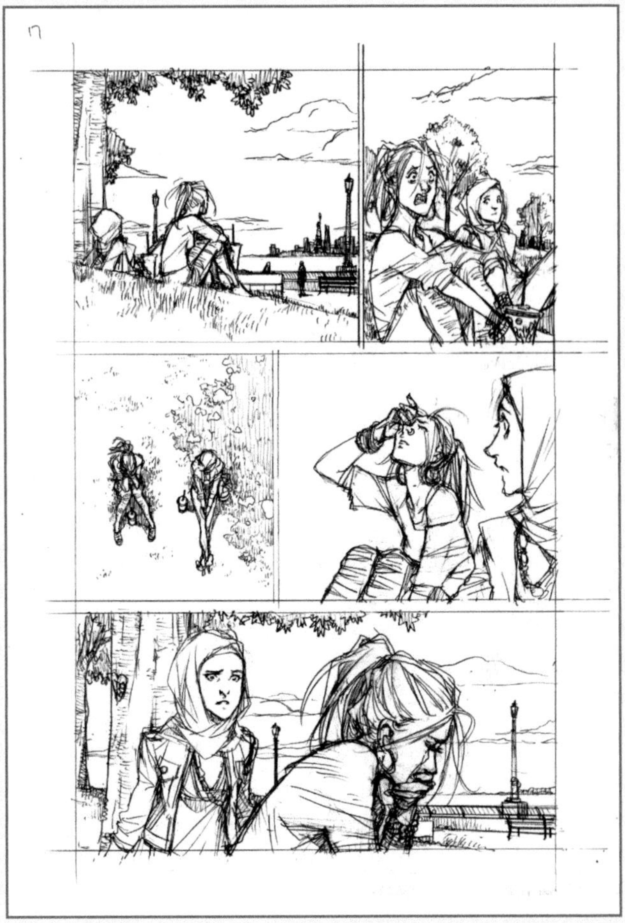

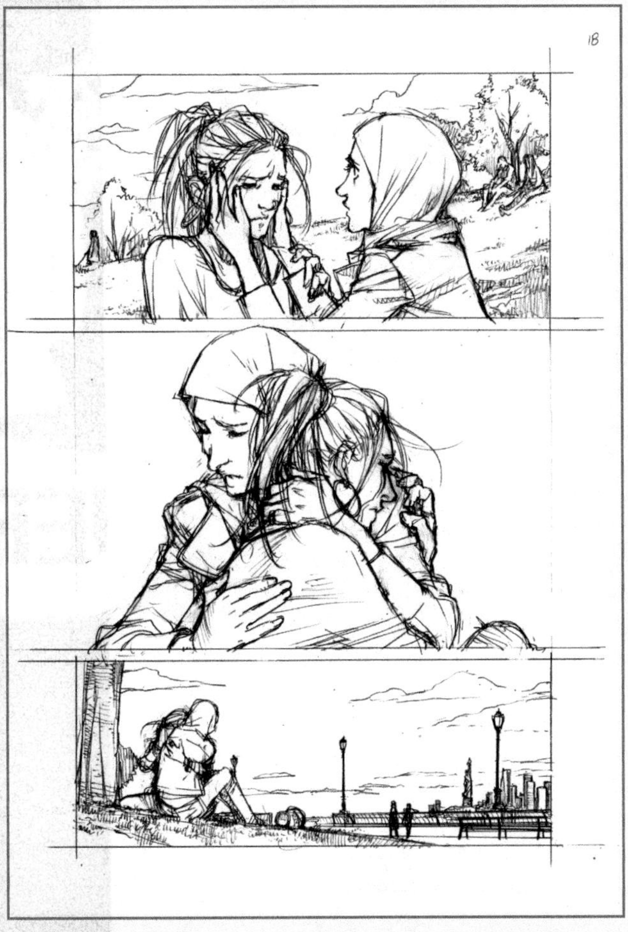

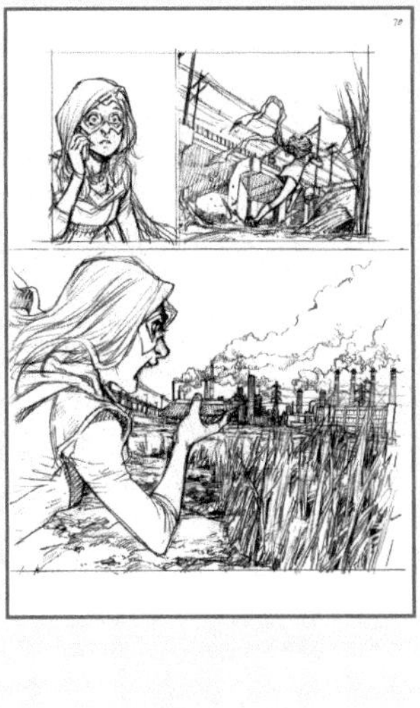

#16 PENCILS
BY TAKESHI MIYAZAWA

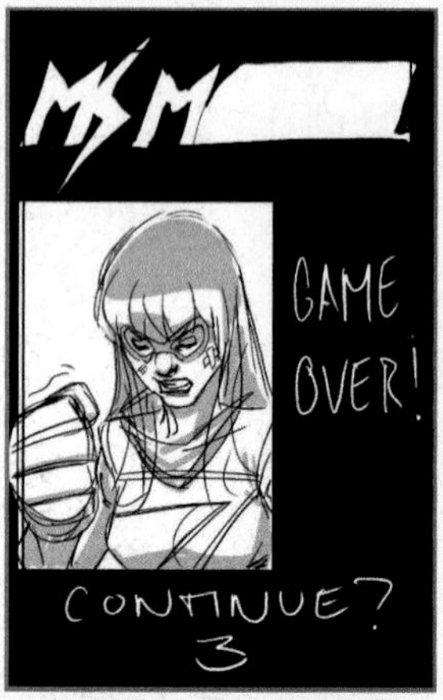
MS M
GAME
OVER!
CONTINUE?
3

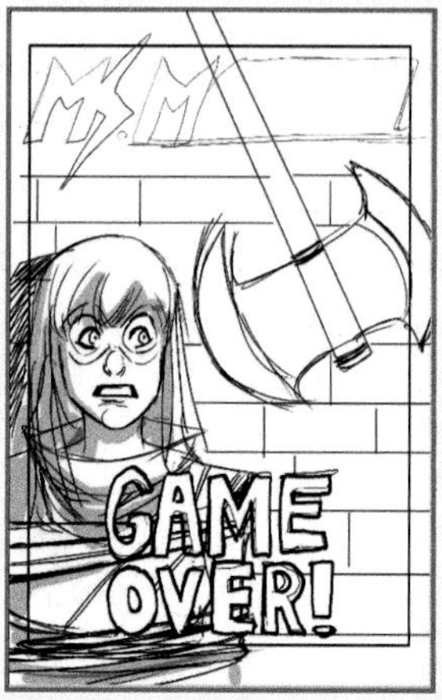
MS M
GAME
OVER!

#17 COVER SKETCHES & INKS
BY NELSON BLAKE II

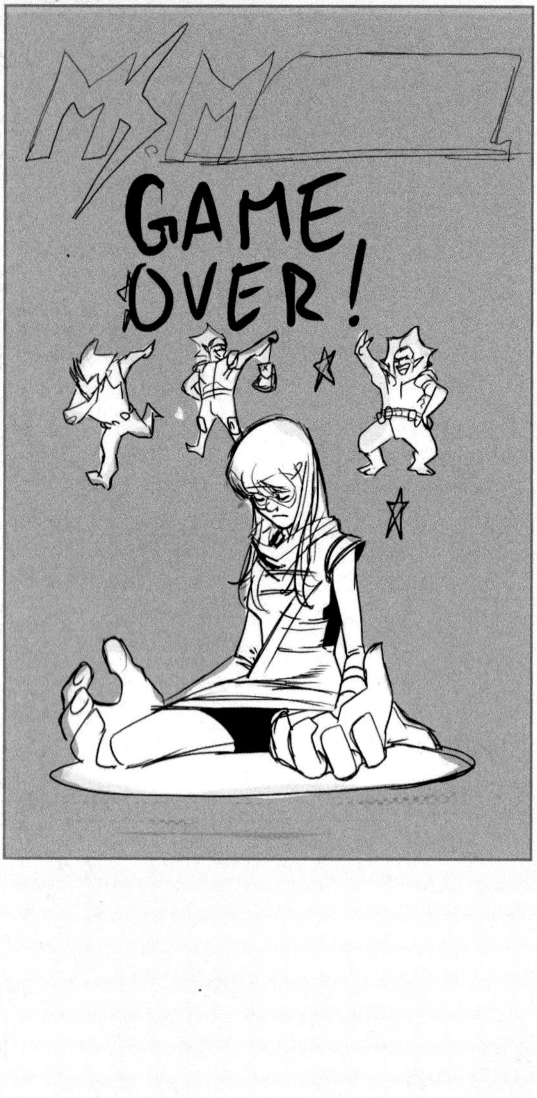
MS M
GAME
OVER!

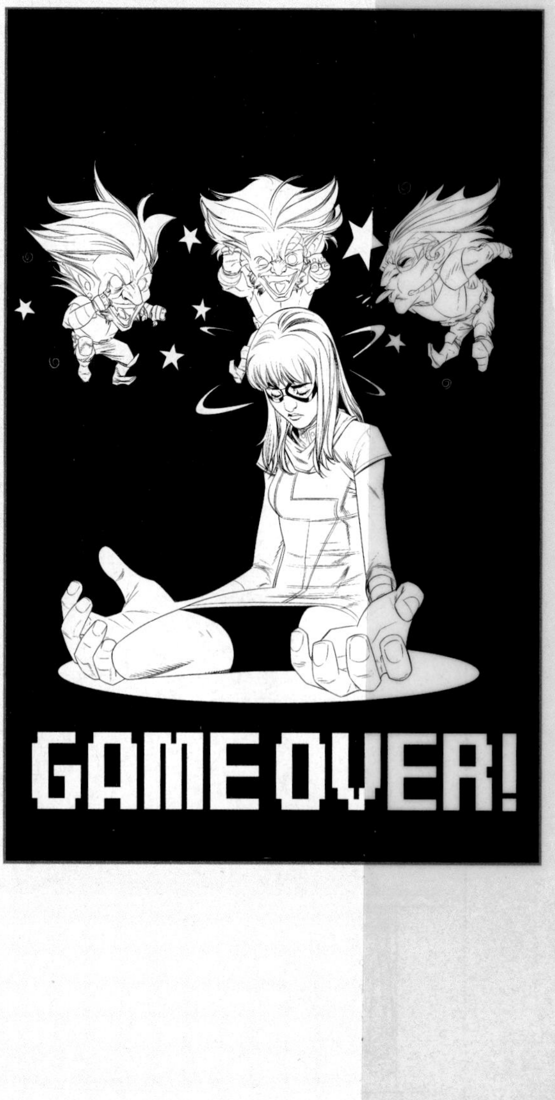
GAME OVER!